MW01592633

MONEY TODAY,
MORE TOMORROW

MONEY TODAY,

MORE TOMORROW

MILTON SMITH
Registered Investment Adviser

WINTHROP PUBLISHERS, INC.
Cambridge, Massachusetts

Library of Congress Cataloging in Publication Data

Smith, Milton
  Money today, more tomorrow.

  Includes index.
  1. Finance, Personal. I. Title.
HG179.S5513   332.024   80-28643
ISBN 0-87626-592-1 (pbk.)
ISBN 0-87626-593-X (case)

© 1981 by Winthrop Publishers, Inc.
  17 Dunster Street, Cambridge, Massachusetts   02138

10 9 8 7 6 5 4 3 2 1

CONTENTS

PREFACE

"I want to put something away for the future. How do I go about it?" "Who can give me advice about my investment plans?" "Where can I go for help?"

These are the kinds of questions you may have if you are beginning to plan for your financial future. Bankers, insurance agents, stock brokers, and real estate agents will be willing to advise you, but what they say will be influenced by their particular areas of expertise. Because my own background spans all of these fields, some corporations and organizations have invted me to conduct seminars and workshops for them. In the course of conducting these sessions, I became aware of the fact that many people do not know what questions to ask to enable them to make the right decisions in selecting investments best suited to their needs. In fact, many of the attendees had difficulty in determining what their needs were!

The questions raised at these meetings—as well as the questions that were not raised (but which should have been)—made me realize that there is a need for simple explanations of the various investment opportunities open to potential investors. Knowing the right questions to ask is more important than knowing the right answers. Questions do not change, but answers do. I therefore began to gather materials that would pose the questions investors should ask and to provide answers to them—based on the current economic climate.

This book begins with some of the questions and answers that I dealt with when I made my presentations to various groups, although I have expanded and added to them.

No author ever writes a book all by himself, but each author must take full responsibility for what is published over his name. I am indebted to many people who shared information with me as I pursued some line of research. My wife Judy and my daughter Leslie were patient and supportive through the long nights and weekends I spent writing this book. To Margaret Henning I owe special thanks. She helped me put my ideas into words, and by her endless questioning "What does that mean?" helped me to make this book easy to read and the explanations easy to understand.

Most of all, I am grateful to the people who attended my seminars. Their questions showed me that what I and other investment counselors take for granted is a mystery to others. I hope this book answers questions and serves as a guide to investment decision-making for those who are trying to plan their financial security.

MILTON SMITH

Beachwood, Ohio

INTRODUCTION

In the past, only corporations and very wealthy individuals had enough money to need advice about managing it—and enough to be able to hire investment counselors. Today, more people than ever before have some money left over after they have attended to their most pressing needs. They, too, can benefit from some investment advice, even if it is limited to planning for retirement. These people still cannot afford to hire someone to counsel them personally, but they can now turn to group sessions, employee seminars, adult education courses, or books. Financial experts who conduct investment seminars do not advise individuals directly. Instead, they provide information so that the participants can make judgments for themselves—which is what this book attempts to do. I will try to explain the intricacies of investments and its specialized vocabulary in language anyone can understand. I have kept mathematical computations to a minimum.

This book is intended for those who would like to put surplus money to work earning a supplemental income, whether they are young adults or are close to retirement. I will explain how the

United States markets work so that potential investors can make intelligent choices.

HOW TO USE THIS BOOK

I have divided the book into three sections. The first section discusses planning for financial security, but only in the most general terms. Anyone who is able to invest some money—no matter how small the amount—should plan his or her financial future. To do this effectively, potential investors should have a broad overview of just what is involved.

The second section deals with the components of investing. Each of the chapters in this section will answer eight questions that investors should ask when considering a specific investment: What is the risk? What is the return? What is the liquidity? What are the taxes? Can the investment be used in retirement plans? Can it be used as collateral? Is it a hedge against inflation? Does it have to go through probate? The answers should meet the investor's financial objectives (see Chapter 1). Section Three deals with investment opportunities for the somewhat more sophisticated investor, but even the neophyte investor will find there answers to questions he might have regarding money management.

Potential investors should begin with a clear picture of their financial profile (see Chapter 3), then outline their financial goals. These goals can change from one period of a person's life to another; initial financial goals will be different from those of later years. Financial goals should be short-range and long-range. Financial objectives for young people should include sufficient insurance to protect a growing family, provide for educating the children, and so on. Later on in life, insurance needs change, housing needs change, and a secure old age becomes the major objective.

This book need not be read through at one sitting because different readers will want to know different things about investments at different times. Investors should refer to it from time to time, however, as investment goals and objectives change and as investment opportunities present themselves. For instance, if you are thinking of taking a new job, read Chapter 14 on retirement plans—even if you are nowhere near retirement. You will be better informed and better able to evaluate the pension plans the new place of employment can offer. If you are thinking of investing in real estate, Chapters 11 and 19 will interest you the most. If you read nothing else, I think you will find Chapter 22 a gold mine of information.

This book is not intended to replace the services and advice of accountants, tax lawyers, investment advisors, insurance agents, stock brokers, or real estate agents. It is an introductory guide to investments which brings together in one place information and explanations about various investment options. The terminology of investing is defined to help you familiarize yourself with the language of investing so that you can understand financial experts and can ask intelligent questions when you don't understand them.

I have incorporated all the latest information and regulations available as I tried to anticipate the needs of readers who are ready to plan for their financial security by investing.

Section One

YOUR FINANCIAL SECURITY

There are two kinds of investment goals: 1) highest return with an affordable risk and highest appreciation; and 2) highest return with the lowest risk and preservation of capital. The importance of an investment changes with the age and obligations of the investor, of course, and the choice of an investment should be based on your situation and objectives. Before you can embark on an investment program, you must have something to invest. You cannot accumulate assets unless you have a systematic savings program.

Save systematically—then invest carefully.

1

SOME QUESTIONS AND ANSWERS

There is a time for accumulating assets and a time to enjoy them. In the period of accumulation, wise investors must familiarize themselves with all aspects of investing and must keep in mind some essential points:

1. The return is in direct proportion to the risk.
2. All investments need time to mature.
3. The importance of any particular investment changes with the investor's age and objectives.
4. To preserve your accumulation, diversify. To speculate, specialize.

In the chapters to come, I will explain specific investment opportunities, compare the advantages and disadvantages of each, and raise and answer the pertinent questions.

"I didn't know." "I didn't ask." "He looked so honest and seemed so prosperous." I have often heard these excuses after an investment did not turn out as expected, but they are not valid reasons for making a poor investment. No one should invest in anything without thoroughly and thoughtfully investigating it, and asking questions is the simplest way to determine the advisability of an investment. But you must know what questions to ask!

Most financial circumstances are variable: economic conditions change, the price of stock rises and falls, interest rates vary, the value of real estate goes up and down, the cost of borrowing money changes, and the value of the dollar does not remain constant. But in an economic system such as ours, certain investment opportunities remain the same and the questions you should ask about them do not change. The two most important questions are: what is the risk and what is the return?

In any investment there is a risk and a return, and the return is in direct proportion to the risk. The less the risk, the lower the return and the greater the risk the higher the compensation that must be paid to induce the investor to take the risk. There is no way around this. Once you recognize and accept this truism, you will be in a better position to ask questions that will have a direct bearing on your investments.

Another important question to ask about an investment is, what is its liquidity? That is, how fast can I get my money back if I need it? How marketable is it—can I easily sell my share of the investment?

Numerous federal and state provisions control investment transactions—truth-in-lending laws, for example. Federal and state securities and exchange commissions (SECs) regulate stocks and bonds. Each state has an insurance department to oversee the buying and selling of insurance within its borders. Banks and the real estate business have their own regulatory agencies. The function of these agencies is not to endorse or recommend investments, but to see to it that the laws of disclosure are strictly adhered to. Proven misrepresentation of facts about investments is punishable by law. There is no reason for investors to be in the dark about any aspect of their investments. Regulations governing investments are open to the public, and sales representatives are trained to answer questions. Sales personnel are experts in their fields and you are not. Investors should never be embarrassed because they don't know as much as the experts, but they should feel foolish if an investment did not do what they hoped it would because they failed to ask questions.

Consider the tax consequences. Do you have to pay taxes annually on the interest or dividends? Can you defer paying taxes to a time when you might be in a lower tax bracket, for example? Is the investment a tax shelter, and do you need one? Is the profit taxable as a capital gain?

Other questions that must be raised are: if you need money, can your investment be used as collateral for a loan? Will your investment have to be probated, or will it go to your beneficiaries without any red tape? Will your investment appreciate, and will the return stay ahead of inflation? Who pays the sales charges? Some investments include the sales charge in the price; sometimes charges must be paid by the buyer, and sometimes by the seller. There is always a sales or distribution charge or a management fee, no matter what the investment is. Ask and compare.

Where can your investment be sold, and what is the procedure? Who is qualified to handle the sale? Stocks and bonds, for instance, may be sold directly by the seller to the buyer. The owner's name may or may not appear on the certificate, depending upon whether the certificate is registered or not. Most sales are made through registered stock brokers licensed to brokerage houses. The stock brokers, in turn, will make the sale to a buyer through stock exchanges. The stock exchanges, along with an Over-the-Counter market (OTC) made up of security dealers who may or may not be members of a security exchange, provide the liquidity for securities.

Insurance is a form of investment, and can be bought from a registered agent or even by mail. Sales charges may be included in the premium. Real estate can be bought directly from the seller or through agents. The commission is usually paid by the seller, but the buyer and seller may split the charge, or the buyer may pay all costs.

Be sure to ask who pays the charges before making any investment. Find out if your investment purchase can be financed if you do not have the total purchase price. Find out if there are any expenses in addition to closing costs.

There are legal ways in which to accumulate assets without paying federal and/or state taxes. Retirement programs are one example. For instance, if your employer has a qualified retirement plan and you are eligible to participate, money is accumulating for which you are not currently being taxed. Your employer may also have an insurance plan that is tax-exempt. Both of these are tax-exempted investments to you. Taxes will be due only when you retire, and by that time, you will probably be in a lower tax bracket.

Social security benefits are not taxable since you will already have paid the taxes when deductions were made from your salary.

If you are self-employed, you can have your own plan (called HR10 or Keogh) which allows you similar tax advantages. The contribution as well as the return are taxable only at the time of withdrawal.

A Tax Deferred Annuity Plan (sometimes referred to as a Tax Sheltered Annuity) covers employees of qualified non-profit organizations. Under certain circumstances, a catch-up provision allows employees to make additional contributions during the years prior to retirement. Funds can be withdrawn at any time, but will be taxed when received. If they are left in the retirement fund, the income is not taxed until retirement. People who are gainfully employed but who are not eligible for any qualified pension plan can have their own Individual Retirement Account (IRA). If the spouse is not employed, the working partner may set up an account for him or her and contribute a certain percentage to it. Withdrawal provisions for IRAs are the same as for Keogh plans.

Thus, pension plans accumulate money for you which is tax-free during the accumulation period. If you have a retirement plan of any kind, you are an investor—even if you didn't realize it. Everyone covered by some kind of retirement plan should understand it. The employer's representative (usually a personnel officer) will answer any questions you might have—in fact, he is obliged to do so.

If you would like to supplement your retirement income or build an estate for heirs, you should investigate investment opportunities. The objectives for the period before retirement are likely to differ from those after retirement. For the period up to retirement, an investment should provide the greatest possible return at an affordable risk and should have the greatest possible appreciation. After retirement, an investment should provide the greatest return at the lowest possible risk, with preservation of capital the foremost consideration. In either case, the return on the investment will depend on the risk associated with it, and the *affordable* risk depends on the investor's age and financial ability. By financial ability, I mean: can the investor afford any possible reverses? How much time is left before retirement to recoup possible losses? Appreciation always represents a risk, and there is no guarantee that any investment will increase in value.

What is a good investment? Any investment is good only if the alternatives, in relationship to the needs of the investor, are neither equal or better. For instance, if you compare the purchase of a bond paying 9% interest to putting the cost of the bond in a bank paying 5%, you will see you may be better off buying the bond. The risk is a bit greater, but is compensated for by the increased interest payment. The alternative of putting the money in the bank reduces the risk since the bank insures its deposits, but the interest payment is lower. Always consider the alternatives before investing.

The investor's primary objective should be to have available at all times a sufficient amount of money to fulfill family obligations. Before even considering any investment, you should have enough insurance to protect yourself and your family, and should have some money set aside for emergencies. Only then can you consider supplementing your income by investing.

For a beginning investor, the first question usually is: "What is the best way to build an investment portfolio?" Bankers will tell you to put your money in their bank. They will say, "Your money is safe—it is insured." Insurance agents will probably recommend increasing your insurance or buying an annuity. They will say, "You will be protected and you will never run out of money." Stock brokers will suggest buying securities which will keep pace with inflation, preserve your capital, and allow you to benefit from your interest and/or dividends. Real estate agents will advise the purchase of real estate telling you that, because land is limited in quantity and the population is expanding, real estate can only appreciate in value. All of these people are giving you good advice—from their point of view. You can talk to friends or friends of friends about investments, but in reality, there is no one good investment; there are only investment advantages.

Whatever the investment, you should choose it on the basis of what it can do for you, taking into consideration your age and your ability to fulfill all obligations and to withstand the stress that sometimes goes with investing. Remember that investments are not carved in stone. You should not sit back and ignore your portfolio; you should be ready to review your investments and buy, sell, and reinvest at the appropriate times. Remember also that there is no investment with a high return and a low risk, that any investment needs time to mature, and that the importance of an investment changes with your age, obligations, and objectives.

How much does it cost to delay your financial planning? As

Figure 1-1 graphically illustrates, if you begin at age 45 you will have to set aside twice as much money each month as you would have ten years earlier to achieve the same result. At age 55, you will have to save more than five times as much.

If you thoroughly analyze the risk, return, appreciation, and preservation of capital aspects of an investment, you should not be surprised at the outcome of an investment choice.

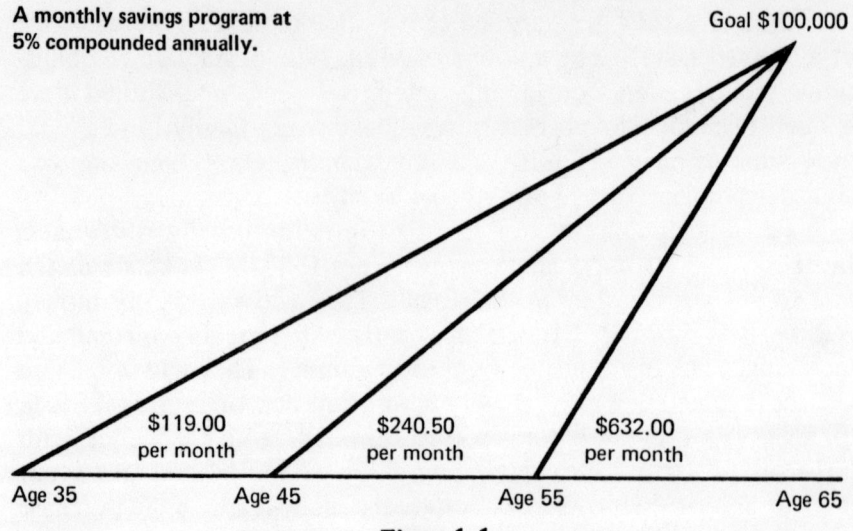

A monthly savings program at 5% compounded annually.

Goal $100,000

$119.00 per month

$240.50 per month

$632.00 per month

Age 35   Age 45   Age 55   Age 65

Figure 1-1

2

THE ACCUMULATION PERIOD: DEVELOPING YOUR INVESTMENT GOALS

Planning for the Future ● *Social Security* ● *Other Pension Plans* ● *Insurance* ● *The First Step Toward Financial Security: Savings* ● *The Next Step: Owning Your Own Home* ● *On the Threshold of Investing: Stocks, Bonds, and Tax Shelters*

PLANNING FOR THE FUTURE

Retirement, which so many look forward to as the "golden years" when they can leave the stresses of the marketplace behind, has become a financial nightmare for many Americans. Inflation is the problem, and it will continue to be so for years to come. If you are at the beginning of your career, you should begin to prepare for a carefree retirement because—barring accidents—modern medicine can almost assure that you will reach retirement age. If you are in your middle years, you should be well along the way toward building a nest egg, since inflation will have eroded the purchasing power of your pension and Social Security benefits.

The principle of retirement planning is simple: set aside some money during your working years so that you will have it when you are no longer earning a salary. A standard rule of thumb is to aim for 60 to 70 percent of your pre-retirement income to maintain your current standard of living. You won't need 100 percent since you will no longer have expenses directly related to working (clothes, transportation, and so on), and senior citizens benefit from a reduced tax rate. A Department of Labor study shows that relatively few retirees attain these percentages, however, let alone provide for an increasing retirement income that will keep pace with inflation.

Because the rate of inflation is impossible to predict from one year to the next, the further you are from retirement, the more difficult it is to predict what your income needs will be by the time you cash your last paycheck. You should, in any case, begin to set aside at least 10% of your income to accumulate as a retirement fund. If you begin early enough, this will become a substantial amount. For instance, if at age 30 you begin to invest a thousand dollars a year in a tax-sheltered, 8-1/2% annual return investment, you will have a fund totalling about $190,000 at age 65. If you begin at age 40, you will have $80,000; at age 50, only $28,000.

Let us assume that your income is $20,000 per year and you are 55 years old. If you take 80% of your income, $16,000 is what you will need a year to maintain the lifestyle you now enjoy. (Remember that you will not need 100% because you are no longer facing the costs of working.) Figure what your pension benefits will be and what your Social Security income will be at retirement and deduct the combined figures from $16,000. What is left over is the amount you will need to meet the $16,000 yearly retirement income. This computation does not take into effect inflation. You can readily see that you will need additional income to maintain a certain standard of living at retirement and you have only ten working years in which to accumulate the funds necessary to produce this additional income.

Knowing how much you will need at retirement will help you make certain decisions—whether to sell your house, move to another climate, and so forth—as well as help you choose the kinds of investments to make.

SOCIAL SECURITY

The moment you obtain a Social Security number, you embark on a retirement program. A percentage of your income is withheld from your paycheck, is matched by your employer, and is placed in a fund to be withdrawn at a certain rate at the time of retirement, lifetime disability, or as an income for your dependents if you should die. Employees of railroads and many state, federal, or local governments have their own separate retirement programs which were initiated before the introduction of national Social Security legislation in 1937. These programs, however, may be incorporated into the national Social Security plan at some time in the future. The exact amount of payroll deduction varies, depending on the employee's salary. Since the inception of Social Security, the percentage contributed by both employer and employee has been raised, as has the maximum income upon which the contribution is based. On January 1, 1937, the rate was 1% from the employer and 1% from the employee's salary, with a maximum salary of $3,000 as the fixed limit. Each put in a maximum of $30 per year, which in 1937 was a considerable sum; $2,000 a year was a good income for a family of four.

An important thing to remember today is that national Social Security was not intended to be a full retirement program, but was designed simply as a means of supplementing whatever other plans you had for your non-working years.

An employer's share of Social Security payments made into the fund is considered a business expense. An employee's contribution is taxable as income, but all of it is tax-free at the time of withdrawal. Of benefits received from state retirement plans, only that portion contributed by the employee is tax-exempt. Some employers may also have pension plans for their workers in which the company makes the total contribution. For eligible workers, the benefits derived from such plans are in addition to Social Security. Benefits from these plans depend upon the employer's contributions, which in turn depend on the employee's age, salary, and length of service. The benefits may also include life insurance, disability income protection, and hospital and medical expenses for the employee, spouse, and dependents up to a certain age. Individual employer pension plans are not compulsory. Employers are not legally bound to provide pension plans for their employees and, if they do, employees may not be required to participate if they do not choose to. Employer pension plans are administered by the employer or an insurance company under the direction of trustees governed by ERISA (Employee Retirement Income Security Act) regulations. They are also accountable to the IRS and the Department of Labor.

Information about any kind of employer pension plan, including Social Security, is available to workers. It is up to the workers to familiarize themselves with all aspects of any retirement plan, whether they contribute to it or their employer makes all the contributions. It is to the advantage of employers to keep employees well-informed about pension programs and other fringe benefits the company offers, since these may help to attract the best employees, satisfy union demands, and contribute to high employee morale. You should read carefully all literature given you about your company's plan, and ask questions about any aspect of it that is unclear.

OTHER PENSION PLANS

All the pension programs mentioned heretofore (Social Security, private employer, non-profit organizations, and so on) are *passive* plans. That is, they are employer-initiated and almost every worker is in a position to take advantage of them. Up to this point, the federal government and/or your employer has taken some responsibility for your financial security. From here on, you are responsible for any additional planning.

If your employer does not have a pension plan, you might consider setting up your own plan, which can have many tax and savings advantages. The Individual Retirement Account (IRA) has been established for those who are gainfully employed but, for whatever reason, are not eligible for any other type of retirement plan. Your contribution to such an account is not taxable, nor is the interest or dividends earned. If your spouse is not gainfully employed, both of you can have individual accounts within the limit of the wage earner's salary.

Those who are self-employed or who are members of a partnership are eligible to participate in the Keogh Plan (also called the HR 10 Retirement Plan). Once such a plan is set up, any workers the self-employed person or partnership hires must be included in the plan.

Employees of a public school system or a non-profit organization are eligible to enroll in a tax-sheltered annuity in accordance with Regulation 403(b) of the Internal Revenue Code of 1954.

These employees may participate in qualified plans offered by insurance companies or in properly established trusts such as mutual funds administered by investment companies. The employer deducts the contribution from an employee's salary and forwards it to the insurance company or designated trust, as in other salary deduction plans. The deduction is not shown on the W-2 form submitted to the IRS for income tax purposes. Payments toward non–tax-sheltered plans, in contrast, *do* appear on the W-2 forms, since the entire earned salary is shown, regardless of what part of it was deducted for a retirement plan. In the case of tax-sheltered annuities, the deduction is not considered taxable when it is earned, but it is taxable as ordinary income when it is finally paid out. As these payments are usually received at a time when taxable income is reduced, the tax advantages of tax-sheltered plans are considerable.

INSURANCE

The purpose of insurance is to cover medical expenses and to meet financial obligations when the policy holder—either through disability or death—cannot. You may be insured against sickness or accident, or you may have life insurance. How much insurance should you have? The benefits should be enough to pay normal living expenses; ideally, enough to support the entire family in the same manner you would if you were not disabled or dead. In the case of disability, Social Security payments can only begin if the disability is potentially a lifetime one.

In the case of death, the benefits of an insurance policy should be sufficient to continue to provide food, clothing, and housing for the family and to assure education for dependent children. There should be enough to support a surviving, non-working spouse, at least until he or she is eligible for Social Security benefits. As a rough guide, death benefits from an insurance policy should be about five to seven times the family's annual income. As income and financial responsibility increase, you should buy additional insurance to adjust death benefits accordingly. On the other hand, as you grow older you may wish to withdraw the cash value of your policies, as you no longer need the family protection you once did.

THE FIRST STEP TOWARD FINANCIAL
SECURITY: SAVINGS

The first thing most people do when planning financial security is to open a savings account with a bank or credit union. Saving systematically is a good habit to acquire and all wage earners should put aside whatever they can from the top of their paychecks before making any expenditures. A definite sum, no matter how small, should be set aside to accumulate for a time when you need it. You should not consider making any investments until you have established some savings. How much is enough? It depends on your own sense of financial security. Many consider a sum equivalent to from three to six months salary sufficient. If you earn $800 a month, for example, between $2,400 and $4,800 in savings will put you in a good position to consider other investments.

THE NEXT STEP: OWNING
YOUR OWN HOME

Once you have reached a stage in life where you have enough income to provide for you and your family, you have some insurance, and you have accumulated some extra money, you are ready to plan for the future by looking at other investment opportunities.

After a savings account, retirement plan, and insurance, the most common next step in planning financial security is to consider the purchase of real estate in the form of a house or apartment. Because its primary purpose is to provide suitable housing, such a purchase is not strictly an investment for income purposes only, but as its value may appreciate (especially in an inflationary period) it may, in the long run, turn out to be a good investment. Whether the property appreciates in value or not, you are building equity against which you can borrow money if you need to. If it does nothing else, purchase of living quarters provides you with a roof over your head. I'll say more about buying and selling real estate later on.

ON THE THRESHOLD OF INVESTING:
STOCKS, BONDS, AND TAX SHELTERS

Let us assume that you have finally "arrived." Your income tax bracket is 30 percent or higher, and you have extra money to invest. You are on the mailing list of financial advisors and "get rich quick" promoters. You are tempted by high-return investments, and the come-ons are hard to resist. How do you evaluate them? What should you look for?

Of course you will want the highest return at an affordable risk, and the highest appreciation on whatever investment you choose. The highest return will enable you to accumulate savings for retirement at the fastest rate, or allow you to enjoy the advantages of an increased income now. The affordable risk should be within the limits you and your family can absorb if the investment turns out to be a partial or even total loss. Your investment should appreciate in value, preferably faster than the current inflation rate. The appreciation will accumulate, tax-free, as long as the investment is not disposed of.

Stocks and Bonds

When you buy a stock, you are buying a share of a corporation—a fractional ownership of a business venture. You are participating in the growth of the company and you receive a portion of its profits in the form of dividends. Of course, companies face risk and there might not be any dividends from the investment. Over 40,000 business ventures currently issue stock and offer you the opportunity to participate. Some companies also issue bonds. State, local, and municipal governments may also issue bonds. While stocks represent fractional ownership, bonds are obligations to pay you the face value at maturity as well as a fixed interest to that time. There is no fixed value for a stock and no fixed rate of dividend payment.

Interest and dividends from stocks and bonds are taxable when received, except that interest from state, local, and municipal bonds are free from federal tax. I will have more to say about stocks, bonds, and other kinds of investments later on. For now, you should note that all investments have certain hoped-for characteristics which you can use to increase the rate at which your assets accumulate.

The increased value of any investment, whether stocks, bonds, real estate, or whatever, is taxable only when the gain is realized. This is what is meant by "capital gain." If the investment is held for more than a year, 40% of the gain (that is, increase in value) is taxable. This means that 60% of the increase in value is tax-free.

Tax Shelters

Taxes, as necessary as they are to pay for the costs of government, put some restrictions on your accumulation of assets. But under some circumstances which are entirely legal, you can defer paying taxes to a later time when you are likely to be in a lower tax bracket. If you are in a high tax bracket, there are shelters that exempt the base investment, but with a higher risk, defer the income tax liability. For instance, when you invest in an insurance policy or annuity, the increase in the cash value is taxable only when received—that is, when it is paid out by the insurance company. Your assets are accumulating, but you are not paying taxes on the increase until you actually receive the benefits.

Gas and oil drilling ventures are another example of legal tax shelters. The actual cost of drilling and developing a well is tax deductible within the year in which the expenditure is made and the amount of this expense can be deducted from your gross income. If a well is successful, the income from it, less the depletion allowance, is taxable. The depletion allowance is a tax deduction permitted as compensation for the reduction of the gas or oil reservoir.

Other tax shelters take advantage of accelerated depreciation and/or borrowing. Examples are real estate, equipment leasing, and cattle feeding and breeding. There are still others which I will talk about later. In these cases, depreciation, interest payments on land, and management, development, and marketing costs may create a tax deduction of as much as 400% over the time of the investment. By assuming risks investors can make a great deal of money simply through the tax savings. For this reason, most states impose "suitability" requirements which must be met before you can participate in such investments. Tax shelters of these kinds are not for the uninitiated. A great deal of careful research is necessary and a lot of "know how" is necessary before considering investing in them.

Another kind of investment is the appreciation-oriented one, and a good example is investment in raw land. The owner receives no income from the undeveloped real estate yet has to pay taxes on it. The taxes are deductible, of course. When the land is sold or developed, hopefully at a higher value than the original purchase price, the increase is taxable as a long-term gain.

You will find a graphic representation of financial goals leading to retirement on page 22. In Chapter 3, on page 32, you will find the other half of this map. If you lay the two maps end to end, you can chart a course for successful, long-range financial planning. But like any map, this one has to be interpreted. You must know where you are and where you are going. You may encounter detours and roadblocks. If you get lost, you must ask for directions.

There are strategies for using basic investment principles to avoid delays in reaching your goals. Mutual funds, for instance, offer the means to combine your financial resources with those of others and let professional money managers do the investing. In limited partnerships, experts will use your monetary resources to increase your worth and (tax) shelter your investment. I will have more to say about all these investment options.

Whatever the route you take, remember: The risk is in direct proportion to the return; and every investment takes time to mature.

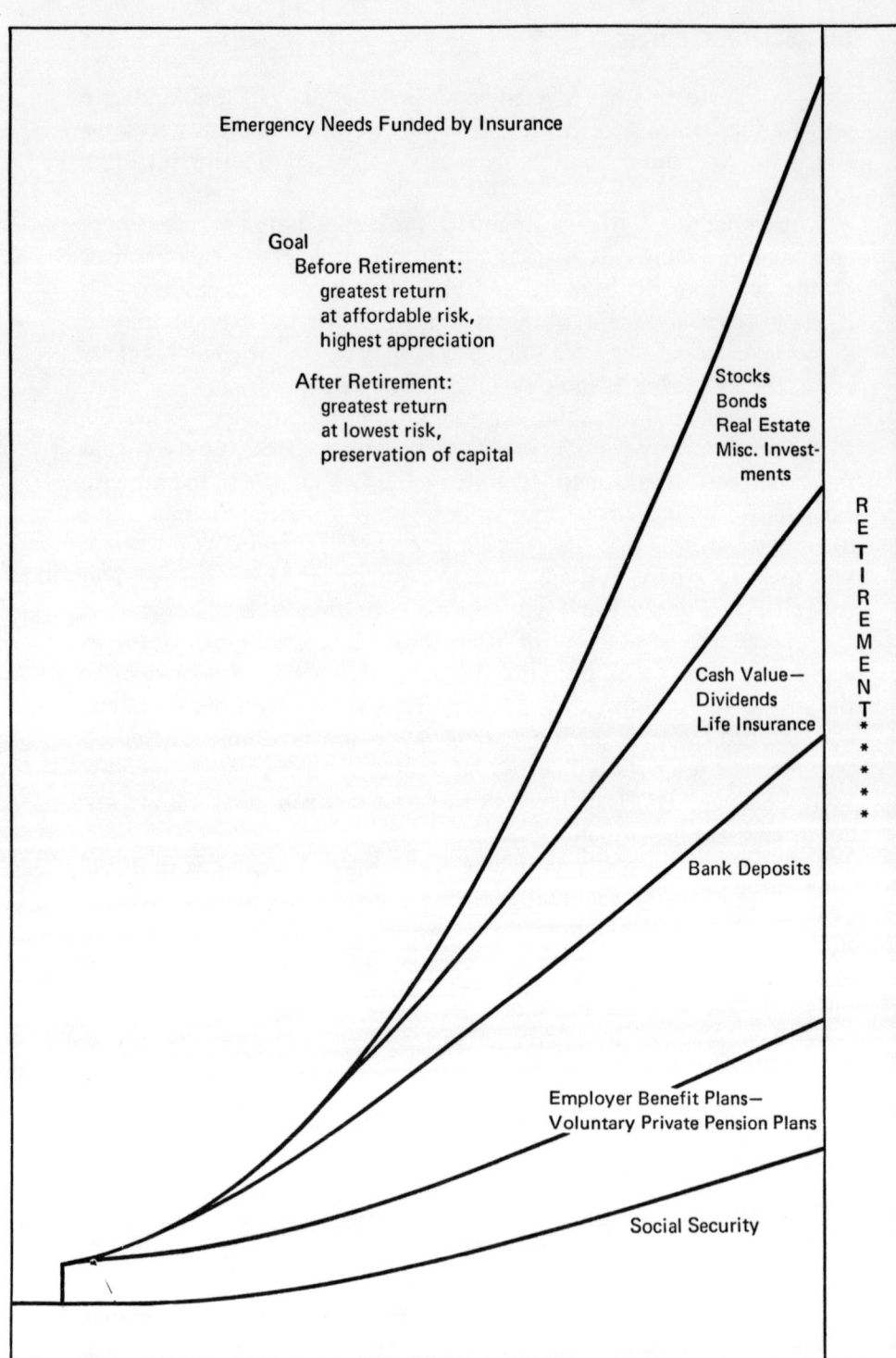

Lifetime Investment Chart (Part I)

3

THE RETIREMENT BENEFIT PERIOD

What to Use for Income • *What Are You Worth?* • *The Cost of Living after Retirement*

As there is a period of accumulation of assets in your life, so there is (or should be) a period when the benefits of a lifetime of accumulation are yours to enjoy. Benefits from investments at retirement will depend upon the accumulation period that preceded it. The main objectives during the accumulation period are to amass enough funds to guarantee a comfortable retirement. At retirement, the objectives change and the emphasis shifts from accumulating to enjoying the fruits of many years of labor. Your major concerns will be to do what you want to do where you want to do it, safeguard your health, and perhaps leave something behind for your heirs. Unfortunately, very few retirees have saved enough to enable them to live in their accustomed manner, even with the help of Social Security and a pension, much less provide for a carefree old age or build an estate.

WHAT TO USE FOR INCOME

From its beginnings, national Social Security was intended to be a supplemental income at retirement, but a lengthened life-

23

span and inflation have eroded Social Security's ability to do what it was meant to do. Social Security, however, may represent the greater part of many a retiree's income. Social Security income is tax-free, but other pension income is taxable as it is received. As your tax bracket after retirement is likely to be lower than it was before, it may be to your advantage to convert your assets into investments that can provide greater income. As a retiree, you are not looking for growth investments; you are looking for income.

Your goal should be to select the investment that will provide the highest return at the lowest possible risk and still preserve your principal. In the accumulation period, you could afford to take some risk in the hope of long-term gain, but at retirement, the time to derive benefit from a wise investment is at hand. Income tax is no longer the burden it was before age 65 and, as a senior citizen, you are entitled to certain tax advantages, such as two personal tax deductions—one as a standard personal exemption and one because you are over 65 years of age. Certain other state and local government benefits also apply to senior citizens such as real estate tax breaks or reduced public transportation fares. As conditions vary depending upon the locality, retirees should investigate these for themselves.

The cash value of life insurance or fixed and variable annuity policies can be turned into lifetime income. Policies offer enough settlement options that policyholders can choose the one best suited for their particular needs. Once an option is selected, however, it cannot be changed. (See Chapter 16 for further information on insurance and insurance options.) Before any of these options is exercised, enough life insurance coverage should be left in force on a paid-up basis in order to pay any last expenses and any estate taxes due after the death of the policyholder. Any permanent insurance policy can be endorsed as paid-up at a reduced death benefit without having to make any more premium payments. As your goal at retirement is maximum income, reduced death benefits are not the same cause for concern they were when your dependents needed protection. You may need the premium payments more for living expenses than you did for buying protection. Only 28% of all life insurance policies currently are terminated because of death, which means that 72% of terminated policies are used to provide retirement income or cash for other purposes. There is such a close connection between converting an insurance policy to income that

that may account for the fact that most pension plans are funded by life insurance companies.

It may also be to your advantage to sell your real estate after retirement since the tax on the capital gain is no longer a deterrent to selling. If you had sold your real estate before you were of retirement age, you would not have the lower tax bracket and tax-deferred benefits you are entitled to at age 65. The money thus realized from the sale of real estate can be put to better use as a source of income after retirement. On the other hand, a real estate investment in the form of a owner-occupied home can provide income in the form of a reverse annuity (see Chapter 19).

Mutual funds are another source of retirement income. Shareholders of the fund can receive fixed, periodic payments. The payments should, of course, be no greater than the return from the fund. If the withdrawals exceed the dividends and capital gain returns, in time the principal will be used up. Throughout this book, I have stressed that fact that the principal should remain intact. For more on mutual funds, see Chapter 12.

If you have been able to set aside enough money during your accumulation period to invest in stocks and/or bonds, or if you have built up a sizeable account at a bank or credit union, the return from these investments will also add to retirement income and will not be subject to as much tax as they were in your working years.

How you build up assets to use at retirement is your own decision; how you use them up is also up to you. There is a time to sow and a time to reap and, in the coming chapters, I will try to provide you with the information you need to let you make up your own mind as to what to sow, how to sow it, and what you can expect to harvest from your efforts.

WHAT ARE YOU WORTH?

Anything of worth has both an intrinsic value, which does not depend upon any outside forces, and an extrinsic value which depends on time, place, and circumstances. A drink of water is of inestimable value to someone dying of thirst, but is worthless to someone who is drowning. The value of a diamond depends upon the size and purity of the stone and the scarcity of diamonds. The intrinsic value of a diamond is nothing at all. It is only carbon that has been subjected to high pressure for a very long time. The extrinsic value is the value people put on it. Food, on the other hand, has an intrinsic value as we could not exist without it. Our homes have intrinsic value, no matter what the real estate market is, simply because they provide us with warmth and shelter from the elements.

The value of real estate is what at any given time the buyer and seller agree upon. If the property is a house, the selling price may be considerably more than the original cost of building it, or (as has happened when a house was built to suit the idiosyncrasies of the original owner) may even sell for less than the original cost. If the property is land, its worth depends upon the use to which it will be put: to graze cattle, for example, or to build a high-rise apartment building. Land under a high-rise building is worth more per square foot than land under a single-family home. Land with water and minerals on it is worth more than land without.

The value of stocks also fluctuates. The price per share offered by one company when it is trying to purchase another may be higher than what the stock is selling for on the open market. The price offered is often the book value of each share rather than the market value. The book value represents the tangible assets of the company divided by the number of shares owned by shareholders, whereas the market value is the amount a buyer is willing to pay and the seller is willing to accept. The book value is often more than the market value, which points up the fact that the value of an item depends upon the buyer's desire to have it.

The same principle applies to just about anything—the value of any commodity is largely determined by what it means to the buyer and the seller. For investors, the use that an investment can be put to should determine the value. A chance to buy a yacht at a fantastically low price is of no use to you if you hate the water—*unless* you can quickly resell it for more than you paid for it.

How to Figure Your Worth

To your employer, your worth is measured by what you can do for him. To your family, your worth is beyond price. Here is a way to think about your financial value to your family. A family that lives on a $21,000 yearly income would need to have $300,000 invested at 7% to realize that same amount annually. You are worth more than you think!

CURRENT ASSETS

Name:

Date:

Home

    Market Value $ _____

    Morgtage Balance $ _____

                               Net Equity Value $ _____

Insurance   Death Benefits   Cash Value

_____ Co. $ _____ $ _____

_____ Co. $ _____ $ _____

_____ Co. $ _____ $ _____

Minus Loans   − $ _____   − $ _____

Total   Net $ _____   Net $ _____

                             Total Cash Value $ _____

Automobiles

    1. Current Value $ _____

       Minus loan balance $ _____

                   Net Market Value $ _____

    2. Current Value $ _____

       Minus loan balance $ _____

                   Net Market Value $ _____

                        Total Market Value $ _____

Savings Accumulation in Banks $ _____

Market Value of Stocks and Bonds $ _____

Market Value of Business Interests $ _____

Market Value of All Other Items Convertible into Cash* $ _____

                      Total of All Assets $ _____

                      Minus Debts $ _____

                      Net Asset Value $ _____

*Furniture, jewelry, silverware, furs, etc.

Before starting out on an investment program, you should have a good picture of your present financial status. The chart on page 27 will help you draw up a financial picture of your present worth. Charting of your assets should be done periodically so you can see how successfully you are keeping up with expenses. The key is that it is not necessarily what you own, but what you do with what you own that determines your worth. You should chart your present indebtedness as well as your assets. You can only draw up an accurate financial picture if you first subtract liabilities from your assets. While they may seem monumental, your debts are probably much less than your total worth. If, however, your debts exceed your resources to pay them, you are in trouble.

THE COST OF LIVING
AFTER RETIREMENT

Will I be able to support myself after I stop working? This is often on the minds of people nearing retirement. Leaving a job with its steady paycheck causes many people anxiety as most people's income will be reduced after retirement. Given the uncertainty of the day-to-day cost of living and soaring inflation, how can anyone project what it will cost to live after retirement?

Social Security has incorporated a cost-of-living provision which increases payments according to increases in the cost-of-living index. A few—very few—corporate pension plans have arrangements to upgrade payments to retirees according to the rate of inflation. Perhaps your own private savings accumulation is sufficient to allow for inflationary increases and to keep even with them. As difficult as it is to predict future income, predicting expenses is even harder.

Tables 3-1 and 3-2 offer a method for estimating current and future expenses. Both use percentages because dollar amounts will vary from person to person. These tables are based on income ranges, however, so that you can find the group appropriate to your income. The income figures were calculated by the U.S. Department of Labor, Bureau of Labor Relations, for an urban family of four at three budget levels, and were based on statistics available for the fall of 1978. By establishing your own budget and selecting the figure closest in the tables to it, you can compare your own spending with that of the average U.S. urban household.

Table 3-1

A Spending Break-down of Annual Budgets for a
Four-person Family at Three Levels of Income,
Urban United States, Autumn 1978.

Components	Lower Budget	Your Own	Intermed. Budget	Your Own	Higher Budget	Your Own
Total Budget	$11,546	$	$18,622	$	$27,420	$
Food: at home and away from home, entertaining	30.95%	$	24.75%	$	21.17%	$
Housing	19.34%	$	22.46%	$	23.14%	$
Transportation	7.41%	$	8.44%	$	7.45%	$
Clothing	7.33%	$	6.5%	$	6.5%	$
Personal care	2.6%	$	2.16%	$	2.1%	$
Medical care (out-of-pocket)	9.22%	$	5.75%	$	4.05%	$
Other consumption: recreation, education, etc.	4.46%	$	5.13%	$	5.75%	$
Other: gifts, contributions, occupational expenses	4.35%	$	4.35%	$	5 %	$
Social Security and disability	6.23%	$	5.76%	$	3.98%	$
Personal income tax	8.10%	$	14.70%	$	21 %	$

The percentages have been computed from figures issued by the U.S. Dept. of Labor, Bureau of Labor Statistics, April 1979. Because of inflation the budget amounts will change, but the percentage break-down should remain approximately constant.

Table 3-2

A Spending Break-down of Annual Budgets for
Retired Couples at Three Levels of Income,
Urban United States, Autumn 1978.

Components	Lower Budget	Your Own	Intermed. Budget	Your Own	Higher Budget	Your Own
Total Budget	$5,514	$	$7,846	$	$11,596	$
Food: at home and away from home, entertaining	31.3%	$	31 %	$	27 %	$
Housing	33.2%	$	36 %	$	38.6%	$
Transportation	6.5%	$	10 %	$	12 %	$
Clothing	4 %	$	5 %	$	5.3%	$
Personal care	3 %	$	3 %	$	3 %	$
Medical care (out-of-pocket)	9.2%	$	10.5%	$	7.2%	$
Other consumption: recreation, repairs, replacements	4 %	$	5 %	$	6.7%	$
Misc. gifts, contributions	4.3%	$	6 %	$	7.5%	$

The percentages have been computed from figures issued by the U.S. Dept. of Labor, Bureau of Labor Statistics, August 1979. Because of inflation the budget amounts will change, but the percentage break-down should remain approximately constant.

By calculating the money available to you after retirement and using Table 3–2, you can find out what the average retired couple spends at the three budget levels. It can be assumed that a couple with an income greater than the highest budget can alter the percentages as they like.

You cannot make comparisons until you know your own budget figures. It is surprising how many people do not know what income bracket they are in or know how much they spend a year to heat their homes. (To determine your tax bracket, divide the total income tax you paid last year by the gross income you earned.) They spend their money for what they need and want until the money runs out, then they either stop spending or go into debt. Although it may seem like a lot of trouble, it is well worth the time spent to keep track of expenditures for one year. This does not necessarily mean recording every penny spent, but major categories such as housing, utilities, medical expenses, transportation costs, and taxes do not demand much in the way of record-keeping effort. You should have some idea of where the major part of your income goes. Once you get in the habit of being systematic and orderly about keeping track of your money, it will not be the chore you think it is. By recording what you have already spent, you can adjust future expenditures so that you can establish a savings program that will enable you to retire gracefully, or to invest in order to obtain extra income.

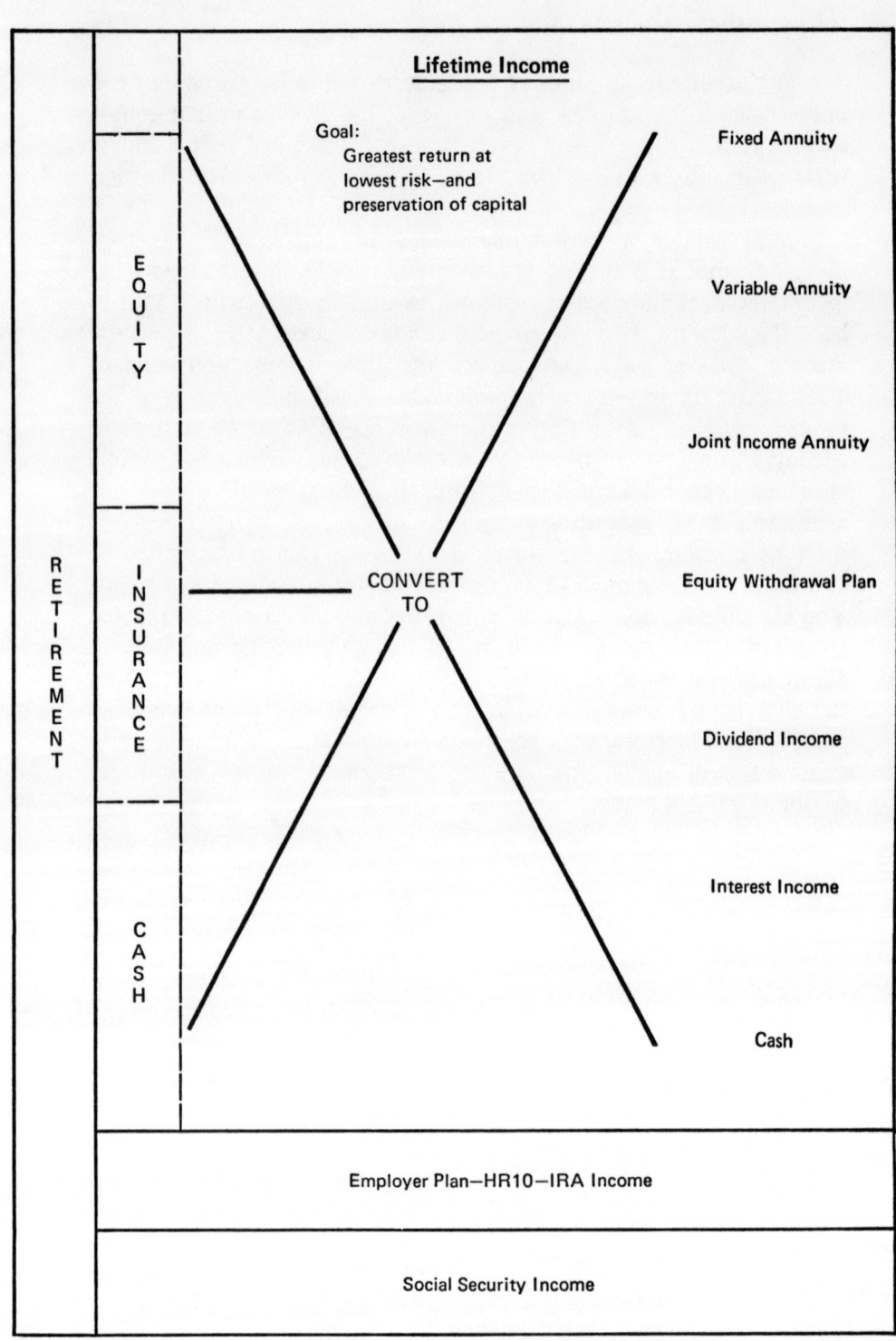

Lifetime Investment Chart (Part II)

4

ON BEING A SENIOR CITIZEN

How to Cope with Retirement ● *What to Do after Retirement* ●
Where to Live ● *How to Finance Your Retirement*

HOW TO COPE WITH RETIREMENT

Retirement can be a traumatic experience or it can be a reward-ing event, and books have been written on the subject of how to cope with it. It is not the purpose of this book to study exhaustively the coping mechanisms of retirees, but let me just say a few words about coping with retirement.

Having seen a member of your family or a friend go through the experience is not the same as living it yourself. As you get closer to retirement, you may have trouble accepting the fact that you have no job to go to. Belonging to a job-related group is satisfying and being severed from such a group can be painful.

The best way to cope with retirement is to be prepared. By being prepared, I mean seriously planning for it and coming to terms with the idea of no longer having a job to go to. One of the best ways to begin preparation is to enroll in pre-retirement programs offered by local groups, schools, or perhaps your place of business. The time to do this has to be decided upon by you yourself, but do not wait until the eve of retirement. Being prepared means gathering all the information, help, and advice you can. An ignorant person is an unprepared one.

WHAT TO DO AFTER RETIREMENT

People whose whole lives have revolved around their jobs suddenly find themselves with little or nothing to do at retirement. Visiting relatives, taking little trips, puttering about a house, going fishing, or playing cards all day sounds wonderful when you are working and have little leisure time. When you no longer have a job to go to, you will suddenly have more time than you know what to do with. Volunteering your time and effort is emotionally satisfying to some, while others cannot conceive of working for no pay. Getting another job, even a part-time one, can present some income tax problems. Be prepared by planning on how you are going to use your free time after you retire. Loafing may appeal to you now, but prolonged loafing can be boring. Retirement is the time to take up the interest you never had time for before. Be prepared by knowing what you want to do—and do it.

So far, I have concentrated on the problems that all retirees must face, but some benfits go along with a senior citizen status. You can wake up anytime you like and go to sleep anytime you want. You can fish all day and play cards all night, if you want. Besides the obvious benefits of filling your time as you choose, there are other advantages of being a senior citizen. Many educational institutions charge no fee or only a nominal fee for their courses. Many theaters give special discounts for golden-agers during certain hours.

Every area of the country has free recreational facilities, museums, libraries, parks, historical landmarks, and other points of interest. Retirees can take advantage of all of these as they might not have been able to do before. If, through careful planning prior to retirement, you also have some money to spend, your sunset years can be truly golden.

WHERE TO LIVE

At retirement, you may want to make a decision about moving to another locality. Whatever you decide, do so with caution. If you move, do not do so simply to get away from where you are, but to be somewhere else. If your present home is too big or too expensive to maintain on a reduced income, or if it keeps you from doing the traveling you have always wanted to do, by all means make the necessary changes to improve your new lifestyle. But first establish what your new lifestyle will be. You may decide to rent an apartment or buy a condominium, but remember that by doing so, you may reduce your worries and living space without reducing your expenses. Your apartment rent costs may go up or the building may go cooperative and you will either be asked to buy or move. Buying a condominium is not rent-free living. You have to pay monthly maintenance charges and possibly other fees. Only careful figuring will help you decide whether staying in the old homestead may not be the most economical choice of shelter for you after retirement.

Moving away from an area in which you have spent most of your life has certain disadvantages. You leave behind friends and neighbors, familiar stores, medical facilities and personnel, and you lose a sense of belonging. True, the old climate may be cold and snowy, but warmer climes may be hot and dry, or uncomfortably humid. The best thing to do is to consider renting your present home and paying a lengthy visit to the place you think you might like to retire to. Spend as much time as you need to get acquainted with the new area. The income from renting your home may be sufficient to finance such a visit. If the new area meets your expectations, you can then consider selling your home. If the new locality is disappointing, you still have your home to go back to.

An important factor in making any kind of move is the quality and accessibility of medical care. As you get older, medical facilities loom large in your life. Moving to that little farm or small town which was the dream of your life may not be practical if it means you will be isolated from hospitals, clinics, and services. Many prescription centers offer reduced rates. Medicare and Medicaid will defray some medical expenses. Federal and local agencies offer a variety of services. Most county governments have a clearinghouse for information on senior citizen services available through the county or state. Some employment agencies will find part-time or even full-time jobs for retirees.

HOW TO FINANCE YOUR RETIREMENT

Social Security, remember, was intended to serve as a supplement to retirement income. By itself, it is insufficient to support retirees and their spouses. Even if you have a retirement pension in addition to Social Security, the income from both may not be enough for you to cover your living expenses and still maintain a comfortable lifestyle, no matter how modest that may be. Unfortunately, the moment of retirement is too late to do much about this.

With your projected Social Security income and your private pension income balanced against your budget estimates (Tables 3–1 and 3–2), it is possible to select the investment return needed to make your retirement comfortable and carefree. If you are some years away from retirement, you have time to allow investments to mature. If you are close to retirement, you should review your investment portfolio to see if any changes need to be made in the light of your changed status. Study the risk, return, and liquidity sections of each of the following chapters. Taking into consideration the money you need, the amount you have saved, and the risk you can afford, you should be able to select the investments that will give you the return you want.

You save all your life for a rainy day—
if it doesn't rain, you are stuck with all that money.

Section Two

ALL THE PARTS THAT MAKE INVESTMENTS WORK

5

A LITTLE ARITHMETIC[*]

Some Investment Alternatives: Savings Accounts, Annuities, Corporate Bonds, and Stocks • *Retirement Investment*

Everyone should save systematically and invest wisely. Putting aside a part of your earnings as a matter of course requires self-discipline; investing wisely requires a bit of know-how. Once you have begun a savings program and gathered some information, you must do some simple figuring to help you decide how much to invest and which investment opportunities to choose. In this chapter I will compare the return on four types of investments to what the same amount of money deposited in a bank would have earned.

Before comparing investment returns, I should say something about how interest on money is figured. Interest can be simple or compounded. Simple interest is paid only once, at the end of the transaction, and is computed by multiplying the principal by the percent of interest by the time period. It is customary for lending institutions to use a 360-day year for figuring interest on periods of less than one year. Compound interest is interest paid on interest. Compounding can be done daily, quarterly, semiannually, or annually. If interest on your savings account is compounded daily, for example, interest will be credited to your account each day, and

*Interest rates used in this chapter are merely representative. The yields given are not necessarily current or anticipated values, which in reality change constantly. The tax bracket of 32% was selected arbitrarily.

this interest will start earning interest the next day. Quarterly, semi-annual, and annual compounding is credited four times a year, twice a year, or once a year, respectively, and begins to earn interest with the following period.

The purpose of investing is to make your money work for you. The return on the investment can be consumed (used up, spent, enjoyed) or can be reinvested. If you reinvest the return, the benefits are compounded while the principal remains intact.

SOME INVESTMENT ALTERNATIVES

Every potential investor should take pencil and paper (or calculator) in hand to translate investment opportunities into actual figures. Let's begin by making some computations. Assume that you have $10,000 to invest for a period of ten years and are in the 32% tax bracket. Let's compare your investment opportunities with the simplest method of making your money work for you—depositing it in a savings bank.

Savings Accounts

If you deposit $10,000 in a bank paying 5% interest, your deposit will earn $500 annually. You will have to pay $160 income tax ($500 X 32%) and your net income will be $340. At the end of one year, your investment value is $10,340 and at the end of ten years, $13,400. At 7%, after taxes of $224, your investment for one year will be worth $10,476 and $14,760 after ten years. Each year, the bank sends you a statement informing you of the amount of interest earned by your deposit for that year. (This is considered ordinary income and must be declared when figuring income tax, whether you withdraw it or not.)

Let us see what happens if you do not withdraw the interest each year but let it compound. The following table shows what your deposit will be worth at the end of ten years, after taxes.

$10,000 for 10 years	compounded	at 5%	at 7%
	daily	$14,049	$16,096
	quarterly	14,029	16,051

semiannually	14,009	16,007
annually	13,907	15,920

You can see that by leaving the interest to compound annually over ten years, you can earn an additional $507, after taxes, at 5%, and $1,160 after taxes at 7%.

Annuities

An annuity is a contract to pay out or receive certain sums at a fixed rate. An annuitant (the person receiving the benefits) purchases or is given an annuity in order to receive periodic income. What if, instead of depositing the $10,000 in a savings account, you used it to purchase an annuity? The annuity has the advantage of deferring payment of taxes to a later date when your tax bracket may be lower. It has the further advantage that the original investment can be withdrawn without taxes being due, and the accumulation left on deposit to continue earning interest. This is a very good way to acquire assets just prior to retirement.

$10,000 annuity	compounded at 7% for ten years
daily	$20,136
quarterly	20,015
semiannually	19,987
annually	19,671

By comparing the return on an annuity with the same amount of money deposited in a bank for the same amount of time, you can see the difference in value.

Corporate Bonds

Suppose you are considering the purchase of a corporate bond and wish to compare its earnings to those of a bank or annuity. Let us assume that the bond has a face amount of $10,000 and a coupon yield of 8% and will mature in twenty years. (Coupon yield is the amount you should receive when you clip a coupon from the bond and redeem it.) To compare the return on this type of investment with the first two, assume that the bond will be sold after ten years of ownership, because we figured the earnings from a $10,000 bank deposit and the same amount in an annuity for that length of time. Remember that the income from corporate bonds is taxable as it is received and you are in the 32% income bracket. The annual coupon yield is $800, which, minus taxes, gives a net income of $544.

$10,000 corporate bond:	Income over a ten-year period	$ 5,440
	If sold at par (the same amount you paid for it)	10,000
	Total received at the end of ten years	$15,440

If the bond is sold at a time when the current interest rate is 6%:

Income over a ten-year period	$ 5,440
Sold at premium (more than you paid for it)	13,330
Total received at the end of ten years	$18,770

If the bond is sold at a time when the current interest rate is 10%:

Income over a ten-year period	$ 5,440
Sold at discount (less than you paid for it)	8,000
Total received at the end of ten years	$13,440

(Current interest rates as they pertain to bonds and further explanation of discount, premium, and par will be discussed more fully later in the book.) Assuming that the risk and liquidity of an investment of $10,000 in a bond are equal to those for any other form of investment, a corporate bond is an advantageous method

of assuring income. Taking into consideration the fluctuation of
the interest rate, a ten-year return on a bond investment can be as
low as that from a savings account, but may be considerably higher.
The same $10,000 invested in a municipal bond of equal quality
would produce lower income (municipal bonds, however, are tax-
exempt) but the annual income and sales proceeds at 32% tax
would be about the same as for a corporate bond. (See Chapter 8
for fuller explanations of the difference between municipal and
corporate bonds.)

The computations outlined above emphasize how important
it is to review a bond portfolio periodically, and to take the time
and trouble to make careful calculations and comparisons. Only
then will you know when you should hold on to your investment
until it matures and when you would be better off trading it in.
Wise investors will be prepared to buy and sell according to their
needs and the condition of the market.

Stocks

In the three comparisons above, the risk and liquidity were
about equal but the returns varied. In the case of stocks, the risk
is higher since neither the value of the stocks nor any dividends is
guaranteed. When the stock is to be sold, its value is the price quoted
on the open market at that time. Considering that neither principal
nor return is as safe as they are in the case of bank deposits, annuities, or corporate and municipal bonds, the total value should
be more than any alternate investment opportunity. Remember,
if the risk is greater, the return should be higher to compensate
for the increased risk.

How much should a $10,000 stock investment sell for? Let's
compare the return with that from a savings bank account—that
is, $13,400:

$10,000 stock	At the end of ten years (assuming that *no* dividends were paid)	should sell for $13,400
	At the end of ten years (assuming a 5% dividend had been paid annually)	should sell for $10,000

At the end of ten years   should sell
(assuming a 7% dividend   for $9,220
had been paid annually)

By comparing the return from the sale of stock to what you would have realized had you kept the same amount of money in a savings account, you can easily figure out whether your stock investment did what you wanted it to.

There is always the chance that the value of the stock would have risen, in which case the total earnings would be higher than those from the bank deposit. This is why investors speculate in stocks. There is always the possibility of appreciation, but you must remember that the long-term gain is taxable when the stock is traded. On the other hand, currently losses up to $3,000 each year are deductible and any excess can be carried over to the following year.

So far I have described investing $10,000 for ten years and paying a 32% income tax and have compared the returns the investment would make with four different investment opportunities. What I have not said is that, unless the $10,000 is an outright gift, one must first earn $14,707 and pay $4,707 in income tax (32%) on it in order to have $10,000 to invest.

RETIREMENT INVESTMENT

Remember that $10,000 represents $14,707 after taxes. To make the comparison equal to our other mathematical comparisons, let's see what would happen to $14,707 if it were deposited in a bank for ten years:

Compounded	at 5%	at 7%
daily	$24,246	$29,614
quarterly	24,172	29,437
semiannually	24,099	29,264
annually	23,956	28,931

The figures look better and better. What would happen if you were able to invest $10,000 *each year* in a qualified retirement plan? Remember that the compounded interest is not taxable until withdrawn. Let us assume that you leave it on deposit to work for you.

Then, $10,000 invested each year for ten years, tax-free, compounded annually, at the end of ten years will be:

$$\$132,070 \text{ at } 5\%$$
$$147,840 \text{ at } 7\%$$
$$156,450 \text{ at } 8\%$$
$$175,310 \text{ at } 10\%$$

It is now obvious by looking at these figures that the return of the after-tax dollar when compared to the return of the before-tax dollar prove that investment in a qualified retirement plan is the wisest, most financially advantageous way to make your money work for you.

Investments take time to mature. As a rule of thumb, one dollar invested at 1% will double in about 72 years. The same dollar invested at 2% will double in about 36 years, and invested at 7% will double in about ten years:

$$\frac{72}{\text{Interest rate}} = \text{Time to double (years)}$$

(This is often referred to as the Rule of 72.)

Which is the best investment for you? Only you can decide by taking into consideration your age, income level, family responsibilities, and how much risk you are willing to take. But you can make your decision easier if you take the time to make a few, simple mathematical comparisons.

Part **I**

DEBT INSTRUMENTS

Debt instruments are the mechanisms for lending or investing, and that is what we do when we deposit money in a bank or credit union, buy an insurance annuity, a corporate or municipal bond, or a certificate issued by the United States government. Investing means putting money into something for the purpose of realizing a profit and/or income. Lending means giving money for temporary use and earning interest on its use. For lending and investing, the expectations are that interest will be paid and the principal will be returned when due.

In Chapters 6 through 9, I will explain debt instruments—what they are, how they work, and what you can expect from them.

There is no investment with a high return and a low risk,
since the return is in direct proportion to the risk.

6

SAVINGS INVESTMENTS: SHORT AND LONG TERM

Banks • *Savings and Loan Associations* • *Credit Unions* • *U.S. Savings Bonds*

BANKS

The stock in trade of banking is money. Banks are used by their customers to store surplus money and to borrow extra money from the bank's reserve. When you deposit your surplus money in a bank, it earns interest and when you borrow money from a bank, you pay interest. The interest you pay for the use of borrowed money is always more than your own surplus money earns; the difference is one of the sources of the bank's income.

You will ordinarily have a choice of three different kinds of banks to choose from: commercial, savings and loan, and a credit union. All three operate similarly, but there are limitations on the kinds of services they can offer. Commercial banks have checking account facilities, for example, while savings and loan banks and credit unions do not.

Before going on to discuss the various banks, we should say something about checks. A check is nothing more than a piece of paper with your signature on it which serves as an order to a bank to pay the bearer the amount written on it. Writing a check is a convenient way of disbursing money, and the cancelled check provides you with a receipt of the transaction. Paying for goods and services by check also saves you the trouble and worry of keeping large amounts of cash on hand.

Accepting a check as payment is a matter of faith. The recipient assumes you have enough money in the bank to cover it and trusts in your ability to make it good if you are overdrawn. All three parties to the transaction—you (the check writer), your creditor, and the bank—have faith in the nation's monetary stability. You have faith that the bank will keep your money safely and return it to you when you want it.

Some firms, especially insurance companies, pay by draft, which is like a check except that the bank will not pay out the funds until the issuer gives final approval. For instance, if the issuer of the draft gives you a draft on his funds for a settlement, let's say, of an insurance policy, the bank will check with the company to make sure that the transaction is approved.

The use of checks increases the money supply without actually increasing the amount of money in circulation. A check may be used to pay for merchandise; it may change hands several times and settle several bills, but only when it is presented for payment at the bank is currency actually being used.

Until recently, money in checking accounts did not earn interest, but now, by shopping around, you can make arrangements for money in your checking account to earn interest.

SAVINGS AND LOAN ASSOCIATIONS

A savings and loan association is like a commercial bank in many ways except that there are legal limitations on its functions. A savings and loan institution may not offer check or draft service, and it may lend only for housing. As compensation for its inability to attract commercial accounts, it is allowed to pay a quarter more

50

interest on its deposits to attract savings accounts. In some states a savings and loan bank may pay your bills for you if you give them instructions by telephone. They may even have an arrangement with a commercial bank whereby the savings and loan depositor can issue checks on the commercial bank and the savings and loan bank will transfer sufficient funds to cover the payment. This arrangement creates, in effect, a checking account that earns interest. Future changes will remove many of the restrictions on savings and loan associations, enabling them to compete directly with commercial banks by giving similar services.

Compounding Interest

Banks pay interest on your deposits in different ways. Some compound daily, some quarterly, and some semiannually or annually. All call their method "continuous compounding," but you will have to find out for yourself exactly how your bank does it. Just ask.

Daily compounding credits interest to your account every day. Quarterly compounding is credited every three months, semiannual every six months, and annual once a year. All start earning interest beginning on the day money is credited to your account. The listing below shows the different interest earnings on $1,000 over one year:

daily	$1,051.11
quarterly	1,050.95
semiannually	1,050.63
annually	1,050.00

You can readily see that daily compounding can make a difference and, in large deposits, the difference can be considerable.

Currently, commercial banks pay 5-1/4% on ordinary bank accounts which have no withdrawal penalty, and savings and loan associations pay 5-1/2%.

Certificates of Deposit

Certificates of deposit were originally used to represent bank deposits between banks. Now, they represent deposits other than those that allow instant withdrawal without a penalty.

Certificates of deposit ranging from three months (the shortest length of time you can buy for) to ten years (the longest time you can buy for) are currently paying 5-1/4% for the short-term certificate to 7-1/2% for the long-term certificate. Again, savings and loan banks can pay a quarter of a percent more.

At present there is a 30-month certificate of deposit which allows savings and loan institutions to pay 1/2% less and commercial banks 3/4% less than the average interest rate of all U.S. Treasury securities. The Federal Reserve Bank establishes the rate at the end of each month. The various institutions set their own minimum deposit requirements. The current maximum annual rate is 12%.

The six-month "money market certificates" issued by commercial banks pay the same interest as 26-week treasury bills, and savings and loans are allowed to pay 1/4% above that. If, however, the interest on a 26-week treasury bill rises to 9% or more, both commercial banks and savings and loan institutions must pay the same. These certificates require a $10,000 minimum deposit.

Because certificates of deposit pay more interest than ordinary deposits, a penalty is imposed for early withdrawal. Those maturing within one year lose three months interest and certificates of deposit maturing after one year are charged a penalty of six-months loss of interest. Deposits of $100,000 or more are not subject to regulations. The withdrawal limit and the interest rate are negotiable.

The Federal Reserve Board regulates the interest rate that commercial banks may pay on their customers' accounts, and it also controls the rate charged to member banks to borrow from it. This latter is called the "discount rate." The rate banks charge their best customers—that is, the "prime rate"—is affected by how much banks have to pay for money they borrow from the Federal Reserve Bank. The Federal Home Loan Bank regulates savings and loan banks and sets the rates they may pay as interest on their customers' deposits.

CREDIT UNIONS

Thus far I have discussed only those banks that most people have access to, but there is another kind of bank that some people may turn to for borrowing money or for saving money. Credit unions were first established by groups of people linked by a common bond or association. Union members, for example, pooled their funds in order to lend them out to other members as needed at a lower interest rate than other lending institutions could offer. It is no longer necessary to belong to a trade union to form a credit union. Well-defined neighborhoods, communities, or rural districts can also establish credit unions. Although their prime function is to lend money to members, they also pay interest on members' deposits. The services of credit unions are now being expanded, and it is expected that many of their services will include those offered by other financial institutions. Credit unions are supervised by the National Credit Union Administration, an agency of the federal government.

UNITED STATES SAVINGS BONDS

When you buy a U.S. savings bond, you are lending money to the U.S. government. Member banks of the Federal Reserve System and the Federal Home Loan Bank may sell EE and HH series bonds which are commonly referred to as U.S. savings bonds. EE bonds are bought at a price (discount) that is less than their full value at maturity, eleven years. They pay 4-1/2% for the first five years and 6-1/2% for the remaining six years.* The bonds can be cashed in at any time, but if they are held for an additional ten years, the interest is paid on the maturity value. HH bonds are bought at par (that is, for the same price as the face value on the bond) pay interest semiannually, and also mature in eleven years. Most employers offer payroll deduction services to make the purchase of these bonds simple and to encourage systematic payroll savings.

EE and HH bonds are not negotiable—that is, they cannot be traded in a market or between individuals—they can only be cashed in.

To sum up, banking practices have developed to fulfill certain needs and to perform certain services. Banks earn an income by pay-

---

*To be competitive with other investment opportunities, the yield and maturity are subject to change. For current information, call your local bank or the nearest Federal Reserve Bank.

ing for the use of your money and by charging customers who need to borrow money. With prudent management and wise investments, banks can increase their income and contribute to the nation's economy. But how safe is your money?

What Is the Risk?

All deposits in institutions chartered by the federal agencies are insured up to $100,000 by either the Federal Deposit Insurance Corporation (FDIC), the Federal Savings and Loan Insurance Corporation (FSLIC), or the National Credit Union Administration (NCUA).

This federal government insurance protection has come about because of the banking crises that occurred during the Great Depression. Many banks collapsed, and many depositors lost their life savings. Up to that time, few controls regulated banking in the United States. Since then, however, the federal government and state governments supervise banking practices very closely. Putting your money in a bank is the least risky of all investments. Because it is relatively risk-free, the return is correspondingly lower.

What Is the Return?

The interest paid varies with each type of account and the amount deposited. The rate, however, is regulated by the Federal Reserve and Federal Home Loan systems, and can be from 5-1/2% up to the same rate paid by Treasury bills. Savings and loan institutions are allowed to pay 1/4% more than commercial banks for the same certificate of deposit of equal maturity and minimum deposit. Credit unions have their own limits on such deposits, which are usually higher.

What Is the Liquidity?

Ordinary deposit accounts have no restrictions on withdrawal, and any amount may be withdrawn at any time without penalty. Certificates of deposit with maturity up to and including one year, impose a penalty for early withdrawal by the loss of three months' interest. Early withdrawal of a certificate of deposit of over one year maturity has a penalty of six months' loss of interest. EE and HH bonds can be cashed in at any time, with no penalty.

What About Taxes?

All interest income received or credited to the account is considered ordinary income for the year in which it was earned. Taxes on the accumulated interest of EE and HH bonds are also ordinary income, and this income must be reported the same as any other ordinary income. Of course, it is taxable only when received.

EE bonds can be converted to HH bonds and the tax deferred on the accumulated interest to a time when the owner may be in a lower tax bracket, such as at retirement.

Can It be Used in Retirement Plans?

Bank deposits qualify for all retirement plans except 403(b). All financial institutions have prototype pension trusts set up which allow the use of their deposits. Banks also offer special U.S. retirement bonds which come only in large denominations and are bought by qualified retirement plans—not by individuals.

Can It be Used as Collateral?

All deposit accounts and certificates of deposit can be used as collateral for loans. A good way to do this is to use long-term certificates of deposit as collateral for a smaller loan for a shorter period. The "spread"—that is, the difference in the interest paid and the interest charged in such a transaction—may only be about 2 to 5%. EE and HH bonds may not be used as collateral.

Is It a Hedge Against Inflation?

Bank deposits and certificates of deposit offer no protection against the loss of purchasing power when the rate of inflation continues to climb.

Must It Go Through Probate?

Bank deposits and certificates of deposit are part of a deceased's estate and may have to be probated, depending upon the account designation. The same applies to EE and HH bonds.

Your Financial Security	Bank Credit Union	Insurance Annuity	Bonds Corp.	Bonds Muni.	Treasuries Commercial Paper	Stocks	Real Estate	Investment Companies Mutual Funds Trusts R.E.I.T.s	Options Futures Warrants
What is the risk?									
What is the return?									
What is the liquidity?									
What about the taxes?									
Retirement plans?									
Collateral?									
Inflation hedge?									
Probate?									

INSURANCE ANNUITIES
AS INVESTMENTS

Single Premium, Tax-Deferred Annuities • Periodic Payment, Tax-Deferred Annuities

---

Insurance is the means by which individuals who sustain financial loss through circumstances beyond their control can receive financial compensation. The benefits of insurance apply to countless situations and circumstances. With insurance, you can provide for your family's ongoing expenses should you die unexpectedly. You can assure yourself of an income should you become disabled and unable to work. You can get your auto repaired if it is in an accident; you can get your house repaired if it suffers damage; you can be recompensed if you are burglarized; and so on. But insurance can also be a savings plan or an investment. In this chapter I will consider insurance as an investment, leaving the subject of insurance for protection for Chapter 16.

Insurance companies play the laws of averages, and the percentages are in their favor. They are betting that nothing dire will happen to you, and you are buying protection because something might.

The law differentiates by the limit of protection offered between insurance used primarily as investment and insurance bought mainly for protection. If the death benefit exceeds each $10 of monthly income of a "ten-year certain settlement option" by a multiple of 100, it is assumed that the policy was bought for protection, and as such, has certain tax advantages that insurance bought as an investment does not.

As an investment, insurance in the form of an annuity policy offers investment provisions not available by any other plan. For instance:

- Any cash value accumulates, tax-free, until withdrawn.
- The original investment can be withdrawn, tax-free.
- A minimum interest rate (varying with the company) is guaranteed for the life of the policy.
- The cash value accumulation may not be attached by any creditor, even in the case of bankruptcy.
- In the event of the insured's death, the benefits are paid directly to the designated beneficiaries without going through probate, thus eliminating any red tape or unwanted publicity.
- The annuitant has various options as to when and in what way to receive the benefits.

In addition, policies contain a provision that allows the insurance company to pay "excess interest," that is, interest above the guaranteed rate if the company earns it. This provision favors the use of single premium, tax-deferred annuities, which are annuities bought with one lump sum. The interest earned by such annuities can make them very attractive, especially if there is the possibility of excess interest.

SINGLE PREMIUM,
TAX-DEFERRED ANNUITIES

An annuity is nothing more than a contract to pay (or receive) a sum of money. In the past, kings, great nobles, and rich merchants would "settle a sum" upon their dependents or favorites to be paid out of their revenues at fixed intervals. In our time, the annuitant (the one who will receive payment) can use the insurance advantages to accumulate tax-free assets and receive a fixed sum of money at a later time. The insurance company uses these contributions to invest in real estate, high quality debt instruments, and other ventures. It is a case of money making money.

Insurance companies can be competitive with other investment opportunities by offering investment annuities that pay currently high, tax-deferred returns. The rates vary, however, and are guaranteed for a limited time only. The limit can be from ninety days to one year, depending upon the insurance company and the prevailing economic conditions. The annuities are usually offered by security dealers who are also licensed to sell insurance. No two policies are exactly alike, and the wise investor should shop around for the best deal.

Some policies have a "front-end load," which means there is a charge every time a payment is made to the annuity, and some have a surrender charge. A surrender charge may apply to any amount withdrawn above a stipulated annual withdrawal—generally 6% of the face value. This charge may decrease on a sliding scale over a certain period after the effective date down to 0%. In addition to a front-end load or surrender charges, there may also be a management fee. When comparing policies, ask about all the extra charges.

Since each plan has its advantages and disadvantages, the purpose of investing in insurance should be carefully thought out and the age and obligations of the investor should be the major consideration.

Single premium, tax-deferred annuities offer a safe way to accumulate savings, particularly as the original investment can be withdrawn without having to pay tax on it again. Remember, the money was taxed before it was invested.

Here is an example of how this type of investment might work:

A person, aged 45, invests $10,000 at 7-1/2%	$10,000
At age 55, the investment will have grown to approximately	20,000
At age 60, he withdraws $10,000, pays no taxes, and still has left	18,400
At age 65, the balance will be	26,100

(See Appendix C: Compound Interest Tables, page 261)

Some insurance companies offer a "variable annuity," which means that the accumulation is not guaranteed. In these annuities, the insurance company invests in high yielding securities or debt instruments but, as there is no way of guaranteeing the return, the variability of such annuities is a risk that the annuitant shares.

Very few single premium annuity policies allow additional contributions once the policy has gone into effect.

PERIODIC PAYMENT,
TAX-DEFERRED ANNUITIES

These policies are just like those described above except that they allow for money to be added by the annuitant on a periodic basis. Their most popular use is in retirement plans, especially 403(b) (see Chapter 14). Some of these policies offer a limited death benefit. When they are paid out, they are taxable as ordinary income. The economic value of the insurance protection is computed by the issuing company based on IRS "PS 58" (see Appendix B) rates of "one year pure insurance protection." PS 58 has been around a long time. Ask your insurance agent to describe it in detail.

What Is the Risk?

Deposits with an insurance company are very secure. The investment practices of insurance companies are closely regulated, and individual state investment rules and regulations are rigidly enforced. Rules and regulations, however, vary from state to state. Moreover, the insurance industry is itself very protective of its reputation and of policyholders' rights. Furthermore, insurance companies operate on the "prudent man" rule—which means that they invest funds entrusted to them as would a prudent person managing his own funds. "Prudent man" is a legal catch-all term which can be proved or disproved in court. Liabilities of any insurance company that finds itself in trouble are readily assumed by other insurance companies in order to protect the entire industry.

Insurance companies are rated by several rating services, of which A. M. Best is the most prominent. (See Chapter 20 for more on ratings and rating services.) A report of any company's activities is available from its agents for the asking. For more about insurance, see Chapter 16.

What Is the Return?

The return from a fixed annuity during the accumulation period varies with each insurance company. The payout during the income period can be between 7 and 10% of the accumulated amount annually. The exact payment varies with the option selected and the insurance company's guarantees. A fixed annuity will guarantee the payment to the annuitant for a fixed length of time—even for a lifetime. A variable annuity will not guarantee the amount the annuitant will receive, but it will guarantee payments according to the current accumulation value.

What Is the Liquidity?

The sum of money accumulated is available at any time to the insured according to the stipulations in the annuity policy. Once a settlement option (except an "interest only" option) is selected, however, liquidity is sacrificed. (See Settlement Options, Chapter 15.)

What About Taxes?

The IRS has a special formula for calculating the taxable portion of a lifetime income plan if the accumulation contains the original investment. The insurance company will make that information available upon request. If the original investment has been withdrawn, all subsequent payments are taxed when received. Remember that the original investment is not taxable again. If the accumulation is the result of a tax-sheltered plan, then all income derived from the plan is taxable when received, except for the value of the pure insurance cost which was taxed during the accumulation period.

Can It be Used in Retirement Plans?

Some annuities and retirement income plans where insurance protection is incidental to the plan, may be qualified to be used for IRA, HR 10 (Keogh) and 403(b) plans.

Can It be Used as Collateral?

Most banks and other financial institutions accept insurance policies as collateral for a loan if enough cash surrender equity has accumulated to cover the loan. All insurance policies and some annuities have a loan provision included in their policies with a specified interest rate indicated which permits the policyholder to borrow against it. Any plan used for a qualified retirement plan, however, may not be used as collateral for a loan, nor may the loan provision in the policy be exercised.

Is It a Hedge Against Inflation?

The return during the accumulation period, because of the "excess interest" provision, can be a hedge against inflation. Once periodic withdrawal has started, however, the payments do not change and during the period of inflation there will probably be a loss of purchasing power. Many people believe that the accumulation and return from variable annuities is a hedge against inflation, but as the returns are not guaranteed, it may not be.

Must It Go Through Probate?

Proceeds from an insurance policy do not have to be probated unless they are payable to the estate. If not payable to the estate, they will be disbursed directly to the beneficiaries upon presentation of the proper papers to the insurance company. The cash value of the insurance is considered part of the deceased's estate when the U.S. estate tax is calculated.

Your Financial Security	Bank Credit Union	Insurance Annuity	Bonds Corp.	Bonds Muni.	Treasuries Commercial Paper	Stocks	Real Estate	Investment Companies Mutual Funds Trusts R.E.I.T.s	Options Futures Warrants
What is the risk?									
What is the return?									
What is the liquidity?									
What about the taxes?									
Retirement plans?									
Collateral?									
Inflation hedge?									
Probate?									

CHAPTER

8

BONDS

Corporate Bonds • *Municipal Bonds*

CORPORATE BONDS

A bond is a written obligation to pay a financial debt within a designated period of time at a stated rate of interest. What you are doing when you buy a bond is lending money at an agreed-upon interest rate. Bonds differ from stocks in that bonds offer a guaranteed interest, whereas stocks do not. Stocks may pay dividends—or they may not. Therefore it is to the advantage of a corporation to issue new stock to raise money rather than to sell bonds. The advantage to the bondholder is that the face value of the bond and the fixed interest payment remain the same throughout the life of the bond, regardless of whether the stock market or current interest rates rise or fall.

The bond certificate specifies a maturity date which can be as long as thirty years, and in some cases is even longer. The interest is usually paid every six months. During the life of the bond, the bond and the interest payments represent a financial burden for the corporation as they are, in effect, loans that must be redeemed.

For this reason, most bonds have a "call date" and a "redemption value" written into them to give the corporation the option of paying off its debt if it finds itself with a financial surplus, has raised money by selling stocks, or can refinance the debt at a lower interest rate. The redemption value will be at "par" or "face value" of the bond plus a premium. The premium is a sort of penalty the corporation must pay to the bondholder for repaying the debt sooner than the bondholder expected. The premium may be up to 3% or higher depending upon the years remaining until maturity.

When you buy a bond, you buy an income at a fixed interest rate with repayment of face value at maturity. Putting it another way, you are buying an investment that will return to you a specified amount at a specified date and which will pay you a specified interest on your principal. The face value of the bond, the date of maturity, and the interest rate cannot change over the lifetime of the bond.

The primary reason for buying bonds is "yield," or return on the dollar invested. The percentage of yield (also called "coupon yield") is stated on the bond certificate and remains the same for the life of the bond. The investor buying a bond should know what the return will be. That amount is easily computed with the following formula:

$$\frac{\% \text{ yield} \times \text{Par}}{100} = \text{Return (\$) annually}$$

For example, a bond with a face or par value of $1,000 and a coupon yield of 9% will return $90 annually:

$$\frac{9 \times 1,000}{100} = 90$$

At any given time, due to various conditions affecting the economy, interest rates (that is, the cost of borrowing money) may change. The change in interest rates for borrowing money does not affect the interest *payment* of the bond because it is fixed and cannot change. But when you are buying or selling a bond, you must consider the current interest rate. Since bond interest payments remain the same, the market value of the bond will change in accordance with the current interest rate for borrowing money. The formula for computing the market value of a bond is as follows:

$$\frac{\text{Coupon yield} \times \text{Par}}{\text{Current yield (interest rate)}} = \text{Current market value}$$

A bond with a face value of $1,000 with a 9% annual yield will bring $1,125 when traded in a market at 8% yield:

$$\frac{9 \times 1000}{8} = \$1,125$$

When you buy a bond the corporation has borrowed money from you. At the time of issuing the bond, the cost of borrowed money was either high or low. At the time the market value of the bond needs to be calculated, the cost of borrowed money has changed, and this change must be taken into account to determine the current value of the bond. If the interest rate is higher than the coupon rate (interest payment rate written into the bond), the market value of the bond is lower than the face value. If your bond pays 8%, for example, and the current interest rate is 9%, no one will buy your bond because they can earn more by investing at the 9% rate. The value of your bond on the market is thus lower than its face value. On the other hand, if the current interest rate is lower than the coupon rate, the market value of your bond will be higher than the face value.

If at the time of trade the bond is sold at face value, the transaction is said to have been made "at par." If it is traded at more than face value, it is done "at premium," and if less than face value, "at discount."

Since the maturity value of a bond is the face amount, a bond bought at discount will result in a higher investment return if held until maturity, and the total yield or "yield to maturity" will be greater than the current yield.

To compute yield to maturity—that is, the yield you would have realized had you held the bond until it matured, and had business conditions remained the same—use the following formula:

Bond bought at *premium:*

$$\frac{\text{Premium (cost above par value)}}{\text{Number of years to maturity}} = \text{Annual premium cost}$$

The annual premium cost subtracted from the annual return is the annual return to maturity.

Bond bought at *discount:*

$$\frac{\text{Discount (difference between cost and par}}{\substack{\text{Number of years} \\ \text{to maturity}}} = \text{Annual discount difference}$$

The discount difference when added to the annual return is the annual return to maturity. To compute the yield to maturity:

$$\frac{\text{Current yield} \times \text{Market value}}{\text{Face value}}$$

This basic arithmetic can help investors in bonds determine the value of their bond portfolios and help them decide whether to trade or to hold until maturity. But the *final* figures are established by the bond market. These values are quoted daily and can be obtained from a stockbroker or from the financial pages of a newspaper.

When trading bonds, you must also take into account another value, called "accrued interest." Bond interest is payable daily, but in fact the interest is usually paid every six months. Because all corporate bonds are registered, the company knows who you, the investor, are and where you live and will automatically send you the money due you. No coupons are clipped as they are in the case of unregistered "bearer" bonds. (Bearer bonds will be discussed more fully in the section on municipal bonds.)

To get back to accrued interest—when trading a registered corporate bond, the holder of record or the owner of the bond on the specific date when interest is due to be paid will receive the interest earned for the past interest period. If the bond is traded before the interest is due, the previous owner is entitled to the interest accrued during the time of his ownership, and the new owner must pay the accrued interest to the previous owner up to the effective date of the sale.

There is another kind of corporate bond which is called "convertible." These bonds can be converted into common stocks at a designated time at a stated conversion rate, and these conversion options are specified on the bond certificate. The inducement to buy convertible bonds is that the conversion rate may be lower than the market price of the common stock at the time of conversion date, and this could mean a nice profit for the bondholder. For the corporation, such conversion means cancellation of the financial obligation represented by the bond. The bondholder has become a stockholder and, instead of being guaranteed return of his original investment, is now taking his chances on the stock market.

What Is the Risk?

A bond represents a debt for the issuing corporation. How secure is the debt? Obviously it can be only as good as the debtor's ability to pay the interest when due and the principal at maturity. There are rating services that analyze the financial position of companies and their ability to meet their obligations (see Chapter 19). It would seem that being owed a debt by a company that is well-managed, is in a stable industry, and has a successful past history represents a low risk. Although corporate bonds are not insured by quasi-governmental agencies as are bank deposits, corporate bonds are well worth the risk to obtain a higher interest. It must be pointed out that a bond issued by a company that is rated lower than "prime" will pay a correspondingly higher interest rate as the risk is greater. Remember, the return is in proportion to the risk.

What Is the Return?

The return should be higher than what a bank will pay, since your deposit in the bank is insured while your bond is not. The return will not change, and neither will the face value of the bond. If the bond is traded any time before maturity, the only change will be in the market value should the current interest rate change. The return can be easily computed. (See page 69.)

What Is the Liquidity?

Bonds are traded on the various exchanges. The higher the rating, the greater the demand for that bond. There is no delay in converting a bond into cash through qualified brokers. The proceeds are available within five business days from the trade date. Bonds underwritten by companies rated "average" or lower or that are in bankruptcy or Chapter 11 of the U.S. Bankruptcy Courts (see Chapter 21), are in demand for speculative purposes. These bonds are commonly referred to as "junk bonds." They are only for the sophisticated investor.

What About Taxes?

Interest income from corporate bonds is considered ordinary income when received and is taxable as such. Profit or loss from the sale of bonds is an ordinary or capital transaction, depending upon the length of time the bond is owned. You must report profit or loss when filing income tax returns; profit is taxable and losses are deductible.

Can It be Used in Retirement Plans?

Bonds may be used in all properly established plans except 403(b). There is some question about whether bonds lower than grade BBB* violate ERISA guidelines.

Can It be Used as Collateral?

Bonds of higher than average grade are usually acceptable as collateral for loans by banks and other financial institutions. The interest payments (coupon yield) are still payable to the bond-holder, which makes bonds excellent collateral for loans. Bond-

*Grading of bonds is explained in Chapter 20, page 231.

holders continue to draw income from them as they would if the bonds were simply lying in a safety deposit box, yet they are able to raise money for other ventures on them by putting them up as collateral for loans. If the bond pays 8% for example, and the bondholder borrows money at 12%, the money borrowed costs only 4%.

Is It a Hedge Against Inflation?

Bonds have always been a safe way to earn income. In inflationary times, however, their longevity does not make them effective hedges against inflation.

Must It Go Through Probate?

Bonds have to be probated just like any other asset. The same evaluation ruling for stocks applies to bonds.

MUNICIPAL BONDS

A municipality is a community that has its own incorporated government to administer its local affairs for the benefit of its inhabitants. How can such a body finance a large project, such as building a school or fire station or replacing sewers? The cost would far exceed the income available through taxation, and the life of the project might be fifty years or more. The municipality can raise additional capital through the sale of "muni bonds." What makes these bonds so attractive to buyers is that, through a reciprocal arrangement with the federal government, the interest is not taxable to the bondholder. This is the result of a 1913 agreement which affirms that a state or municipality will not tax federal installations such as Post Office buildings, armed forces locations, and other structures that lie within its boundaries, and the federal government will not tax income derived from state or municipal financing. This puts municipal financing in a very advantageous position with respect to corporate financing. A rule of thumb is that it is better for a person who is in the 32% or higher tax bracket to invest in tax-exempt bonds, and those people in a lower tax bracket to buy corporate bonds. When buying bonds, consider your tax obligations before deciding what is best for you. (See Table 8–1, page 78.)

Municipal bonds may be issued by states, counties, cities, educational institutions, school districts, and by specified authorities and agencies to build and improve parks, hospitals, streets, electric and gas facilities, and anything else necessary for the public good. Municipal bonds may or may not be registered. If they are registered, the owner's name and address are on record. If they are unregistered, they are called "bearer" bonds, that is, they belong to whoever has them in hand. Bearer bonds have specifically designated sections called "coupons" attached to them. These coupons are clipped at certain intervals and presented for payment at particular banks, or even to the treasurer of the issuing body.

Municipal bonds are issued in $5,000 denominations, although there are some with $1,000 par value. Interest is payable every six months.

There are several types of municipal bonds. "General obligation" bonds are backed by a pledge from the issuer with his "full faith and obligation" regarding payment of interest and principal when due. These bonds are usually paid off from revenue from taxes collected so the tax base and future possible tax income of the community or authority issuing the bonds is a factor in the quality rating. Other kinds of bonds are backed by specific pledges, such as the income from a gasoline tax or assessments for special purposes. Revenue bonds are backed by the income from revenue-producing projects such as airports, hospitals, educational institutions, or commercial enterprises. Bonds may be issued by "authorities." Inhabitants or visitors to New York City, for instance, are used to seeing notices declaring that some authority or other (N.Y. Port Authority, N.Y. Transit Authority) is undertaking construction of a project. They are called authorities because their charters begin by saying "Authority is vested in . . . ." These authorities may issue bonds for the construction or improvement of tunnels, turnpikes, or other enterprises which they have the "authority" to develop and manage.

The computation of current market value, current yield, and yield to maturity for municipal bonds is the same as for corporate bonds.

What Is the Risk?

In all cases, the underlying project as well as the good faith and obligation of the issuer has a bearing on the quality of the bond. The rating from Standard & Poor, Moody's, or Dun & Bradstreet rating services is very important to the marketability and yield. During the 1929–1932 depression, less than 2% of municipal bonds defaulted in their payments, and less than 1/2% failed to pay at all.

It is also possible for the issuing body or individual bondholder to buy insurance to guarantee interest and principal against default and nonpayment. The insurance premium is very inexpensive because of the past good performance of municipal bonds. Such insurance generally runs from about $0.50 to $1.50 annually for each $1,000 of the face value of the bond. Insured bonds enjoy a higher credit rating, which calls for a lower coupon rate. The saving in interest payment for the issuer is by far greater than the cost of the insurance.

What Is the Return?

The return depends upon the rating given the bond by the rating services. The higher the rating, the lower the risk and the in-interest rate. The going interest rate for borrowing money fluctuates with the availability of money and the economic climate, but the interest rate specified by the bond does not change.

As I mentioned before, the interest rate on a municipal bond is lower than that offered by a corporate bond of comparable quality. But remember that the return is not taxed by the federal government as are corporate bonds. A state may tax income derived from bonds issued by other states, however, and this tax possibility should be determined before you buy an out-of-state bond. Having to pay a tax reduces the return of any investment.

What Is the Liquidity?

Municipal bonds, especially those with a rating of average or better, present no liquidity problems. There is a ready market for them.

What About Taxes?

The interest income from municipal bonds is not taxable by the federal government or the state issuing them, and their tax advantages are obvious. Some states may, however, tax the income from bonds that are issued by other states.

Can It be Used in Retirement Plans?

From the standpoint of quality and liquidity, municipal bonds can be used for all retirement plans except 403(b). As their return is not taxed, however, it doesn't seem logical for any retirement program to include them in a portfolio, since a retirement plan is already exempt from taxes during its accumulation period.

Can It be Used as Collateral?

Municipal bonds are not generally acceptable as collateral for loans since the interest is tax-exempt. Banks do occasionally make exceptions and accept them as collateral, however.

Is It a Hedge Against Inflation?

Municipal bonds are generally a safe and solid means to consistent income. Although the income remains the same, periodic review of your bond portfolio is a must during an inflationary period.

Must It Go Through Probate?

Bonds are subject to the same probate rules and regulations as other securities.

Your Financial Security	Bank / Credit Union	Insurance Annuity	Bonds		Treasuries / Commercial Paper	Stocks	Real Estate	Investment Companies / Mutual Funds / Trusts / R.E.I.T.s	Options / Futures / Warrants
			Corp.	Muni.					
What is the risk?									
What is the return?									
What is the liquidity?									
What about the taxes?									
Retirement plans?									
Collateral?									
Inflation hedge?									
Probate?									

Table 8–1

Comparable Tax Yield

You can establish the equivalent taxable yield by
finding the intersection of the tax-exempt bond
yield and your income tax bracket.

% Bracket	25	27	28	29	31	32	34	36	38	45	50	55	60	62	66	70
4.50	6.00	6.16	6.25	6.34	6.52	6.62	6.82	7.03	7.26	8.18	9.00	10.00	11.25	11.84	13.24	15.00
4.60	6.13	6.30	6.39	6.48	6.67	6.76	6.97	7.19	7.42	8.36	9.20	10.22	11.50	12.11	13.53	15.33
4.70	6.27	6.44	6.53	6.62	6.81	6.91	7.12	7.34	7.58	8.55	9.40	10.44	11.75	12.37	13.82	15.67
4.80	6.40	6.58	6.67	6.76	6.96	7.06	7.27	7.50	7.74	8.73	9.60	10.67	12.00	12.63	14.12	16.00
4.90	6.53	6.71	6.81	6.90	7.10	7.21	7.42	7.66	7.90	8.91	9.80	10.89	12.25	12.89	14.41	16.33
5.00	6.67	6.85	6.94	7.04	7.25	7.35	7.58	7.81	8.06	9.09	10.00	11.11	12.50	13.16	14.71	16.67
5.10	6.80	6.99	7.08	7.18	7.39	7.50	7.73	7.97	8.23	9.27	10.20	11.33	12.75	13.42	15.00	17.00
5.20	6.93	7.12	7.22	7.32	7.54	7.65	7.88	8.13	8.39	9.45	10.40	11.56	13.00	13.68	15.29	17.33
5.30	7.07	7.26	7.36	7.46	7.68	7.79	8.03	8.28	8.55	9.64	10.60	11.78	13.25	13.95	15.59	17.67
5.40	7.20	7.40	7.50	7.61	7.83	7.94	8.18	8.44	8.71	9.82	10.80	12.00	13.50	14.21	15.88	18.00
5.50	7.33	7.53	7.64	7.75	7.97	8.09	8.33	8.59	8.87	10.00	11.00	12.22	13.75	14.47	16.18	18.33
5.60	7.47	7.67	7.78	7.89	8.12	8.24	8.48	8.75	9.03	10.18	11.20	12.44	14.00	14.74	16.47	18.67
5.70	7.60	7.81	7.92	8.03	8.26	8.38	8.64	8.91	9.19	10.36	11.40	12.67	14.25	15.00	16.76	19.00
5.80	7.73	7.95	8.06	8.17	8.41	8.53	8.79	9.06	9.35	10.55	11.60	12.89	14.50	15.26	17.06	19.33
5.90	7.87	8.08	8.19	8.31	8.55	8.68	8.94	9.22	9.52	10.73	11.80	13.11	14.75	15.53	17.35	19.67
6.00	8.00	8.22	8.33	8.45	8.70	8.82	9.09	9.38	9.68	10.91	12.00	13.33	15.00	15.79	17.65	20.00
6.10	8.13	8.36	8.47	8.59	8.84	8.97	9.24	9.53	9.84	11.09	12.20	13.56	15.25	16.05	17.94	20.33
6.20	8.27	8.49	8.61	8.73	8.99	9.12	9.39	9.69	10.00	11.27	12.40	13.78	15.50	16.32	18.24	20.67
6.30	8.40	8.63	8.75	8.87	9.13	9.26	9.55	9.84	10.16	11.45	12.60	14.00	15.75	16.58	18.53	21.00
6.40	8.53	8.77	8.89	9.01	9.28	9.41	9.70	10.00	10.32	11.64	12.80	14.22	16.00	16.84	18.82	21.33
6.50	8.67	8.90	9.03	9.15	9.42	9.56	9.85	10.16	10.48	11.82	13.00	14.44	16.25	17.11	19.12	21.67
6.60	8.80	9.04	9.17	9.30	9.57	9.71	10.00	10.31	10.65	12.00	13.20	14.67	16.50	17.37	19.41	22.00
6.70	8.93	9.18	9.31	9.44	9.71	9.85	10.15	10.47	10.81	12.18	13.40	14.89	16.75	17.63	19.71	22.33
6.80	9.07	9.32	9.44	9.58	9.86	10.00	10.30	10.63	10.97	12.36	13.60	15.11	17.00	17.89	20.00	22.67
6.90	9.20	9.45	9.58	9.72	10.00	10.15	10.45	10.78	11.13	12.55	13.80	15.33	17.25	18.16	20.29	23.00
7.00	9.33	9.59	9.72	9.86	10.14	10.29	10.61	10.94	11.29	12.73	14.00	15.56	17.50	18.42	20.59	23.33
7.10	9.47	9.73	9.86	10.00	10.29	10.44	10.76	11.09	11.45	12.91	14.20	15.78	17.75	18.68	20.88	23.67
7.20	9.60	9.86	10.00	10.14	10.43	10.59	10.91	11.25	11.61	13.09	14.40	16.00	18.00	18.95	21.18	24.00
7.30	9.73	10.00	10.14	10.28	10.58	10.74	11.06	11.41	11.77	13.27	14.60	16.22	18.25	19.21	21.47	24.33
7.40	9.87	10.14	10.28	10.42	10.72	10.88	11.21	11.56	11.94	13.45	14.80	16.44	18.50	19.47	21.76	24.67
7.50	10.00	10.27	10.42	10.56	10.87	11.03	11.36	11.72	12.10	13.64	15.00	16.67	18.75	19.74	22.06	25.00
7.60	10.13	10.41	10.56	10.70	11.01	11.18	11.52	11.88	12.26	13.82	15.20	16.89	19.00	20.00	22.35	25.33
7.70	10.27	10.55	10.69	10.85	11.16	11.32	11.67	12.03	12.42	14.00	15.40	17.11	19.25	20.26	22.65	25.67
7.80	10.40	10.68	10.83	10.99	11.30	11.47	11.82	12.19	12.58	14.18	15.60	17.33	19.50	20.53	22.94	26.00
7.90	10.53	10.82	10.97	11.13	11.45	11.62	11.97	12.34	12.74	14.36	15.80	17.56	19.75	20.79	23.24	26.33
8.00	10.67	10.96	11.11	11.27	11.59	11.76	12.12	12.50	12.90	14.55	16.00	17.78	20.00	21.05	23.53	26.67
8.10	10.80	11.10	11.25	11.41	11.74	11.91	12.27	12.66	13.06	14.73	16.20	18.00	20.25	21.32	23.82	27.00
8.20	10.93	11.23	11.39	11.55	11.88	12.06	12.42	12.81	13.23	14.91	16.40	18.22	20.50	21.58	24.12	27.33
8.30	11.07	11.37	11.53	11.69	12.03	12.21	12.58	12.97	13.39	15.09	16.60	18.44	20.75	21.84	24.41	27.67
8.40	11.20	11.51	11.67	11.83	12.17	12.35	12.73	13.13	13.55	15.27	16.80	18.67	21.00	22.11	24.71	28.00
8.50	11.33	11.64	11.81	11.97	12.32	12.50	12.88	13.28	13.71	15.45	17.00	18.89	21.25	22.37	25.00	28.33

TAX-EXEMPT YIELDS

9

THE MONEY MARKET

United States Securities • *Commercial Paper*

UNITED STATES SECURITIES

The United States government conducts certain aspects of its financial affairs as if it were a giant corporation. It sells what are commonly called "Treasuries" just like corporations sell securities in order to raise money. These Treasuries represent the nation's indebtedness. Short-term Treasury bills are those that mature in less than one year, usually three months and six months. Long-term Treasuries are issued either as bonds or as notes, and are interest-bearing rather than sold at a discount from par value. These bonds or notes have longer maturities than do the Treasury bills. Notes carry initial maturities ranging from one to seven years, and bonds are issued with maturities ranging from one to twenty-five years. Both notes and bonds pay interest semiannually and are redeemable at par value on maturity.

Some federal agencies also issue securities, the majority of which are also financial obligations of the U.S. Treasury. They carry an implied guarantee by the federal government. The six most commonly traded government agency securities (there are many others) are:

Cooperatives (Co-Ops)

Co-Ops were first organized under the Farm Credit Act of 1933 to benefit farmers who were suffering from the effects of the Great Depression. Banks became part of these Co-Ops and provided service loans to eligible agricultural cooperative associations owned and controlled by farmers.

Federal Land Banks

Land banks are the oldest of the federal agencies. Since 1917, they have been making first mortgage loans to farmers or ranchers for rural real estate and for agricultural or credit needs.

Federal Home Loan Banks

These operate as a credit reserve system for institutions that encourage home ownership.

Fannie Mae

This is a popular name for the Federal National Mortgage Association, which is a government-sponsored corporation owned entirely by private shareholders. Its purpose is to lend money to institutions for the purpose of making mortgage money available. It serves as a secondary market for the Federal Housing Administration (FHA), Veterans Administration (VA), or Farmers Home Administration insured or guaranteed mortgages. Fannie Maes provide liquidity for mortgage investments by buying mortgages when other sources of money are in short supply and selling mortgages when funds are plentiful.

Ginnie Mae

This is the popular name for the Government National Mortgage Association. Ginnie Mae shares some functions with Fannie Mae, but its main purpose is to help finance more housing by making real estate mortgage investments attractive to all kinds of investors. A Ginnie Mae certificate represents a share in a pool of FHA and/or VA mortgages. The GNMA issues a security that is backed by mortgages that "pass through" the mortgage payments to the security owner. In short, Ginnie Mae investors own a government security that has as its collateral government guaranteed mortgages.

Federal Farm Credit Bank

The Farm Credit system provides credit and other services to farmers, ranchers, and their cooperatives. It also provides services to harvesters and producers of aquatic products, rural home-owners, and some farm-related businesses. Loans can be from twenty-four hours to forty years. They are secured by land, buildings, equipment, livestock, and other agricultural or aquatic assets. These banks obtain funds from the sale of bonds, and the system is supervised by the Farm Credit Administration.

In each chapter of Section Two, I have discussed the risk, return, liquidity, tax, retirement plans, collateral, inflation, and probate aspects of the particular investment. Table 9–1 answers risk, tax and liquidity questions a potential purchaser of U.S. Treasuries might ask. The table does not answer any questions about retirement plans, collateral, inflation, and probate an investor in U.S. Treasuries might have, so I will discuss them now.

Can It be Used in Retirement Plans?

All U.S. Treasury bonds can be used in retirement plans of any kind.

Table 9-1

Money Market Security	Minimum Denomination	Life of Issue	Subject to Federal Tax	Risk	Liquidity (Secondary Market)
Banks for Cooperative Bonds	$5,000	6 months to (currently) 3-1/2 years	Yes	No expressed liability assumed by U.S. gov't.	Yes
Certificates of Deposit	$100,000	30 days to 5 years	Yes	Issuing Bank	Yes
Export/Import Bank Debentures & Participation Certificates	$5,000	3 to 15 years	Yes	Full faith and credit of U.S. gov't.	Yes
Farmers Home Administration Insured	Varies: $ 25,000, $ 100,000, $ 500,000, $1,000,000	5 to 15 years	Yes	Full faith and credit	Yes
Federal Home Loan Bank Bonds	Older issues $5,000; new issues $10,000	1 to 20 years	Yes	No expressed liability assumed	Yes
Federal Intermediate Credit Bank Bonds	$5,000	9 months to 4 years	Yes	No expressed liability assumed	Yes

Security	Denomination	Maturity		Backing	
Federal Land Bank Bonds	$1,000	13 months to 5 years	Yes	No expressed liability assumed	Yes
FNMA Capital Debentures	$10,000	5 to 25 years	Yes	No expressed liability assumed	Yes
FNMA Debentures	Varies: $ 1,000, $ 5,000, $10,000	18 months to 25 years	Yes	No expressed liability assumed	Yes
Gen'l. Services Administration Participation Certificates	$5,000	30 years	Yes	Full faith and credit	Yes
GNMA Federal Home Loan Mortgage Corp.	$25,000	2 to 25 years	Yes	Full faith and credit	Yes
GNMA, FNMA Bonds	$25,000	5 to 20 years	Yes	Full faith and credit	Yes
GNMA Participation Certificates	Some $ 5,000, most $10,000	8 to 20 years	Yes	Full faith and credit	Yes
GNMA Pass-throughs	Min. $25,000; multiples of $5,000 thereafter	30 years; 12 years average life	Yes	Full faith and credit	Yes

Table 9-1–*Cont.*

Int'l. Bank for Reconstruction and Development Bonds	$1,000	5 to 25 years	Yes	No expressed liability assumed	Yes
Postal Service Bonds	$10,000	25 years	Yes	No expressed liability assumed	Yes
Small Business Administration Debentures	$10,000	10 years	Yes	Guaranteed by SBA; Gen'l obligation of U.S. gov't.	Yes
Tennessee Valley (TVA) Authority Bonds	$1,000	5 to 25 years	Yes	No expressed liabilty assumed	Yes
Treasury Bills	$10,000	3 months to 1 year	Yes	Full faith and credit	Yes
Treasury Notes and Bonds	$500 older issues; $1,000 and $10,000 recent issues	12 months (currently) to 25 years	Yes	Full faith and credit	Yes

Can It be Used as Collateral?

All U.S. Treasury bonds are acceptable as collateral for a loan.

Is It a Hedge Against Inflation?

The interest rate and market value of any U.S. Treasury bond change as they do for other kinds of bonds. Except for those of short maturity, therefore, treasury bonds cannot be considered a hedge against rising inflation rates.

Must It Go Through Probate?

Treasuries are treated the same as any other asset and must be probated.

COMMERCIAL PAPER

Very often large corporations or their financial institutions (such as General Motors Acceptance Corporation or General Electric Credit Corporation) have short term cash shortages or surpluses. The time involved may only be 24 hours or up to 120 days. The surplus or shortage may be from $100,000 to several millions. By issuing or buying commercial paper, these situations can be easily resolved at a currently acceptable interest rate. Such trades can be made through investment banks or brokerage houses.

What Is the Risk?

Commercial paper represents an unsecured loan. The rating and the ability of the issuing corporation to pay interest and principal when due is the risk when buying such investment.

What Is the Return?

The interest rate is the commercially acceptable rate to the issuer and buyer, considering the maturity term.

What Is the Liquidity?

An active trading market exists with other corporations, commercial banks, mutual funds, insurance companies and pension funds.

What About Taxes?

Interest when received is taxable as ordinary income.

Can It be Used in Retirement Plans?

Commercial paper can be used in retirement plans if the paper meets the "prudent man" criterion. The large amounts involved limit the use to larger pension funds.

Can It be Used as Collateral?

Yes, but their life span limits their use.

Is It a Hedge Against Inflation?

Because of their short lifespan, the money can be reinvested at a higher interest rate during a rising interest rate period.

Must It Go Through Probate?

Yes, just like any other asset.

Your Financial Security	Bank Credit Union	Insurance Annuity	Bonds Corp.	Bonds Muni.	Treasuries Commercial Paper	Stocks	Real Estate	Investment Companies Mutual Funds Trusts R.E.I.T.s	Options Futures Warrants
What is the risk?									
What is the return?									
What is the liquidity?									
What about the taxes?									
Retirement plans?									
Collateral?									
Inflation hedge?									
Probate?									

Part **II**

EQUITY INSTRUMENTS

It is possible to invest and to own at the same time. When you purchase a home or other real estate or buy shares in a company, you are investing in something, and at the same time you are buying part or all of it. The part you own is the equity you have in the investment. Whether you are buying a small slice of a large company, a large slice of a small company, or making a down payment on a piece of real estate, you are risking your cash, of course. However, there is undeniable value in owning something.

The next two chapters discuss equity instruments in the form of stocks and real estate.

The market will go up or down—
but not necessarily in that order.

10

STOCKS: OWNERSHIP IN
COMMERCE AND INDUSTRY

Stocks represent ownership in a corporation. After they are issued by the company in the form of certificates, stocks can be bought and sold at any time. The value of each share is determined by what a buyer is willing to pay for it and what a seller is willing to sell it for. Stocks, almost more than anything else, are governed by the old law of supply and demand. Many circumstances influence the market value of a stock. The price of a stock represents the future worth of the company, and that is always speculative. The many thousands of companies that are owned by millions of shareholders are in various stages of growth and profitability, but profitability does not necessarily mean dividends for the stockholder. A company may invest its profits in its own growth, and this is reflected in an appreciation of its stock. This increases the stock's *book* value, but may not always result in an increase in *market* value.

Some corporations are very profitable and pay out a large portion of their profits as dividends, either in the form of cash or as additional shares. Some companies show no profit and may even show a loss. The value of their stock is not appreciating, even though the companies seem to have everything going for them. All this is reflected in the price buyers are willing to pay and sellers are willing to take.

One measure of comparing stocks with each other is the price/earning ratio (P/E). This shows the price a buyer is willing to pay for each dollar of earnings per share of the company. This ratio—sometimes called the "multiple"—is the price of the stock divided by the actual current earnings per share. Do not make the mistake of confusing a company's earnings with the dividends it pays out. Earnings are what a company realizes in the course of doing business, but out of earnings a company must pay expenses and taxes before figuring profits. Another measure of comparison is the averages for the stock market as a whole; in other words, how are *all* listed stocks doing? One of the best known indexes is the Dow Jones, which represents thirty industrial stocks, twenty transportation stocks, and fifteen utilities stocks of corporations traded on the New York Stock Exchange. Other indexes include Standard & Poor, representing 500 different stocks, and Value Line Investment Research, representing about 1,700. There are other stock exchanges besides the New York Stock Exchange and these have their own ways of measuring the daily changes in the market according to the actual stocks traded. None of these methods can be used to forecast with any certainty the behavior and fluctuations of stock market prices, much less individual stocks.

The stocks I have referred to so far are known as *common stocks.* Corporations also issue *preferred stocks.* Preferred stocks are those with fixed dividends which must be paid to the preferred stockholders before any dividends are paid to common stockholders. There are also *cumulative preferred stocks,* which means that if a dividend is omitted, the cumulative omissions must be paid in full before dividends are paid to common stockholders. Yet another type of preferred stock may be converted into common stock at a future date at a fixed price.

The first time a company offers stock for sale to the public (prime offerings) the offer must be accompanied by a prospectus. The prospectus must give all pertinent facts about the corporation—such as who the officers are, how much it is capitalized for, what business the company is in, and so on. The prime offering lasts until all the stock issued has been sold. The prospectus of a first offering of stock will tell you a great deal about the corporation. To learn more about established companies, especially those listed on the various exchanges, consult their quarterly reports and their audited annual reports. These reports are easy to come by—your stock broker can help you, as can any large public library.

Analysts employed by brokerage houses and investment services constantly review these financial reports and often are the first to spot changes—favorable or otherwise—in a company's operations. Their opinions are available to the public through the services of a stockbroker. Standard & Poor, for instance, issues reports on most publicly traded corporations. In other words, information about any listed corporation is available to you, but many people find it difficult to understand the information, so they rely on the advice of their stockbroker.

What Is the Risk?

Common stocks do not guarantee the payment of dividends. A company's size, maturity, and past performance, along with the talent and ability of its management reduce the risk of adverse and unexpected situations. Each company is rated by a rating service. Dun & Bradstreet, Standard & Poor, Dow Jones, and Moody's give a reliable but not guaranteed measure of present and future performance. The fluctuation of the market value of a security (in this case stocks) also represents a risk in itself. Holding a security for an extended period of time minimizes the effects of the market's daily ups and downs, and the average value of the stock is likely to increase.

Any money held in the care of a brokerage house, as well as any securities placed in their care for safekeeping, are insured by the Securities Investor Protection Corporation (SIPC) up to $100,000—20% in cash and the rest in securities. As an added protection, most brokerage houses subscribe to a private insurance plan which extends protection up to $500,000 for each account.

What Is the Return?

The return from stock investments varies with general economic conditions as well as with the performance of the corporation issuing the stocks. Dividends can range from zero to as much as 10%, and more. The return can also influence the price of the stock. If a corporation has been paying 5% of the cost of the stock as dividends, and if it cuts the dividend or, for whatever reason, pays less than it had been paying, the market value of its stock may go down. Conversely, increasing the dividends makes the stock more attractive, and its value may go up.

Sometimes a company will split its stocks to decrease the price of each share and thereby improve the likelihood of investment. For instance, in the case of a two-for-one split, another share will be issued to a stockholder for each share the stockholder owns. What a stock split does is increase the number of shares outstanding. Stock splitting does not increase the profitability of the corporation, it simply divides the value of each old share over a greater number of shares. What this means to the stockholder is that he/she now owns two shares for every one he held before the split. It has been demonstrated that stocks trading in the $30 to $50 per share range are most likely to attract the average investor, and thus increase stock-ownership of the corporation.

What Is the Liquidity?

Stocks traded on the exchanges can be readily bought and sold. (For more information on the exchanges, including over-the-counter (OTC) transactions, see Chapter 14.) Supply and demand for stocks depends upon the quality of the issuing corporation and on general economic conditions. Under normal circumstances, proceeds from the sale can be received within five business days if traded through regular channels. When you buy stocks, you must pay for them within five business days.

What About Taxes?

At present, the first $200 of dividends received each year is exempt from federal taxes, $400 if husband and wife own stock jointly. Profits realized from a short-term (one year or less) equity sale (stocks held for one year or less and then sold), are taxable as ordinary income. Losses up to $3,000 may be deducted from your federal income tax each year. Losses in excess of $3,000 can be carried over to the following year. Forty percent of the profits from stocks held longer than one year is taxable as ordinary income. Ideally, losses on your stocks should be made up by profits, and long-term losses can be balanced out as $2 for each $1 of short-term loss. Your stockbroker, accountant, or the IRS will give you further information.

Stock dividends (additional stock paid out in lieu of cash) are not taxed when received. If a corporation owns stocks in another corporation, 85% of the dividend received is tax exempt.

Can It be Used in Retirement Plans?

Stocks may be used in all retirement plans except 403(b), provided that they are set up in a trust account usually made available by a bank. The cost of setting up a qualified trust account varies from bank to bank. Your stockbroker will be glad to help you.

Can It be Used as Collateral?

Some banks and investment houses will accept stock certificates as collateral for a loan. The collateral value may vary from 50% to as high as 80% of the market value of the stock. Some stocks are not acceptable at all, especially speculative stocks. It is advisable to check the competitive interest rates.

Is It a Hedge Against Inflation?

The value of stocks can, as a whole, be considered a hedge against loss of purchasing power. There is, however, no guarantee that this will be so at any given date in the future. Long-term ownership of selective stocks and periodic review of a portfolio are prerequisites in trying to keep pace with inflation.

Must It Go Through Probate?

A portfolio of stock holdings becomes part of the estate of the deceased and must go through probate, if for no other reason than to transfer ownership to the beneficiary. There are specific rules for evaluating securities to establish tax liabilities of the estate and to set a fair market value for the beneficiary. A lawyer, trust officer of a bank, or the IRS should be consulted.

Your Financial Security	Bank Credit Union	Insurance Annuity	Bonds Corp.	Bonds Muni.	Treasuries Commercial Paper	Stocks	Real Estate	Investment Companies Mutual Funds Trusts R.E.I.T.s	Options Futures Warrants
What is the risk?									
What is the return?									
What is the liquidity?									
What about the taxes?									
Retirement plans?									
Collateral?									
Inflation hedge?									
Probate?									

11

REAL ESTATE: OCCUPANCY
AND INVESTMENT

Real Estate Financing • *Buying versus Renting* • *Condominiums and Cooperatives* • *Commercial Property*

Real estate can be defined as land and anything on it (buildings, appurtenances), under it (minerals, water), or in the air space over it. There are two reasons for purchasing real estate: occupancy and investment.

As an occupant, you may be a renter or an owner/occupant. Renters pay a charge for occupancy which may or may not include utilities. Renters are not liable for any losses, maintenance, or repairs, but neither do they participate in any gains or appreciation of the property. They are responsible for any damage to the dwelling and have an obligation to keep the premises fit for occupancy and to behave in a responsible manner. There may or may not be a lease. If there is a lease, the obligations and responsibilities of both landlord and tenant are spelled out. The absence of a lease, however, does not absolve either party of responsibility or obligation to each other, and there are laws in each state to protect both parties.

Real estate ownership is documented by a deed and registered in county or state records. The owner is responsible for taxes and assessments levied against the property. During the years immediately after World War II and well into the 1960s, it was common practice for a young couple to buy a small house with a minimal down payment. After about five to eight years, the property appreciated sufficiently, the equity increased, and wages rose enough to enable the couple to buy a larger, more expensive home. The new home, with the proceeds from the sale of the first home, could be financed by a mortgage with an interest rate not much higher than the original mortgage. The owner-occupant was in a highly rewarding financial position.

Since then, however, the interest rate has greatly increased, lending institutions require a much larger down payment, and construction costs have risen so much that today's young couple cannot benefit from home ownership to the extent that their parents did. Land is limited and as the population grows, there will be more and more users of land. The value of land and buildings keeps going up, and so do their costs. As people will always need a place to live, the question of whether to be an owner-occupant, renter, or real estate investor arises. The answer will depend upon individual needs, finances, and goals.

REAL ESTATE FINANCING: SOME BASICS

Some basic facts should be kept firmly in mind when you consider any real estate investment. The monthly mortgage payment by the mortgagor (the one who borrowed the money) includes an interest payment for the use of the money and a repayment of the loan. Since the monthly payment is a fixed amount, as the principal declines the percentage of the payment which goes for interest decreases and the amount that is applied to the loan principal increases.

The interest paid is tax-deductible, and the reduction in the face amount of the loan can be considered an enforced savings because the equity in the house is correspondingly increased. The equity thus accumulated can be converted into cash if the home is sold or refinanced. Refinancing the home would incur additional charges and would, most likely, be done at a considerably higher interest rate than the original mortgage. Thus, you should consider refinancing for ready cash only as a last resort.

BUYING VERSUS RENTING

It may be helpful to begin by comparing the costs of renting and buying.* Let's assume that we are dealing with a single-family home valued at $50,000, with real estate taxes of $1,200 annually and with a twenty-five year mortgage of $40,000 at 9% interest. The down payment was $10,000 and utilities and insurance run $1,380 annually. The monthly mortgage payment is $335.68 and $240 per year is allocated for normal upkeep. (We are not assuming any major remodeling or repairs.)

Before we can make a comparison, we must do something about the down payment of $10,000. Although this is a one-time cash outlay, we must figure it in annual costs of home ownership, and we can best do this by figuring what this sum would have earned had it been invested rather than used as a down payment to buy a home.

If the $10,000 had been invested at 4%, tax-free, it would have earned $400 annually. Because it was not, we can consider the $400 as an expenditure.

Total Annual Cost of Owning a Home

Down payment	$ 400
(Monthly) payments	$4,028
Insurance and utilities	$1,380
Taxes	$1,200
Maintenance	$ 240
	$7,248

After ten years of ownership, the mortgage balance will be $33,080. You have actually paid $40,280 in monthly payments in that time, of which $6,920 will have gone toward reducing the mortgage debt, and the balance of $33,360 will have been paid in interest.

Although the monthly payments remain constant, the allocation to interest decreases and the reduction of the mortgage debt

*These figures are not based on actual costs, current or future, or a particular area.

101

increases. Therefore, the average annual interest payment over the first ten years is $3,336 (33,360 ÷ 10), and the mortgage reduction $692 (6,920 ÷ 10).

Let's assume that you are in the 32% income tax bracket. Your total *annual net* cost would be:

Down payment	$ 400
(Monthly) interest payments (3,336 − 32% tax)	$2,268
Insurance and utilities	$1,380
Taxes, deductible less 32%	$ 816
Maintenance	$ 240
	$5,104

By owning your living quarters and benefiting from the income tax deduction you are allowed, you are ahead $2,144, and have increased the equity in your home by $692 each year.

It is well worth the time and effort of any owner or prospective owner to compile such figures in order to have an exact picture of the advantages of owning.

CONDOMINIUMS AND COOPERATIVES

"Condominium" and "cooperative" are terms that are sometimes confused. A condominium is an individually owned unit in a multi-unit structure. An owner owns only his or her unit. A cooperative is a multi-unit structure which is owned cooperatively, but occupied individually. Ownership of a co-op means part-ownership in a corporation set up to control the structure. A co-op owner shares in the building and the land on which it is situated, while a condominium owner owns only his or her unit outright.

As individually-owned, detached housing becomes more and more expensive and as land becomes increasingly scarce, more and more people are buying condominiums or buying into cooperatives. The purchase price is generally less than that of a single-family house, and there may be some benefits that people enjoy such as a swimming pool, party room, parking, and well-tended grounds that require no effort on the part of the individual owner.

Windows are washed, snow is shoveled, and grass is cut—by someone else. The manager or a committee of owners assume the responsibility for maintaining common areas and for repairs and upkeep. The condominium or cooperative owner pays a share of the costs of these services.

If there is a mortgage, the interest is tax-deductible just as it would be for a house. Condominium insurance is less expensive than a home-owner policy, but more expensive than a tenant policy. If condominium owners pay their own utilities, these are generally lower than the same expenses in a single home. In addition to mortgage payments, unit owners must contribute to a fund for building management, insurance, repairs and maintenance, and to a replacement fund. These fees can be quite high. Prospective owners should check to see that they will have a voice in administering these responsibilities.

The occupant agreement which you as a condominium owner must sign should state that unpaid fees can be put as a lien against your unit. Too many liens from too many units, however, can result in reduced cash flow to pay for day-to-day operations. Recent experience has shown that some owners of condominium units are remiss in paying their monthly shares. This neglect places an undue burden on other occupants. Liens on condominiums may be satisfied only when the unit is sold. Some occupant agreements specify that only owner-occupants are welcome, or may state that the other tenants have the right to approve condominium rentals. (Cooperative apartments have their own rules and regulations and their occupant agreement stipulations should be thoroughly investigated prior to purchase.)

Condominium owners should chart the costs of ownership in the same way that single-family home owners do, but they must add in the amount of the monthly contributions to the common fund when doing the figuring.

Whether owning a unit in a multi-unit building or owning a detached house, the average length of ownership of a dwelling is ten to thirteen years, according to mortgage records. During that period, the value of the property will have increased or decreased. It will most likely decrease in value if a large proportion of homes are on the market in an area at the same time, or if the property has been neglected. The value will increase if the property has been well maintained and if there is a shortage of housing.

No two properties are exactly alike, and there is no such thing as a typical neighborhood or typical buyer. There is, thus, no sure way to predict whether property will appreciate or depreciate. During an inflationary period, the cost of housing will rise and during a deflationary, recession, depression, or even stable period, the average cost will decline—if for no other reason than depreciation as the building ages.

Although in this book I will not attempt to advise readers which investments are better than others, it does appear that owning your own home has great advantages over renting, in spite of the risks involved. Yet, for many people, renting is the only alternative. By looking once again at the comparison figures, it is obvious that owning costs almost as much as renting, except that at the end of a period of time the renter has only rent receipts, while the owner has accumulated something in the form of enforced savings represented by the equity in his home. The homeowner renting that same $50,000 house I talked about earlier, rather than living in it, will charge approximately 1% of the market value as rent—$500 per month, or $6,000 per year.

Mortgage interest rates change depending upon the availability of money and the economic climate. A lender may require different size down payments from different borrowers, and requirements vary from one to another. (See Chapter 19 for more on mortgages and real estate financing.) Sometimes a lender may also require that the morgage be protected against default by a commercial insurer. The procedures described below apply to all real estate transactions, whether they are residential, commercial, or industrial.

COMMERCIAL PROPERTY

Commercial and industrial real estate is generally an investment. Commercial means "for profit" and includes such things as stores, offices and warehouses. Industrial properties are used for production or manufacture. Commercial or industrial properties are not used as living quarters. Before committing themselves to financing a commercial real estate venture, lenders will analyze the physical condition of the property, its suitability for the intended use, and the ability of the user to maintain the property to obtain the maximum return.

Once financing has been arranged, all real estate—commercial as well as residential—must go into escrow. Escrow is a legal term applied to a deed, other written instrument, or other property entrusted to a third party to be delivered to a named party when a specified act has been completed (clearance of a real estate title, for example). The word comes from "scroll" because at one time everything was handwritten on linen or parchment (and later paper) that could be rolled up.

Escrow arrangements are usually administered by a bank or title company. Their duty, as the disinterested third party, is to assure that all provisions of the purchase contract between the buyer and seller are carried out. The seller is to give a "free and clear" title with all taxes and assessments, as well as outstanding utility bills, paid up to the date of transfer. The buyer must present the purchase price, which includes both the down payment and necessary financing. The buyer's lender may also ask for a valid insurance policy protecting the property against fire, theft, vandalism, and liability. The lender may also ask for title insurance, which is protection against undetected liens or claims on the property. The parties to the real estate transaction pay any charges incurred to fulfill their obligations, and any escrow fee is usually shared equally by the two parties.

For real estate property investment to be profitable, the mortgage payments and taxes should be less than half of the rental income. Management, maintenance, repairs, replacement, insurance, utilities, and other miscellaneous expenses should also be less than half of the income so that the two percentages combined leave a surplus for the owner.

Since the purchase is an investment, the owner is entitled to a depreciation allowance. Depending upon which depreciation plan is applied, the investment should show a paper loss. (Depreciation schedules are complex and I will not go into them here. You should consult with an accountant for details.) If the property is owned by a corporation, this paper loss can be carried forward on the books. If the property is owned by an individual or partnership, the loss can be charged against the owner's income. It is this kind of bookkeeping that makes real estate investment a tax shelter.

The advantages of depreciation and paper loss do not last indefinitely. The monthly mortgage payments, paid out of the income the property produces, serve to liquidate the mortgage. After about seven years, the part of the mortgage payment that applies to reduction of the debt and is considered profit for tax purposes should equal the depreciation. From that time on, the investment will most likely show an annual, increasing paper profit which is taxable. If the property is owned by a corporation, the profit can be applied to past losses until it is used up. If the property is owned by an individual or partnership, the profit is taxable income.

What Is the Risk?

Real estate is usually what is called a highly leveraged (in-debted) investment; that is, it is generally financed by heavy borrow-ing. The more you owe, the more you risk.

Apartment investment for rental use, or investment in commer-cial or industrial structures to be rented to a business enterprise is somewhat risky because whether the building is damaged or even destroyed depends upon the actions of the tenants.

Location, type of structure, utilities, aging, weather, population movement, change in zoning and neighborhoods, and availability or shortage of tenant occupancy all influence the value of property. Expenses of maintaining a rental property can rise faster than in-creases in rental income.

Diversification in different types of real estate tends to mini-mize risk, but it requires large financial commitment and bookkeep-ing assistance. Apartment buildings and industrial-commercial structures have particular kinds of management problems. These should be thoroughly investigated before you decide on any invest-ment in them.

What Is the Return?

The return on real estate investment can be expected to be high because the initial risk is great. The return is somewhat more predict-able than returns on other types of investment because rents and taxes remain steady—at least within a given year.

What Is the Liquidity?

Liquidity is a major disadvantage in real estate investment. It takes time to build up equity to a point when refinancing can be considered, and refinancing may not be worthwhile if borrowing rates have gone up. Also, real estate cannot be sold as rapidly as other kinds of investments if you need cash on short notice.

What About Taxes?

In the early years of ownership, real estate is a tax shelter. The maximum profit can only be made from the sale of the property, and if it is a long-term investment it is taxed as such. A private residence can be sold and a similar one bought without a capital gains tax being imposed if the transaction takes place within eighteen months.

Senior citizens benefit from certain privileges when selling their real estate. If the seller or the seller's spouse is fifty-five years of age or older, and if either has lived in the house three of the last five years, the first $100,000 of the profit is not subject to tax. Commissions and closing costs, as well as any expenses incurred in improving the property within ninety days of the sale, can be deducted from the selling price to arrive at the net profit. The $100,000 profit exemption is a "once-in-a-lifetime" privilege for both owners, however, and cannot be used again. Senior citizen privileges may become more liberal and more numerous in the future, and these should be explored as the opportunity arises.

Can It be Used as Collateral?

Real estate is acceptable as collateral for a loan providing that sufficient equity has been built up to cover the loan amount. Obviously, a lender will not approve a loan for $10,000 if only $2,000 of the mortgage on the property has been paid off.

Commercial banks, savings and loans associations, insurance companies, administrators of pension plans, and ordinary investors consider loans secured by real estate as very safe investments. By matching property—whether a home or commercial or industrial property—with a qualified prospective owner, the lender is assured of a return of interest and principal over a fixed period of time. The lender (mortgagee) will advance to the prospective owner (mortgagor) the balance of the purchase price over the down payment.

The mortgagees will not lend more than a percentage of the appraised value of the property. Should the mortgagor default in making payments as agreed, the mortgagee has the right to foreclose and sell the collateral (the real estate property, in this case).

Can It be Used in Retirement Plans?

Real estate, except for financing, should not be used in a retirement plan since it is already a tax shelter. You can, of course, use real estate investments as a source of income after retirement if you are willing to take on the problems that go along with the management of rental property.

Is It a Hedge Against Inflation?

An inflationary period is a favorable time to invest in real estate, since the mortgage will be paid off in ever-cheapening dollars. Thus, real estate has proved to be an outstanding hedge against inflation.

Must It Go Through Probate?

Normally, real estate must go through probate.

Your Financial Security	Bank / Credit Union	Insurance Annuity	Bonds (Corp. / Muni.)	Treasuries / Commercial Paper	Stocks	Real Estate	Investment Companies (Mutual Funds / Trusts / R.E.I.T.s)	Options / Futures / Warrants
What is the risk?								
What is the return?								
What is the liquidity?								
What about the taxes?								
Retirement plans?								
Collateral?								
Inflation hedge?								
Probate?								

Part III

HYBRIDS AND OTHER THINGS

In the previous chapters, I have discussed debt and equity instruments. A third kind of investment—which I call a "hybrid"—is a mixture of the two, and aims to offer the best of both. Mutual funds and trusts (also called investment companies), for example, may be made up of both debt and equity instruments to take advantage of the best characteristics of each.

I will also discuss other things—options, futures, and warrants—in this section. These are claims to a product, commodity, equity, or debt and can also be part of an investment portfolio.

To preserve your assets, diversify;
to speculate, specialize.

INVESTMENT COMPANIES

Mutual Funds: Open-End, Closed-End, and REITs • Unit Investment Trusts

---

MUTUAL FUNDS

Mutual funds are investment companies that pool the funds of many investors who do not wish to manage their money themselves. The mutual fund invests the money in securities that it selects for the "mutual" benefit of its investors. Mutual funds offer investors the ultimate in diversification, even for a very small contribution.

Mutual funds have been in existence since the early part of this century. They are regulated by acts of Congress passed in 1933 and 1940 and amended in later years. These regulations specify that investment companies (the legal term for mutual funds) may not invest more than 5% of their capital or assets in any one company or own more than 10% of a company. In order not to be taxed directly, they must distribute at least 90% of their income after deducting the expenses of running the company to the shareholders. All income (dividends) is ordinary income to the shareholder, but any gains or losses are capital or long-term transactions and are taxed as such.

As a matter of disclosure, investment companies must state

their objectives and expenses and name all persons associated with their management. They must also provide a prospectus to any person to whom the investment is offered.

There are two kinds of mutual funds: open-end and closed-end.

OPEN-END MUTUAL FUNDS

These funds make a continuous offering of new shares to investors at net asset value (plus a sales charge) and stand ready to redeem any shares at net asset value as determined by the market value of the securities they hold. Open-end funds have a sales charge or "load" when bought, but no charge when redeemed. There are some funds that have no charge when bought or sold and some which have a surrender charge. All have a management fee. When selecting a fund, you should know in advance what all charges will be.

Funds with a sales charge can be bought from representatives licensed by the National Association of Security Dealers (NASD), who may work for the fund itself, or from a stockbroker or an insurance agent. All are licensed in the state where the transaction takes place. "No load" funds are sold directly to the prospective purchaser, and the management may redeem shares from any fund shareholder at no charge.

The daily market price of mutual funds appears on the financial pages of a newspaper. The net asset value (NAV), or redemption value, is shown as "bid." The sale price—that is, the price the fund will sell each share for—is shown as "ask." The difference between bid and ask is the sales charge, or "load." If bid and ask are the same, there is no charge when you buy into the fund.

The fund managers try to achieve the objectives outlined in the prospectus by maintaining a portfolio or trading on the market in the type of securities that will be of the greatest benefit to the fund and the shareholders. Income objectives can best be achieved by specializing in high-income stocks or bonds, or a combination of the two. It is most unlikely that high income and maximum growth can be gained from the same fund (Fig. 12-1).

Before investing in a fund, you should review its objectives and past performance to make sure that it meets your personal financial needs and plans. The same criteria you would use yourself to select

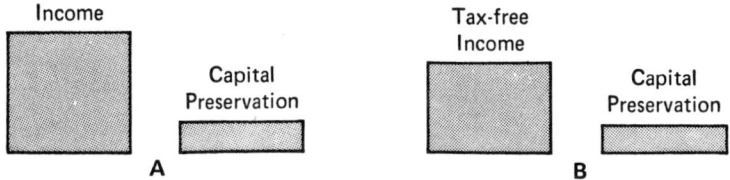

A and B represent the objectives of trusts that aim to generate income, either taxable or tax-free, and still preserve capital.

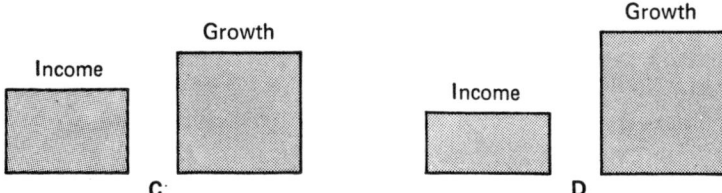

C and D portray fund policies which are to produce some income and corresponding growth with only a moderate risk.

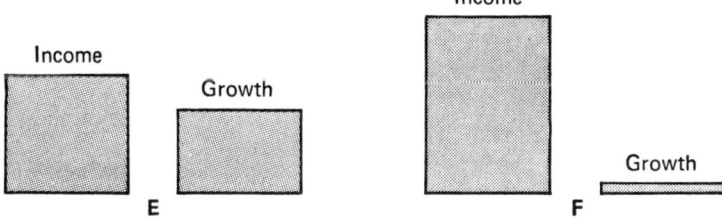

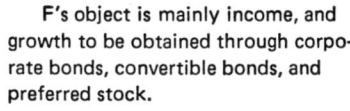

E is most likely a corporate bond fund which seeks maximum income with growth in excess of the current inflation rate.

F's object is mainly income, and growth to be obtained through corporate bonds, convertible bonds, and preferred stock.

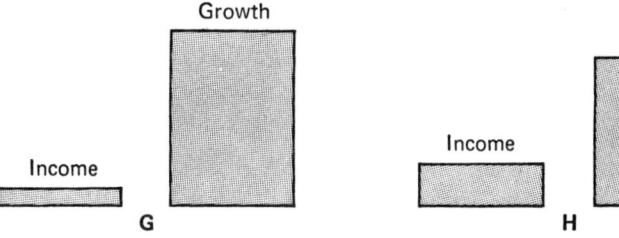

G seeks maximum growth with income only an incidental objective. Growth can be obtained by buying certain common stocks, warrants, options, and bonds that may appreciate during favorable interest fluctuation.

H shows growth objectives with some income. The portfolio making up this fund probably contains more conservative securities than F or G.

Figure 12-1

stocks and bonds should be used in selecting a mutual fund investment company, since the companies deal in the same securities and are subject to the same fluctuations of the stock market as you are. A major advantage of being a mutual fund shareholder is the convenience of having experts make the decisions for you.

Some funds invest in companies representing special interests, such as gold or silver mining, foreign enterprises, exploration and environmental development, and so on. New mutual fund investment companies can be created for any situation that may arise—with the speculation that such ventures entail. There are also mutual funds that deal in tax-exempt bonds, and those that are made up of short-term debt obligations. These latter are called cash management funds. A fund with the obligation of writing options is organized to do just that. Some funds invest primarily in utility stocks. So you see, there are many different kinds of funds appealing to many different kinds of investors. Only you can choose the right one for you.

The success of any fund depends upon the management's ability to select and trade securities and upon the market's actions as a whole. Some management organizations have as many as ten different funds under their overall supervision, with each fund having a different objective. It is possible to transfer assets from one fund to another within the same management company, but not more often than once each year. Any charge for such transfer will be minimal (currently about $5.00).

Mutual funds lend themselves very favorably to systematic savings on a periodic basis, and contributions can be as low as $10.00. Considering the fluctuations of the market value of stocks, buying periodically and consistently averages out the cost of the investment. This is called "dollar averaging." It is also possible to reinvest dividends and capital gains distributions when they are declared, but both are taxed during the year paid, even when the proceeds are reinvested.

Other funds take advantage of certain corporate tax privileges. Corporations that own stock in other corporations do not have to pay taxes on 85% of the dividends received. This privilege allows such a fund to reinvest that tax-free amount in the fund itself, thus increasing the value of each share owned by a shareholder. Since these shares can be redeemed at any time, the gain or loss can be treated as a capital gain or loss by the shareholder.

Mutual funds offer the benefit of another feature called the "withdrawal plan," whereby the fund will pay a fixed monthly or quarterly or even semi-annual amount to its shareholders, if they prefer. If the pay-out does not exceed the return, the assets of the fund will never be exhausted. Obviously, if long-term income is the investor's objective, return and payments must be closely balanced out.

What Is the Risk?

The risk in being a shareholder of a mutual fund investment company is not greater than that of owning a diversified portfolio of stocks and bonds. The objectives of each fund are clearly stated in its prospectus, as is the investment policy. The management's ability to manage can be compared with the performance of other funds with similar objectives.

What Is the Return?

The return is a direct reflection of the securities in the portfolio. Once again, the management's ability to produce the hoped-for dividends and appreciation of its holdings is critical.

What Is the Liquidity?

An open-end fund will buy back its outstanding shares at net asset value (NAV) any time they are presented. The net asset value is established each trading day (each fund has its own specific time each day) by each fund. This figure represents the actual total market value of the securities held by the fund divided by the actual number of shares outstanding. The proceeds are usually available within five business days from the date of the redemption.

What About Taxes?

Dividends are classed as ordinary income, and are taxed when received. Capital gains or losses are treated as long-term investments, and are taxed accordingly. An end-of-the-year statement from the fund will give the shareholder the necessary tax information. Returns from a fund dealing in tax-exempt bonds are not taxed by the federal government, but may be taxed by the state in which the shareholder resides—particularly that portion of the income derived from bonds issued by municipalities in other states.

Can It be Used in Retirement Plans?

Mutual funds can be used for all retirement plans, including 403(b), if set up in a qualified trust. The fund itself will make the necessary arrangements.

Can It be Used as Collateral?

Some banks and other financial institutions may accept mutual fund shares as collateral for loans.

Is It a Hedge Against Inflation?

The portfolio of securities in a mutual fund reflects the ability of its managers to meet inflationary forces. Obviously, growth stocks are better suited for that purpose than bonds, although bonds can be sold at a time when their market value is at a premium.

Must It Go Through Probate?

The same probate rules and regulations that apply to securities also apply to mutual funds.

CLOSED-END MUTUAL FUNDS AND REITS

Closed-end mutual funds obtain their initial capital—the money to invest—by selling a fixed number of shares at a set price on the open market. These funds are thus like corporate stock shares. A commission is charged for each trade which must be paid by the buyer and seller.

The capitalization of a closed-end mutual fund remains constant unless new shares are issued. The management invests the money in ways it expects will help it achieve the intended objectives. The net asset value (NAV) and the overall market averages cause daily changes in the market price of each share.

By far the greatest number of closed-end funds are in real estate investment trusts (REIT). These funds invest in high-yield mortgages such as real estate construction and/or development, and short-term mortgages. They can attain a high return with good liquidity, which is a plus, since good liquidity is usually not available with ordinary real estate investments. Other REITs may invest by buying real estate properties outright. The return on such investments is likely to be lower than would be the case if the REIT held mortgages, but the chances for appreciation are greater. REITs are a diversified real estate investment and normally require a smaller financial commitment than conventional real estate investment.

What Is the Risk?

The risk of being a shareholder of a closed-end fund is the same as that of an open-end fund. Shares of a real estate investment trust limits the money "at risk" to the amount actually invested.

What Is the Return?

The return is a direct reflection of the investment in the fund's portfolio, no matter what it consists of—stocks, bonds, real estate, or mortgages.

What Is the Liquidity?

Shares of a closed-end fund can be traded on the various exchanges any time there is a market, just like any other security. The proceeds are normally available within five business days from the date of trade.

What About Taxes?

Dividends declared are ordinary income when received. Profits from the sale of shares are ordinary or long-term income, depending upon the length of time the shares were owned.

Can It be Used in Retirement Plans?

Closed-end funds can be used for all retirement plans, except 403(b).

Can It be Used for Collateral?

Certain banks and financial institutions may accept mutual fund shares as collateral for loans.

Can It be Used as a Hedge Against Inflation?

The portfolio of securities in the fund reflects the ability of the fund to meet inflationary forces. Investments in real estate are generally believed to be a good hedge against inflation.

Must It Go Through Probate?

The same probate rules and regulations that apply to securities also apply to closed-end funds and REITs.

UNIT INVESTMENT TRUSTS

A unit investment trust is formed to obtain current income through investment in a diversified portfolio of tax-exempt municipal or taxable corporate debt obligations and preferred stocks. The main objective of these trusts is income and preservation of capital.

The sponsor of such a trust may be an investment house or brokerage firm which will assemble a portfolio consisting of a predetermined number of securities of various values and maturities, all with current high yield. The life of the trust is limited, but may be as long as twenty-five years for a long-term trust, or ten to twelve years for a medium-term trust. There are some shorter-term trusts. The underlying securities may be rated BBB or better by at least two rating services. If they are rated lower than BBB, the return may be higher, but the risk is greater.

The sponsor will market these trusts in the form of trust units. The units can be bought from representatives licensed by the NASD. The representatives may work for a brokerage house or insurance agency, but all have to be licensed in the state where the transaction is executed. A sales charge is included in the cost of each unit. Once the trust is sold out, another is formed. These various trusts are designated as series with consecutive numbers and the name of the sponsor. The portfolio of securities is turned over to a trustee, usually a bank, for administration. Unit investment trusts thus differ from open-end or closed-end funds in that they do not have their own management. The trustee holds the certificates, collects the interest when due, and disburses the income to the unit holders monthly, quarterly, semiannually, or annually. If a debt obligation that is part of the portfolio is called for liquidation, the trustee will distribute the proceeds to the unit holders in proportion to their share of the trust ownership.

Each unit represents (and each unit holder owns) an undivided interest in the underlying securities and net income of the trust. An evaluator will price the total trust each business day at the close of trading at the various exchanges. (For computing yield, see the corporate bonds section in Chapter 7.)

The unit price of a trust is about $1,000. This amount will fluctuate with the market value just as bonds do. Some sponsors price each unit at about $100, and may stipulate the minimum number of units a purchaser must buy. When you buy units in a trust, in addition to the market price, you will have to pay an "accrued interest" cost, like that on bonds. The accrued interest charge is the amount that accrues before the transfer date of ownership and the interest due date.

Corporate trusts are made up of corporate debt obligations and/or high quality corporate preferred income securities. The income from such trusts is taxable. Some trusts contain government-guaranteed mortgages, the income from which will consist of a return of the principal as well as interest. The interest is taxable, but the return of the principal is not. This kind of trust is comparable to a mortgage. Some trusts consist of tax-exempt bonds, the income from which is not taxable; however, the income is proportionately lower than from corporate bond trusts. Some sponsors allow you to reinvest income from their tax-exempt bond trusts in their tax-exempt bond fund at no charge.

What Is the Risk?

The risk is a direct reflection of the quality of the debt obligations making up the trust. Ratings from at least two rating services are stated in the prospectus. The principal and interest of tax-exempt municipal bond trusts can be insured by either the issuer or the individual unit owner. If insured by the issuer, the rating of the bond will rise by one position, but the interest rate will be lower because the underlying bonds will have a better rating by virtue of the insurance protection.

What Is the Return?

The return is what the average underlying securities are currently paying. The amount will remain constant unless there is a change in the bonds held in the trust. Municipal bond trusts have a lower return than corporate bond trusts of equal quality because they are exempt from federal taxes.

What Is the Liquidity?

Although the sponsor and trust are not obligated to do so, they will buy back any trust unit offered to them at the current market value. The trade can be handled through a brokerage house or insurance agency that is a member of NASD at no cost to the seller. Proceeds are normally available within five business days from the date of trade.

What About Taxes?

Income from corporate bond trusts is taxable as ordinary income when received. Income from tax-exempt bond trusts is tax-exempt from federal income taxes. State taxes may have to be paid on that portion of income derived from obligations issued by other states.

Can It be Used in Retirement Plans?

Trusts may be used for retirement plans, except 403(b). There does not seem to be any particular advantage to putting tax-exempt trust units into a retirement plan, since the return is not taxable anyway.

Can It be Used as Collateral?

Trust units are accepted by some banks as collateral.

Can It be Used as a Hedge Against Inflation?

The value of trust units as a hedge against inflation is the same as that of bonds.

Must It Go Through Probate?

Investments in trusts and mutual funds are under the same rules and regulations as other securities and debt obligations—that is, they are part of the deceased's estate and must be probated, unless they are owned jointly.

Your Financial Security	Bank Credit Union	Insurance Annuity	Bonds Corp.	Bonds Muni.	Treasuries Commercial Paper	Stocks	Real Estate	Investment Companies Mutual Funds Trusts R.E.I.T.s	Options Futures Warrants
What is the risk?									
What is the return?									
What is the liquidity?									
What about the taxes?									
Retirement plans?									
Collateral?									
Inflation hedge?									
Probate?									

13

OPTIONS, FUTURES, WARRANTS: THEIR ROLE IN INVESTMENT STRATEGY

Stock Options • *Real Estate Options* • *Futures* • *Warrants*

Options, futures, and warrants have one thing in common: they speculate on the future. They are all contracts to sell or buy a commodity at a given price within a specified time. Futures and options are used as a hedge against a price change, while a warrant is an inducement to buy.

An option is just that—an option or choice of doing or not doing something or buying or not buying something. Options have expiration dates and until the option expires, the option owner has exclusive control over whatever the option covers. In real estate, an option means that a speculator has purchased the privilege of exercising a choice (option) to buy a specific piece of real estate or not to buy it as long as the option is in effect. Until the option expires, no one else can purchase that particular piece of real estate. I will say more about real estate options later. Options are also used in other industries and businesses, such as publishing and entertainment, and are also available in the securities field.

STOCK OPTIONS

There are two main types of options in the securities business: "calls" and "puts." A call is the right to *buy* a fixed number of shares of stock at a stated price within a specified period of time. It is the right to "call for stock" and pay the agreed upon purchase price for it. A put is the right to *sell* a certain number of shares of stock at a specific price within a fixed period of time. The put buyer is obligated to "put" the stock up for sale.

Call Option

In the case of a call option, the call writer (investor) sells the right to sell a fixed number of securities at the specified price (strike price) within a definite period of time—usually about nine months from the date of initiation of the option and ending on the third Friday of the ninth month, at 2 P.M. Chicago time.

The speculator (call buyer) buys the right by paying a premium to the call writer through a stockbroker. The call writer receives the premium, which reduces the cost of the underlying security. If the market value of this underlying security does not go above the strike price, the underlying security remains the property of the call writer. If the market value goes above the strike price, the call writer will have to sell the securities at the strike price. Speculators of course hope that the strike price will be above their cost, including premium, so that they make a profit on the deal.

The risk for call writers is that the market value of the underlying security may rise when they have sold their right to sell it for a lower cost.

The buyer of the call option believes and hopes that the market value will increase above the strike price. An owner of a call option has the right to "call," and the writer is obligated to deliver (sell) the security at the strike price. The buyer has the advantage of buying the security at a lower price and selling it at the current price, thereby realizing a profit. In this case, the value of the option has also increased, due to the difference between the strike price specified in the option and the actual or current value. The speculator can sell the option to a third party before it expires and realize a profit in that way also.

By buying an option, the speculator controls a specified number of shares of the underlying stock by paying only about 10% of its value for it. Thus, a greater return is possible on a smaller investment. By not exercising the option (right to buy), the speculator cannot lose more than the investment.

Any dividends paid to the holder of record of the underlying security go to the owner of the stock, not the option buyer.

It is also possible for option writers to speculate. They may sell an option *without owning the underlying stock.* In this case an option writer guarantees to deliver a certain amount of stock at a fixed price within a certain period of time. If the stock goes down (below the strike price), the option writer makes a profit. If the security is called when the stock goes up, the writer has to go to the market and buy the security to deliver at the strike price.

Selling an option while owning the underlying security is considered selling a "covered option." Selling an option without owning the underlying security is called a "naked option."

Put Option

Put options work the same way as call options. Sellers of put options sell the right to buy securities at a specific price within a definite period of time. The seller of the put option is obligated to buy and the buyer has the right to sell. The buyer pays a premium to the seller for this right. Buyers of put options insure themselves against a loss should the value of the stock go down.

Call and put options are paper transactions. They are placed through a stockbroker and can be had on many securities. Only options on specific securities can be traded on the various exchanges, however, and this gives the options liquidity. Options traded "over-the-counter" lack the liquidity that should be a major concern in any investment.

Call and Put Strategies

Since calls and puts are used to insure against losses in a fluctuating market, combinations of both have been devised to minimize losses and to maximize gains, no matter what the market does.

Straddle. If you buy a straddle, you buy a call and a put on the same stock. To sell (write) a straddle, you sell a call and a put. The expiration date and the strike price are the same for both the call and the put.

Call spread. In this case, you buy a call and sell a call on the same security, but the strike price and/or expiration date are different.

Diagonal spread. You are buying and selling the same security, but with a different strike price and a different expiration date.

Combination. You buy a call and put on the same security, or sell a call and a put at the same time on the same security with the same expiration date and strike price.

Variable hedge. Selling one more call for each 100 shares owned.

There are other combinations of call and put, but only those security owners who can afford to speculate should get involved. The Securities and Exchange Commissions as well as reputable brokerage houses are very careful about allowing only financially qualified option traders to participate. All too often the trader takes credit for successful transactions, and losses are blamed on the broker. Either way, speculating in options is tricky.

REAL ESTATE OPTIONS

Suppose someone in the homebuilding business thinks it will be possible to turn a profit by constructing a house on a certain plot of land. The builder does not know whether there is a market for the style, price, and location of the type of house he or she has in mind, and also does not own the parcel of land. The builder can buy an option on the lot if the lot owner is thinking of selling. Builders can buy one lot and the option to buy a number of additional lots adjacent to the original lot if the area is not built up and is open to development. They are ready then to build on the lot they own. Should the house prove to be difficult to sell, they are not bound to go through with the purchase of the optioned lots. They will have lost only the option premium. The landowner is free to sell the lots to another developer. The payment of the premium compensated the landowner for not having the land available for sale to someone else while the option was in effect.

Here is another real estate option application: a real estate trader has a rental prospect for a building that is for sale. Having that prospect under lease would make ownership of that building profitable. The real estate trader can buy an option on the property to buy it at a specific price by a specific date, and will pay the current owner a premium for keeping the property off the market. If and when the rental agreement is signed, the trader can go through with the real estate property deal and buy the building as agreed. Should the rental agreement not go through, the trader loses only the option cost. It is sometimes possible to buy an option on property and sell it (the option) at a higher price before it expires to someone who is anxious to have the property. Options on real estate will be bought for speculation if it is suspected that an airport will expand, a shopping center will be built, or a highway will be constructed. Sometimes the deals go through and sometimes they don't. Owners of real estate options take their chances.

FUTURES

Mr. McDonald grows corn on his farm and is ready to plant his next crop. The price of corn is running about $2.20 a bushel,* and he predicts that he must get at least that when he harvests it to cover all his costs and to assure himself a profit. Anything can go wrong—or right. The weather may be unfavorable or perfect. The value of the dollar may rise or fall. Other corn-producing areas may have good or bad yields. Many factors can affect the price of corn on the market. How can Mr. McDonald protect himself today? In the past, a farmer took his chances; today he can sell his future crop by posting a "good faith deposit" with his broker.

Before Mr. McDonald can sell, someone must buy. Mr. Miller processes corn. He has customers who depend upon him to supply them next year at the same competitive prices as today. It seems logical that Mr. Miller and Mr. McDonald should get together, and they do. Mr. McDonald commits himself to deliver a fixed quantity of corn at a pre-arranged price by a specified date. If everything goes well, he has assured himself a fair profit and has guaranteed himself

---

*Not necessarily the current market value.

no loss. On the other hand, the price of corn may go up, and he will have sacrificed the chance of making a larger profit. Be that as it may, he has secured himself a buyer for his crop at a price he is willing to sell for.

Mr. Miller has also assured himself a reasonable profit, and has guaranteed to meet his customers' needs at a competitive price by also posting a 5% good faith deposit to show his sincerity in fulfilling his end of the bargain. If the price of corn drops, he is locked in to buy at a price agreed on in advance. His competition could buy cheaper and sell cheaper, but this is the risk he takes. Both parties have arranged for themselves a hedge against an unexpected variation in the price of corn. These kinds of arrangements provide a stabilizing influence on price, supply, and demand.

Mr. McDonald and Mr. Miller do not know each other; they did not come to agreement over the McDonald back fence or Mr. Miller's desk. They made the necessary arrangements through a commodity broker. The whole transaction is a paper one, but is nonetheless binding on both.

Futures can be contracted for any commodity that does not currently exist in a form attractive to buyers, but that will in the future. Beef, soybeans, pork bellies, cotton, sugar, chickens, fruits, and coffee, as well as crude oil, gold, Swiss francs, and U.S. Treasury bills are some examples of commodities that are bought and sold by futures contracts. There are many exchanges that deal only in futures.

To participate in such trades, it is not necessary to be either a producer or a processor. Speculators are willing to buy and sell futures contracts. They also put up a good faith deposit. If the current market value of the underlying commodity is greater than the price stated in the futures contract, the value of the futures goes up. If the value of the commodity goes down, the futures contract is worth less. By the expiration date, the speculator must either sell the futures contract or take physical possession of the commodity. The last thing a speculator wants is actual possession of a herd of cattle or carloads of wheat.

When speculators cannot take physical possession and sell their contracts they may have to do so at a lower price than the purchase price. If they cannot deliver the commodity they contracted to deliver, they must buy the contract back at a possibly higher price. Remember that they only paid about 5% on the contract and have put themselves at risk for the remaining 95%.

Trading in futures gives those who are in production, consumption, importing, or wholesaling the opportunity to protect their profit margins, establish costs, and reduce the risk of commodity price fluctuation. Investors who are in none of these businesses can also trade in futures, but their objective is strictly to take advantage of the vagaries of the market.

WARRANTS

Another option—which is not, however, looked upon as such—is the warrant, or "right." Warrants are usually issued as an inducement to buy a new issue of stocks or bonds. The issuer of the security will attach a warrant (or right) to buy additional shares—usually common stocks at a fixed price on or within a fixed date—of the security. These warrants may be detached from the security after an announced time and sold separately. They may be negotiable. The market price of the warrant will reduce the cost of the security bought. The value of the warrant will change with the variation of the market value of the underlying stock and the conversion price stated on the warrant certificate.

What Is the Risk?

Options, futures, and warrants depend on market fluctuations, so their success or failure cannot be predicted. For the investor, they can be a hedge against possible losses. The speculator is in the position of controlling a greater amount than invested and, if lucky, can realize a much greater return at the risk of losing a proportionately smaller sum.

If the security goes down, or is "flat"—that is, not moving—speculators will lose. Call writers, on the other hand, will gain if the underlying security is not being called and they can keep the premium. Speculators can gain if the value of the underlying security rises. Consequently, they can call in the stock or sell the option. Call writers will gain, but not as much. Their returns will be limited, since they have lost the opportunity of selling their stock at the higher market price once they lose control of the stock.

Investors are at greater risk if they write an option without owning the underlying security—that is, when they have written a "naked option." In futures, with only about 5% of the contract on deposit, 95% is at risk. This may be a very high risk for an ordinary investor.

Warrants may be worthless at their expiration date if the exchange or conversion price is the same or lower than the market value of the stock. If the warrant was an inducement to buy, the original purchase itself should be the justification for owning the stock. A warrant bought on the open market is subject to the same vagaries as an option.

A real estate option may not represent a risk, but it can be a hedge against greater losses. Real estate options may or may not be negotiable.

What Is the Return?

The return in relation to the investment can be very high in proportion to the amount invested.

What Is the Liquidity?

Options, futures, or warrants can be readily traded if they have a market value. There are twelve major commodity exchanges in the U.S. Futures offered by reputable brokerage houses should present no trading problem. Options are traded by most national and regional exchanges. Options traded over-the-counter, however, are not very liquid, and you should appraise these carefully before you get involved with them.

What About Taxes?

Trading in options, futures, and warrants requires special tax treatment by the IRS, and these rules are subject to change. Your broker and/or accountant is best qualified to give proper information.

Can It be Used in Retirement Plans?

The "prudent man" rule precludes trading in options, futures, and warrants with the possible exception of covered calls or buying puts. Check with the Retirement Plan Prototype (see Chapter 15).

Can It be Used as Collateral?

Options, futures, and warrants cannot be used as collateral for a loan.

Is It a Hedge Against Inflation?

Options, futures, and warrants are no hedge against inflation because of their short life before expiration.

Must It Go Through Probate?

The handling of options, futures, and warrants may present special problems for the executor of an estate, but they must be treated like estate assets and are subject to probate.

Your Financial Security	Bank Credit Union	Insurance Annuity	Bonds Corp.	Bonds Muni.	Treasuries Commercial Paper	Stocks	Real Estate	Investment Companies Mutual Funds Trusts R.E.I.T.s	Options Futures Warrants
What is the risk?									
What is the return?									
What is the liquidity?									
What about the taxes?									
Retirement plans?									
Collateral?									
Inflation hedge?									
Probate?									

SPECIFICS OF INVESTING

The next chapters will discuss the specifics of various kinds of investments. These have been divided into segments that could be grouped together, but certain kinds of information and explanations cut across all lines and could not be specifically categorized. In Chapter 22 you will find specific information about such things as joint ownership, how to verify a signature, explanations of default and bankruptcy, and so on. If you have not found what you are looking for elsewhere in this book, Chapter 22 may clear up any confusion you may have regarding the intricacies of investments.

There are no stupid questions,
only stupid answers.

14

REGULATORY AGENCIES

Stock Exchanges • Over-the-Counter (OTC) Stocks • The Federal Reserve System • The Securities and Exchange Commission • Other Federal Agencies and Associations • What is Money?

STOCK EXCHANGES

I have said before that for every buyer there must be a seller. In stock trades, any corporation has a fixed number of shares, and only those "for sale" can be "bought." As with any other kind of transaction, if sellers know a buyer for their product, they can effect a sale without an intermediary agent. With stocks, such sales and purchases are rarely possible, so a central market was the logical way to bring buyer and seller together, and stock exchanges came into being.

The biggest securities market in the United States is the New York Stock Exchange. About 75% of all exchange transactions are handled there. The American Stock Exchange and the many regional exchanges handle the balance. The exchanges provide a place for their members to conduct business. The New York Stock Exchange currently has 1,366 members, most of them officers or directors of brokerage houses who will act for their houses in buying and selling securities for their customers. Member-brokers who have the same security to offer compete against each other in selling their securities to prospective buyers (other member-brokers) for the highest price. The buyers, of course, try to buy at the lowest price. Stock exchanges can be compared to auctions and, as a matter of fact, they are often referred to as "auction markets."

Various member-brokers have delineated for themselves certain functions and areas of expertise. For instance, "specialists" are brokers who specialize in certain stocks and, by doing so, are able to maintain a fair and orderly market in the securities in which they specialize. "Commission brokers" execute orders for the clients of their firms, and the client pays the firm a commission for the service. "Two-dollar" brokers execute orders for members who may be too busy to do it themselves and are paid a commission by the broker-member—and it is not two dollars. There are also "registered traders" who trade for themselves—that is, for their own accounts. All of these specialists may trade for themselves or their own accounts, but a client's orders take precedence.

Memberships in stock exchanges are called "seats," and are limited. They can be sold to individuals who meet certain exchange requirements; the sale price is negotiated between the seller of the seat and the buyer.

Securities listed on the New York Stock Exchange must meet certain specifications. Currently, one of them is that at least one million shares must be publicly held and there must be at least 2,000 shareholders who own a hundred shares or more. The market value of all the shares must be at least $16,000,000. There are other requirements, such as a limit on the minimum earnings for the past three years, certain strengths and stability of the company, and future earning capability. A company may no longer be listed if it does not meet minimum requirements. Listing requirements on the American Stock Exchange and the regional exchanges are not quite as rigid as they are for the New York Stock Exchange. Most companies listed on the New York Stock Exchange are also listed on the regional exchanges, but very few are listed on the New York and the American exchanges at the same time. Those that are are referred to as "dually listed." Smaller companies, or companies doing business in certain regions only, may only be listed on the regional exchange in their area.

OVER-THE-COUNTER (OTC) STOCKS

There are also companies that are not formally listed at all. Stocks in these are traded "over-the-counter." Individual brokerage houses may maintain an inventory of such securities, and will sell them to other brokers who have interested customers. Maintaining such an inventory is called "making a market," and brokers who handle the securities making up such an inventory are referred to as "market makers" of those stocks. They buy stocks for their inventory and sell stocks from it acting as brokers for their clients or as dealers with other brokers. As dealers they can trade from their inventory as a principal, in which case they take a mark-up and their profit and sales expenses (commissions) are included in the mark-up. The dollar amount of this mark-up does not have to be shown on the confirmation slip, but the dealer's position as a principal must be disclosed. When they act as brokers or agents for their clients, the commission must then be shown along with the disclosure of the dealer's position as a broker.

As there may be several market makers dealing in the same security who are located all over the country, a nationwide telecommunication network allows buying agents to know the "ask" price of a security from other market makers. They will then negotiate with one or more to get the best price for their clients. A selling agent, of course, will negotiate for the best "bid" price for a client. Such negotiations make the over-the-counter market a "negotiated market," which is different from the "auction market" of the various exchanges. The difference between the bid price a market maker is willing to pay and the ask or selling price is the maker's profit.

Securities sold over-the-counter are known as "unlisted securities," and include all new issues just going public; mutual funds (closed-end funds); many bank and insurance stocks; corporate, municipal, and government bonds; and foreign securities.

All transactions—whether negotiated over-the-counter or auctioned on the exchanges—are regulated by the Securities and Exchange Commission. Salesmen, agents, registered representatives, and account executives are registered with it, as are the various exchanges themselves. The National Association of Securities Dealers

(NASD) cooperates with the SEC in regulating all over-the-counter transactions and the sales personnel involved in them.

Only after passing a New York Stock Exchange examination can a person work as a broker for a member of that exchange. All other exchanges also honor this examination. Many insurance agents take the NASD test to be able to sell mutual funds.

THE SECURITIES AND EXCHANGE COMMISSION

The Securities and Exchange Commission (SEC) was created by Congress in 1934. It is an independent, bipartisan, quasi-judicial agency of the United States government. Its purpose is to protect the public against misrepresentation, manipulation, and fraudulent acts and practices in the purchase and sale of securities. Securities laws and regulations are designed to facilitate informed investment analyses and prudent and discriminating decisions by the investing public. In the final analysis, however, it is the investor, not the commission, who must make the ultimate judgment of the worth of securities offered for sale.

Before a security is offered to the public, it must be registered so as to provide disclosure of financial and other information, on the basis of which investors may appraise the merits of the securities. Securities that do not have to be registered are those issued as private offerings to a limited number of persons or institutions and not to the general public, or securities issued by municipal, state, or federal and other governmental agencies.

The SEC also supervises the trading of securities and requires the registration of security exchanges (stock exchanges) as well as broker-dealers (brokerage houses) and their agents (account executives or registered representatives). It is the duty of the commission, under the laws it administers, to investigate complaints or other infractions and violations in securities transactions, and to prosecute if necessary. It has the power to make surprise audits of brokerage houses and subpoena their records and other documents.

The commission is not a collection agency for investor losses. It has only the right to investigate all complaints, but it has the power to revoke or suspend the registration of everything and everybody under its jurisdiction. There are also state SECs which license those doing securities business within its boundaries. These state SECs may revoke or suspend any license for violation upon the findings of the federal SEC.

The SEC is thus the prosecuting agency of the U.S. government, as well as the adviser in proceedings for reorganization of debtor corporations in which there is a public interest (see Chapter 22).

THE FEDERAL RESERVE SYSTEM

The Federal Reserve System was established on December 23, 1913, by the Federal Reserve Act. The system was designed to give the country an elastic currency, to provide facilities for discounting commercial paper, and to improve the supervision of banking practices. The Federal Reserve System was thus created to help the nation achieve its economic and financial objectives within the framework of national goals and objectives as established within the legislative and executive branches of the United States government. In the economic sphere, the "Fed" (as it is sometimes referred to) helps to achieve these goals by its influence on the availability and cost of bank reserves, bank credit, and money in circulation.

Almost 5,600 commercial banks are members of the system. The primary functions of the system's Board of Governors are to formulate monetary policy, to supervise and regulate the activities of member commercial banks, and to oversee the Federal Reserve Bank. The board is responsible for establishing maximum interest rates that member banks may pay for savings and time deposits. The similar responsibility for setting ceiling rates payable by non-member commercial and savings banks and by insured savings and loan associations, respectively, rests with the Federal Deposit Insurance Corporation and the Federal Home Loan Bank Board. The structure of ceiling rates so established contributes to equitable competition among banks (commercial) and thrift institutions (savings and loan associations) for interest-earning deposits from the public. The Securities Exchange Act of 1934 and its subsequent amendments also authorize the Board of Governors to regulate the use of credit for purchasing or carrying securities. In exercising this responsibility, the board imposes limitations on the amount of such credit that may be extended to brokers and dealers (Regulation T), banks (Regulation U), and other lenders (Regulation G).

By statute, the Federal Open Market Committee (FOMC) is responsible for determining what transactions the Federal Reserve Bank will conduct in the open market by buying and selling U.S. government securities, Federal Agency securities, or banker acceptances. In this manner, the Federal Reserve System absorbs and releases bank reserves and thereby controls the money supply. The operation of the Federal Reserve System is conducted through a nationwide network of twelve Federal Reserve banks.

National banks (they always have "national" as part of the name) are chartered by the Comptroller of the Currency, who is an official of the U.S. Department of the Treasury. All national commercial banks must belong to the Federal Reserve System. Banks chartered by the various state banking departments may belong if they meet the necessary requirements.

Banks that become members of the Federal Reserve System must assume several important obligations: they must maintain sufficient monetary reserves on hand to meet the requirements established by the Board of Governors. Such reserves may be either deposits at their Reserve bank (these do not draw interest) or cash in their own vaults. They must remit at par for checks drawn against them when presented by a Reserve bank for payment. They must comply with various federal laws, regulations, and conditions of membership regarding the adequacy of capital, mergers with other banking institutions, establishment of branches, relations with bank holding companies, interlocking directorates, loan and investment limitations, and other matters. If the member bank is chartered by a state, it is subject to general supervision and examination by the Federal Reserve System.

Benefits accompany membership in the Federal Reserve System. For example, when they are temporarily in need of additional funds member banks may borrow from the Federal Reserve banks, subject to criteria for such borrowing (customarily called "discounting") as set by statute and regulation. Member banks may: use Federal Reserve facilities for collecting checks, settling clearing balances, and transferring funds by wire to other cities; obtain currency as needed; share in the informational facilities provided by the system; and participate in the election of six of the nine directors of the Federal Reserve bank for their district.

OTHER FEDERAL AGENCIES
   AND ASSOCIATIONS

The Federal Home Loan Bank was established in 1932 as an independent federal agency. It charters all federal savings and loan institutions, also referred to as thrift institutions. All such chartered banks belong to the Federal Home Loan Bank. In addition, banks chartered by various states may join voluntarily. The designation "federal" identifies a bank that is federally chartered. These thrift institutions comprise the country's major source of funds to finance the construction and purchase of private housing. There are currently about 4,200 such institutions in the U.S.

The Federal Home Loan Bank Board also serves as the Board of Directors of the Federal Home Loan Mortgage Corporation, which was established by the Emergency Home Finance Act of 1970 to operate a secondary market in conventional mortgages. "Secondary market" here means the resale of mortgages by the mortgagor to another investor. The Federal Savings and Loan Insurance Corporation insures the deposits in institutions chartered by the Federal Home Loan Bank.

A Federal Credit Union is a cooperative association organized to promote thrift among its members and to accumulate a fund from these savings to make needed loans to members for useful purposes at reasonable interest rates. It is not a government agency, but it is chartered and supervised by the federal government through the National Credit Union Administration. Membership is limited to persons having a common bond of occupation or association, and to groups within a well-defined neighborhood, community, or rural district. The Federal Credit Union Act, which was passed in 1934, provides for the chartering and supervision of Federal Credit Unions. Its general provisions are similar to those of many state credit union laws, and are based on the best experience gained under state laws that preceded its passage by Congress. Since 1934 there have been amendments to update the Federal Credit Union Act. For instance, legislation enacted in October of 1970 provides that share accounts (equivalent to deposit accounts in other banks) in federal credit unions are insured by the National Credit Union Administration (NCUA).

Among other restrictions, the surplus funds of the credit union may be invested only in obligations of the federal government or its agencies; in obligations of the Federal National Mortgage Association; in shares of central credit unions; in loans to other credit unions; and in shares or accounts of institutions insured by the Federal Savings and Loan Insurance Corporation or the Federal Deposit Insurance Corporation, or in shares of federally insured credit unions. All Federal Credit Unions are supervised and periodically examined by the National Credit Union Administration.

As has been said before, not all banks, thrift institutions, and credit unions are chartered by the federal government. However, all states charter counterparts that have the same functions and loss protection as the federally chartered ones.

Federal Insurance Agencies

Deposits in institutions chartered by the federal government are insured by the Federal Deposit Insurance Corporation (FDIC), the Federal Savings and Loan Insurance Corporation (FSLIC), and the National Credit Union Administration (NCUA). State chartered institutions joining the federal organizations are also insured through the same agencies. Other state chartered institutions are not obliged to belong, and are not compelled to insure their deposits. They do have their own insurance, however, and the deposits are insured to the same extent as the federally sponsored plans. Since all banks provide equal protection it is not necessary for potential depositors to investigate each one's coverage. But any institution that carries deposit protection is only too happy to inform depositors by prominently displaying the appropriate emblem. If you do not see it, ask about it.

The maximum protection limits are the same for all accounts, regardless of the size and regardless of whether the deposit is in a commercial bank, savings and loan institution, or credit union. Each account is insured up to $100,000. If two people have a joint account and each one has a separate account, together they have three accounts and their maximum protection is a total of $300,000.

Money and securities entrusted to brokerage houses are insured by the Securities Investor Protection Corporation (SIPC). This is a government-sponsored insurance program under the supervision of the Securities and Exchange Commission. Maximum coverage is $100,000, of which $40,000 can be in cash and $60,000 in securities. In addition, some brokerage houses may voluntarily extend their protection to a total of $500,000.

The SIPC is a non-profit membership corporation which receives its revenue from those brokers and dealers who are required, by law, to be members. SIPC does not protect customers against losses resulting from fluctuations in securities prices, but is an instrument for the orderly distribution to customers of their securities and cash balances within the limits provided by law in the event of the financial demise of a SIPC member broker or dealer.

WHAT IS MONEY?

Everybody knows what money is—especially when they don't have any. If money grew on trees and was free for the picking, no one would put any value on it and would not accept it in exchange for goods and services. Ultimately, what makes money valuable is its scarcity and the guarantees backing it up by the issuing government. If money is seen simply as a medium of exchange, cattle, shells, or beads would do just as well—and, in fact, have done so. But where does money come from and how does it enter our economy? This is a serious question and many books have been written on it. I will try to discuss it in the simplest terms possible.

All we really want to know about money is how much in goods and services it will buy and how we can get enough of it to buy what we want and need. We all know about government mints where money is stamped out in the form of coins or printed as paper dollars. The amount of money—its volume—must be controlled by the issuing government to make it scarce and thereby more valuable. In the past, governments have printed much more money than they could guarantee in the hopes of solving their economic ills, but have only succeeded in debasing their currency and bringing financial ruin on themselves. So much money was printed in Germany after the First World War that it took a wheelbarrow full of it to buy a loaf of bread or a postage stamp. After the German inflation of 1923, the new "rentenmark" currency survived because the amount the government issued was restricted.

There are two kinds of money: currency (paper money and

coins) and deposits in checking accounts (called demand deposits because you can get your money back on demand). One dollar in currency and one dollar in a demand deposit are convertible into each other.

When a check is cashed, the amount of money on deposit is reduced and the amount in circulation is increased. The money a government issues is a liability for it and money in demand deposits are bank liabilities. The real value of money is the confidence people have in it. Everyone assumes that "something" stands behind it to guarantee its value. This something is the amount of gold and silver bullion a government stores in its vaults. Gold is the one thing all governments over the ages have agreed would support their money.

Before August of 1971, the U.S. Treasury Department bought and sold gold for a fixed price in terms of U.S. dollars. By the end of 1974, the U.S. gold stock stood at almost $12 billion. After August 1971, the United States could no longer peg the price of gold to the U.S. dollar because the rest of the world's banking systems refused to sell us gold at our price. The reason for this was that the value of their money began to exceed the value of ours. We had to allow the price of gold to "float" and find its own buying and selling price. Up until 1974, it was illegal for a private person in the United States to own gold. Now the ordinary citizen can trade in the world's open market, just as governments do.

Control of the amount of money in circulation, therefore, is essential if its value as a scarce commodity is to be maintained. The actual worth of money, however, can only be measured by what it will buy, and this worth varies inversely with the general level of prices. If the amount of money in circulation grows faster than the rate at which the output of goods and services can be increased—prices will rise. There will be more money chasing fewer commodities. Any increase in prices reduces the value of money even though the monetary unit is "backed" by sound assets. If, on the other hand the volume of money in circulation does not keep pace with the production of goods and services, prices will fall. There will not be enough money available to buy all those goods and services.

How large should the money supply be in order to handle all the transactions of an economy without affecting prices? The answer depends on how money is used. Some holders of money spend it quickly and the money goes back into circulation; others hold onto their dollars by saving them. If too many people hold on to too much money, not enough will be in circulation to conduct business.

It is the job of the Federal Reserve banking system to know how much money there is in circulation and how much needs to be in circulation at any given time. Before going on to discuss how the Federal Reserve bank operates, let's say a little bit more about money.

The creation of money (not the actual minting and printing) takes place in commercial banks. Accounts increase when customers deposit currency and checks, and when the proceeds of loans made by banks are credited to the borrower's accounts. Banks can go on building up deposits by increasing loans and investments so long as they keep enough currency on hand to redeem whatever amounts the holders of demand deposits want to convert to currency.

By law, all banks that are members of the Federal Reserve system must maintain deposit balances at its district Federal Reserve bank equal to its deposits for a seven-day period ending every Wednesday. When a bank finds that it does not have enough cash on its own vaults to cover its demand deposits, it borrows from these reserves. The reserves deposited with the Federal Reserve Bank are assets to the bank, but liabilities to the Fed. When commercial banks borrow from the Federal Reserve bank, they are charged an interest called the "discount rate." The Federal Reserve system attempts to control the flow of money by raising the discount rate to discourage borrowing or reducing it to encourage borrowing.

The Federal Reserve system obtains money by buying it in the form of Treasury bills from a dealer in U.S. securities. It pays for these securities by checks issued on itself. The securities dealers deposit these checks in their own account with a commercial bank which sends it on to the Federal Reserve bank for collection and immediate credit to the commercial bank's account at the Federal Reserve bank. Thus the commercial bank has reserves on deposit with the Federal Reserve bank which did not exist before and money has been created in the form of demand deposits which, as we have seen earlier, are immediately convertible into currency.

Bank deposits must be supported by reserves and the Federal Reserve system's influence over money rests on its control over the aggregate volume of reserves and the conditions by which member banks may gain access to these reserves. The volume of money does not change, only the way money circulates and how much it costs to borrow it. You buy money when you borrow and sell it when you lend.

There is much more to understanding how money and the

United States Federal Reserve system operates than I can possibly say here. I urge investors to find out all they can about what money is and how it works. The Federal Reserve Bank of Chicago publishes a pamphlet called *Modern Money Mechanics* and copies are available from the Research Department, Federal Reserve Bank of Chicago, P.O. Box 834, Chicago, Illinois, 60690. The booklet explains in detail how currency and bank deposits are handled by the U.S. Federal Reserve system.

15

RETIREMENT PLANS

ERISA • Corporate Pension Plans • Vesting • Pension Benefit Guaranty Corporation • Keogh (HR 10) • Simplified IRA/Employer IRA • 403(b) • Individual Retirement Account (IRA) • IRA Roll-Over • Investment Possibilities • Employee Stock Ownership Trust (ESOT) • Receiving Pension Benefits

---

In Chapter 3 I talked about the retirement benefit period. In this chapter I will discuss specifics of the various pension plans. As I have noted before, qualified pension plans are a very important means to accumulate assets toward those "golden years" of secure, comfortable retirement. During the working years, the initial investment and its growth from wise investing are not taxed. In the past, managers of pension funds were not held as accountable as they are today. To increase the benefits to workers and their beneficiaries the laws, rules, regulations, and limitations are constantly being adjusted and amended. By periodically reviewing this chapter you can evaluate your own situation and perhaps decide when and how any of these plans can best serve you in assuring you and your family a financially carefree retirement.

ERISA

Before the enactment of the Employee Retirement Income Security Act in 1974 (commonly known as ERISA), there were no strict laws protecting participants in most pension plans. Excessive privileges were granted to some pension fund officials, while the workers paying into the fund had few rights. Money paid into some pension plans was wiped out by mismanagement of the fund. Before 1974, there were only a few pension plans that could meet today's standards. Since then, any contribution to an ERISA-approved pension plan has been protected by legislation.

ERISA's purpose is to protect the interests of workers and their beneficiaries regardless of age, sex, religion, or race. While it does not demand that an employer set up a pension plan for its employees, it has drawn up guidelines for funding, participation, and vesting requirements for all qualified pension plans. ("Vesting" means "ownership of benefits or rights." I will say more about it later on.) ERISA requires that you be given the right to certain pension benefits you have earned, even though you leave that job before retirement. ERISA also provides for persons who are gainfully employed who happen to work for a company without a retirement program, or who are in business for themselves, to make their own arrangements for participating in pension plans.

CORPORATE PENSION PLANS

Any employer's decision to set up a plan is voluntary. Most companies have such plans to attract the best working force and to show concern for the welfare of their employees. Once a corporate pension plan is set up, however, its execution is mandatory under ERISA. A company cannot decide to do away with a pension plan once it has established one, and once established it is very difficult to change unless the changes are to the employee's benefit.

Basically, there are three types of pension plans:

Defined Contribution

1. Profit-Sharing: contributions are fixed to a percentage (not to exceed 15%) of the profits of the employer and credited to the employee on an equitable basis.
2. Contributions may be tied to the amount of compensation paid to the employee. Contributions may be in cash and/or stocks with a stated maximum value.

Defined Benefit

3. Certain benefits may be explicitly defined with contributions calculated to meet these needs.

Once a plan has been established, it must be administered. The administrator may be anyone designated by the corporation (sponsor) or the fiduciary (trustee) of the plan. The duties of the administrator include filing the necessary reports with the Department of Labor, the Internal Revenue Service, and the Pension Benefit Guaranty Corporation. The fiduciary is anyone who controls the assets of or has discretionary power over the plan. Fiduciaries are required to discharge their duties solely in the interests of the workers and beneficiaries for the exclusive purpose of providing them with the benefits to which they are entitled and to defray reasonable expenses of the plan. If fiduciaries breach any responsibilities imposed on them by ERISA they are personally.liable for any losses to the plan under law. Although they may receive reasonable reimbursement of properly incurred expenses, they cannot be paid if they are already receiving a salary from the employer or union whose plan they are overseeing.

ERISA is very specific about the participation of eligible employees in a pension plan. They and their beneficiaries must receive a summary plan description in easily understandable language within 90 days of eligibility and no later than 120 days after the plan is subject to reporting and disclosure provisions. Employees must be advised of any change in plan description, and annual reports, statements of accrued benefits, and all pertinent data must be available for inspection at any time.

Generally, employees become eligible to participate in a corporate retirement plan when they have reached the age of twenty-five and have given at least one year of full-time service or a thousand hours to the company. No one may be discriminated against, but certain plans may exclude new employees who are within five years of retirement.

VESTING

Vesting means that an employee has a "vested" interest in a pension plan—that is, undisputed ownership of certain pension benefits. In some plans, full vesting may require three years of service, but vesting privileges are usually extended after one full year. If a plan sponsor (the corporation) is sold to another company, the workers' pension time accrued and vesting privileges can be carried over to the new company's pension plan. If workers move from one company to another, ERISA provides that their benefits go with them. They may leave their accumulation with their old company if their plan allows it, transfer it to the new company if their plan will accept it, or transfer it into an IRA "Roll Over."

The following are specific ERISA vesting rules:

1. Full vesting after ten years of service if there are no partial vesting stipulations.
2. Graded vesting with 25% after five years, plus 5% for each additional year up to ten years of full service, with an added 10% for each year thereafter. Full vesting (100%) is attained after fifteen years.
3. The "rule of 45," which is based on age and service, and which means that the employees' vesting provisions must be 50% if they have at least five years of service and their age and length of service total forty-five. In addition, 10% for each year over that must be included.

Under any of the options, an employee must be at least 50% vested after ten years of service and 100% after fifteen years. Profit-sharing, stock bonuses, and money purchase plans in each year's contributions vest separately but must provide 100% vesting not later than the end of the fifth plan year. Some plans require the employee to contribute a small amount which the employer matches one-for-one, or one dollar for every two dollars. In that case, the employee's contribution has already been taxed, so the return accumulates tax-free. The employer's contribution must also vest no later than five years after payment has been made.

All pension plans have trustees—several people who jointly direct the affairs of the plan. The trustees may invest the assets of the fund any way they deem to be in the interests of the workers and their beneficiaries. Trustees must at all times act according to the "prudent man" rule. This is a legal term that is difficult to define exactly, but it can be used in a court of law to show that someone has or has not acted cautiously and wisely. In the case of a pension fund's assets, no more than 10% may be invested in the employer's securities or in real estate.

PENSION BENEFIT GUARANTY CORPORATION (PBGC)

When the defined contributions to a pension plan depend upon the profits of the employer—as, for instance, in the case of profit-sharing—the employer's responsibility is to fulfill the commitment to the plan. But sometimes this responsibility may be impossible to meet during adverse business conditions, bankruptcy, or other factors beyond the company's control. To provide for these contingencies, ERISA provides the services of the Pension Benefit Guaranty Corporation, which is supported by employers offering pension plans that involve defined contributions and defined benefits. PBGC is under the direct supervision of the U.S. Department of Labor and its role is to protect the vested interest of participants in pension plans. In case of default on the part of the employer, PBGC will guarantee and make good the worker's vested interest up to a statutory maximum. It is empowered to attach up to 30% of the employer's assets to compensate itself for such losses.

KEOGH OR HR 10 PLAN

This plan originally became a law under the Self-Employed Individuals Tax Retirement Act of 1962. (ERISA incorporated it into its fold by making certain changes.) The plan was established to create a retirement program for the benefit of sole-proprietor and partnership businesses and their employees. The establishment of pension plans is not mandated by law for such concerns, but is a voluntary act by the owner-employees. Participation in it means that small proprietary businesses can have the same pension benefits as large corporations.

Two types of plans are available:

1. The *defined contribution plan,* which provides for an individual account for each participant, with the benefits based solely on the individual's share of contribution. If the contribution depends on the employer's profit, it is also called

a profit-sharing plan. If the contribution is geared to the employee's income, it is referred to as a money-purchase pension plan. As a money-purchase plan, it may be co-ordinated with the employee's potential Social Security income.

2. The *defined benefit plan,* which stipulates the benefits which will be paid at the time of retirement. It depends upon both the contributions and on good investment performance to meet that goal.

Employees become eligible to participate in both types of Keogh plans at age twenty-five with at least three years of full-time service, and become fully vested with any contribution made in their behalf. The administrator of the plan is usually the sole proprietor or partner, with their accountant assuming the responsibility of filing the required forms with the IRS and Department of Labor.

The maximum that can be invested is 15% of the compensation (salary), not to exceed $7,500 each year for each participant. The percentage applicable to each participant must be the same. For example, if a proprietor-partner earns $50,000 a year and contributes $5,000, or 10% of his earnings each year, everyone else in the business must use the same percentage—10%. Those earning $750 a year or less may invest 100% of their earnings; when they earn more, their contribution percentage reduces to the same as that for other participants.

The trustee for a Keogh Plan may be a bank, individual, or insurance company. Whichever one serves this function, it must meet the "honesty bond" regulation and set up a proper trust agreement. Each one of the trustees is accountable for his or her part of the trusteeship of the plan.

Employees may voluntarily contribute an additional 10% of their salaries, not to exceed $2,500 annually. This voluntary contribution is taxable at the time paid in, but the growth is tax-deferred.

Some banks have an Approved Keogh Plan Prototype Agreement. This is a trust agreement that specifies all rules and regulations prescribed by ERISA to which the bank will conform. The sole proprietor or partner does not relinquish the right to control and supervise, but the trustee assumes the responsibility to protect the plan's assets. Trustees are responsible for losses, however, only if they were due to their own neglect or fault.

Under a Keogh Plan, no withdrawal may be made prior to age 59-1/2 and withdrawal must be begun before age 70-1/2. The only exceptions are the disability or death of the participant. Unauthorized premature withdrawal will result in an excise tax of 10% of the amount taken out in addition to the regular income tax imposed. The ten-year income averaging tax benefit can be used if the accumulation is withdrawn in a lump sum, or the lump sum can be "rolled over" into an IRA roll-over account.

Defined contribution plans can take advantage of many investment opportunities, such as buying an annuity with life insurance as an incidental benefit. U.S. retirement bonds are also available through these plans. Most investment companies—that is, mutual funds—have a qualified trust agreement that also meets the standard for investing in their funds. Brokerage houses use a bank Keogh Prototype Trust Agreement, and all equity products meeting the "prudent man" rule may be used in this manner. Any stockbroker, insurance agent, or bank representative will be happy to offer their services and advise on such plans.

In setting up plans for other than owner-employee programs, an accountant is the best source of information. IRS Publication 560, "Tax Information on Self-Employed Retirement Plans," is very comprehensive and may be obtained from the Department of the Treasury, Internal Revenue Service.

SIMPLIFIED IRA OR EMPLOYER IRA

This plan is so new that at the time of this writing no printed instructions have been issued. Congress enacted this retirement program to help small businesses provide a pension for their employees. The plan does not require employers to report to the U.S. Department of Labor or the IRS. The employer has no fiduciary responsibility, since each plan is in the employee's own name. The contribution is included in the employee W2 tax reporting form, but employees can deduct that amount from their gross income when they fill out their 1040 Federal Tax Form, thus reducing their income tax assessment.

The simplified IRA or employer IRA must be initiated by the employer. Maximum contribution is 15% of the employee's income, not to exceed $7,500 a year, and the percentage may vary with each employee. Employers may reduce their IRA contribution by the amount of Social Security payments. The employer may have more lower-paid employees than higher-paid ones, but no discrimination may be made in favor of higher salaried employees. Any employees receiving less than $1,500 in employer contributions may add the difference themselves if their financial situation so warrants.

Savings accounts, mutual funds, annuities, securities or insurance policies may be used as qualifying investments. The sponsors of these plans—banks, mutual fund investment companies, insurance companies, or brokerage houses—will provide the necessary management services.

As in the Keogh Plan, withdrawal cannot start prior to age 59-1/2 except in cases of disability. Withdrawal must begin by age 70-1/2. Penalties for early withdrawal are the same as for the Keogh Plan—i.e., 10% of of the amount withdrawn in addition to the ordinary tax payment. After age 59-1/2 the proceeds are considered ordinary income, but employees can take advantage of a five-year income-averaging provision. All employees age twenty-five or over who have served for three of the preceding five years are eligible. Employees are 100% vested when contributions are made in their behalf. No voluntary contributions are permitted.

This plan's simplicity makes it attractive to many small business employers. Although no U.S. government publication has been issued as yet, institutions that offer qualified investments can help in setting up such a plan. Accountants or qualified lawyers who have access to the latest information can also help.

403(b)

If you are a qualified employee of a public school system or a non-profit, tax-exempt 501(c)(3) organization operated exclusively for religious, charitable, or educational purposes you are eligible to participate in a tax-sheltered program under Section 403(b) of the Internal Revenue Code. Your employer must purchase the plan for you and will deduct the contributions from your salary. Your contribution will not be shown on your W2 form and you will, therefore, not be reporting it to the IRS and will not be taxed for it. There is a limit, called the "exclusion allowance," for the amount that can be contributed. The following simple formula can be used to

arrive at the annual exclusion allowance for an employee of a qualified employer who has been contributing to a retirement plan such
as State Teacher Retirement Plan or Public Employee Retirement
Plan.

$$\text{Average annual contribution} = \frac{(A \times B) - (5 \times C)}{B + (5 \times D)}$$

where

A = Annual salary
B = Total years of past service
C = Total employer contribution, past and projected future
D = Future years of service (to date of retirement)

To make the computation easy, let's use $10,000 even though it
isn't a realistic wage. If you are earning $10,000 a year, have worked
for a public museum or public school system for ten years, expect to
work for twenty more, and your employer contributes $1,000 per
year, the first part of the equation will read:

$300,000 (10,000 $\times$ 30) – $150,000 (5 $\times$ 30,000)
= $150,000

The second part will be:

10 + 100 or 110

Thus:

$$\frac{\$150,000}{110} = \$1,363.63 \text{ as your annual contribution}$$

An additional limitation of the annual contribution is the lesser
of the above exclusion allowance or 20% of the salary.

In general, most tax-sheltered annuity programs are defined
contribution plans. As of January 1, 1978, an employer's contribution to an employee's account cannot exceed the lesser of 25% of the
employee's annual compensation or $30,050. This dollar limit
changes with the cost-of-living index.

There is also a special "catch-up" provision for employees of educational institutions, hospitals, and health service agencies who want to contribute the amount they were eligible to put aside but did not do so earlier in their working careers. This can only be done in the year of separation from the institution, and there is a limit to the amount that can be contributed in that year. The Internal Revenue Service is very explicit in explaining ways to take advantage of this deduction (see IRS Publication 571). It is to the qualifying employee's benefit to defer federal income taxes to the time of retirement when tax payments could be greatly reduced.

Until a few years ago, only tax-sheltered annuities could be used for such tax-deferred investments because by law only those plans that could guarantee a lifetime income were eligible. This limited plans to insurance companies. Also, fixed or variable annuity or retirement policies with incidental benefits qualified for such tax shelters. The insurance cost of the death benefit was not tax-deductible, since it was considered a current economic gain and the value of this gain was taxed as ordinary income. The loan provision in insurance policies does not apply.

When ERISA allowed mutual fund investment groups to set up a qualifying trust for tax-sheltered investments, this opened up a new investment possibility. Now tax-sheltered participants have the opportunity to set aside all or part of their exclusion allowance in a mutual fund, a fixed annuity, or a variable annuity. Remember that mutual funds have various investment objectives, fixed annuities guarantee a future accumulation, and variable annuities are a combination of both. It is possible to split a tax-sheltered retirement contribution among these various investments, or to switch from one to the other, but no more often than once a year. Many mutual funds that have varied investment objectives permit changing from one to another for little or no charge.

Employers must make participation in 403(b) available to all employees, but they do not have to assume any responsibility for the wisdom of the selection or the correctness of the exclusion allowance. This is a responsibility of the employees, who are in control of their investment. Neither employers nor employees are required to report payments into the plan. All or part of the accumulation can be withdrawn in case of disability or financial need prior to age 59-1/2. "Financial need" has never been defined, so withdrawal is almost at the participant's discretion.

Periodic or lifetime income payments from insurance companies as well as withdrawal plans from mutual funds are available on retirement. The money received is taxable as ordinary income during the year received. If a lump sum payment is requested, the five-year averaging method may be applied. If desired, all or part of the money may be invested in a roll-over IRA.

For more information, check with your stockbroker, insurance agent, mutual fund representative, or employer. As I said before, IRS Publication 571 is very detailed. Publication 506, "Computing Your Tax Under the Income-Averaging Method," is also helpful. These publications are available from your Internal Revenue service or the Superintendent of Documents, U.S. Government Printing Office, Washington, D.C. 20402. A good public library also has these and other government documents on file.

INDIVIDUAL RETIREMENT
ACCOUNT (IRA)

If you are gainfully employed but your place of work does not have a retirement plan, you can initiate your own individual retirement account in which you can contribute up to 15% of your salary, not to exceed $1,500 each year. As there are no fixed requirements for your yearly contribution, you can contribute any percentage you want up to the maximum limit. Your contribution is not taxable when made, but it is deducted from your gross income by making adjustments on Form 1040 when filling out your income tax. If your spouse is not gainfully employed, both of you may participate by contributing 15% of the worker's salary, with the upper limit extended to $1,750 for both or $875 for each IRA account. You can invest with a bank, credit union, insurance company, mutual fund, or brokerage house that has the facilities to offer qualifying services. Or you can take advantage of U.S. government retirement bonds. You cannot contribute to two IRA accounts at the same time, but you can, however, have one IRA and one roll-over IRA.

If you have your own individual retirement account and become eligible to participate in another pension plan, you can leave your accumulation in the IRA account or transfer it to your new plan (if they accept IRA assets, and most do) or you can transfer the assets into another roll-over IRA. The limitations are the same: withdrawal may begin before 59-1/2 only in cases of disability; otherwise a penalty of 10% of the withdrawn amount is imposed. As in other such plans, federal income taxes must be paid if the funds are withdrawn before age 59-1/2. As in the other such plans, withdrawal must begin before age 70-1/2 and no contributions are accepted after age 70-1/2. Lump sum withdrawals are eligible for the five-year income-averaging method of tax payment. For further information, see U.S. Government Publication 590, "Individual Retirement Arrangements, Tax Information on."

ROLL-OVER IRA

If you elect to receive a lump sum payment from a retirement plan—corporate, Keogh, 403(b), or IRA—because of job termination, plan discontinuation, because your employer is going out of business or has been taken over by another company, or for some other reason—you may transfer the accumulation into a roll-over IRA account. Only cash may be rolled over, and this must be done within 60 days of receiving the proceeds. No roll-over is permitted after age 70-1/2. No additional contributions may be made to an existing roll-over IRA account. A roll-over IRA account is thus a "holding" mechanism for a pension fund accumulation which can't be administered, for whatever reason, by any other method. If you are still of working age, however, gainfully employed, and want to contribute to a retirement plan, a regular IRA is to your benefit.

Assets in a roll-over IRA account may not be used as collateral for a loan. These assets, however, may be invested in accordance with your trust agreement through a stockbroker in a "self-directed" plan with a bank as a trustee. Or they may be invested in mutual funds or credit unions, banks, or insurance companies, or in fixed or variable annuities or endowment policies. U.S. government retirement bonds are also a possibility. Assets in a roll-over IRA account may be "rolled over" into another Keogh Plan, a regular IRA account, or a corporate retirement plan. Once rolled over, you cannot return these proceeds into another roll-over IRA account.

If roll-over must be made, a special retirement distribution formula exists which should be investigated before the actual withdrawal is made. A tax expert or the IRS can provide this information.

INVESTMENT POSSIBILITIES

In previous chapters I dealt with the retirement applications for each investment I discussed. To make the right selection, however, various factors should be taken into consideration, not the least of which is time available to maturity. Other conditions affecting retirement application of investments are the total of assets accumulated and the need for income after retirement. Income taxes due after retirement are not a major factor for most people as Social Security income is not taxable when received and senior citizens have special tax benefits.

Individuals who must make their own pension provisions starting with small amounts ($1,500 annually in IRAs or up to $7,500 in Keogh) usually deal with banks. Insurance companies, however, offer annuities that lend themselves very well to investments that guarantee a fixed income after retirement. Mutual funds are also available for adding periodic contributions and have the benefit of having their investment objectives all spelled out. The advantages of all three opportunities should be investigated, and there is no reason why two—or even all three—should not be considered, provided of course that a sufficient amount is being invested.

With large amounts such as might be expected to be accumulated with corporate pension plans or even some Keogh plans, you should also consider the investment opportunities offered by brokerage houses.

The creation of huge assets by pension funds has increased the opportunity for a wide range of investment possibilities. Brokerage houses and insurance companies have special departments to service pension accounts. Many brokerage houses have expanded into insurance or have combined their services with those of insurance companies. Selective real estate financing (mortgages) lends itself very well to pension plan investing, and, of course, banks have investment trusts for pension money. It is to the benefit of future retirees and/or their beneficiaries to take advantage of these various investment opportunities.

Any accumulation in a qualified retirement plan will be distributed to the beneficiaries as designated by the deceased participant. The first $5,000 of the benefits paid out is not taxable, whether it is received in a lump sum or as an annuity. For further information, see U.S. Government Publication 448, "A Guide to Federal Estate and Gift Taxation."

EMPLOYEE STOCK OWNERSHIP TRUST
OR PLAN (ESOT/ESOP)

Whether it is called an Employee Stock Ownership Trust or Plan, this is an ERISA qualified retirement program. It is an ESOP when it forms part of a retirement plan, the balance of which includes a profit-sharing or stock bonus plan. An ESOT, on the other hand, is a trust that may be set up only for the benefit of employees and their beneficiaries, and only the employer's securities, stocks or marketable obligations may be used.

Both ESOT and ESOP work like this. The employer is a closely-held corporation having an established profit-sharing plan for its employees. "Closely held" means that most of the stock is owned by family members and key administrative personnel; there is no open or public market for the stock. No one is selling, so no one can buy. If a number of shares are pledged to a cooperating bank, the bank will advance an agreed upon sum of money to acquire the stock from the corporation or stockholder, holding the stock as collateral. The employees' profit-sharing plan will then retire the loan with proceeds from the plan. What has happened is that the stock owners will have received cash for their stocks and the bank holds a loan against the ESOT(P). The stocks are not on the open market. ESOT(P) will repay the loan to the bank with their profit-sharing proceeds and will thus own the stock. The loan is being repaid with *before*-tax dollars. Interestingly enough, the contributions the employer makes to the pension fund are considered an expense and are, therefore, tax-deductible for the corporation. In time, the trustees acting for the trust may become directors of the corporation by virtue of the fact that they own a large block of its stock.

If the ESOT(P) accumulates enough money, it may buy the stock directly from the corporation, bypassing the bank and its loan. The trust is not limited to buying only shares of the corporation; it may also buy annuities and insurance and maintain a cash account.

At the time of retirement, the trust may only distribute stocks or shares in the parent corporation to the participant. If the corporation is well run, and if the employees are interested in and contribute to its well-being to the best of their working ability, the firm will be profitable.

If the retirees prefer to sell their shares of vested interest rather than live on the dividends, they could offer their stocks to the trust or to any other interested buyer. It is important to note that the employees have the right to do as they wish; they own a "put" option. (See chapter 12 for more on put options.)

In any employee stock ownership trust or plan, the value of the stock involved must be determined each year by a professional appraiser. The price of the security must be at a fair market value. With all the built-in protections and benefits, there is no doubt that an ESOT(P) can be of great benefit to the owner of a closely held corporation, as well as to the employees. Both owners and employees have a genuine interest in the welfare of the corporation, and the employees come close to being entrepreneurs.

For more information, consult the Federal Register, Department of Labor, Office of Employee Benefit Security, the Department of the Treasury, Internal Revenue Service, and Employee Stock Ownership Plans. Although there is not much else in the literature at present, accountants and lawyers are aware of ESOT(P) and should be able to provide help and advice.

RECEIVING PENSION BENEFITS

At the time of retirement, workers have several options for receiving their pension benefits. If the worker and spouse choose to select a lifetime income option, the pension plan can buy an annuity for them. Or the plan may have a provision whereby the employee may leave the benefits with the plan for later withdrawal, or may choose a lump sum payout if the plan allows it. If taken in cash, a ten-year tax-averaging method can be used to pay any taxes due. Or you might take advantage of roll-over IRA.

In any event, you should be familiar with all facets of your pension plan. Your employer must provide you with all the information you need and must explain any part of it that is not clear. For more information, read "Often-Asked Questions About the Employee Retirement Act of 1974," published by the U.S. Department of Labor, Labor-Management Services Administration, Washington, D.C. 20216. It is free for the asking. For ten-year averaging of taxes at the time of retirement, consult an accountant or tax specialist or IRS Form 4972, "Special Ten-Year Averaging Method."

Remember that information is available, and an informed person is always in a better position to make decisions than an ignorant one. There are answers to your questions, but first you must ask the questions.

16

INSURANCE FOR PROTECTION

Life Insurance: Permanent or Cash Value • Term Policies • Riders • Lapsed Policies • Settlement Options • Guarantees • Variable Life Insurance and Minimum Term Deposit • Interest-Adjusted Cost • Property Insurance: Understanding and Reading Your Homeowners Policy

---

The concept of insuring against possible loss has been around for a long time. Marine insurance, for instance, can be traced back to Italian traders of the fifteenth century and life insurance is known to have existed in England as early as 1583. All forms of insurance may be defined as a method whereby a large group of individuals reduces or eliminates a possible economic loss to its members. The idea is to spread the cost of such a loss, which would normally fall upon a single individual, over the members of the group who are exposed to the same hazard. Not all risks are insurable and buying insurance is not the only method of dealing with possible risks, but it is the one best known to most of us. What we do when we buy insurance is to add a portion of our financial resources to a pool during a time when we are in the best position to do so. It is to be returned to us later as specified.

LIFE INSURANCE

Life insurance is an important component of everybody's family protection and financial planning, but few people understand it well. It has been claimed that life insurance is never bought, only sold. What is it, then, that is being sold to us?

First, let us discuss who sells life insurance. Almost all life insurance policies today are sold by two types of companies: mutual companies wholly owned by *policyholders,* and stock companies owned by *stockholders.* In a mutual company, the policyholders participate in the financial surplus of the company; in a stock company, the stockholders have a claim on any surplus (profit). Surplus, of course, means what is left over after claims are paid and expenses deducted from the amounts collected as premiums.

The surplus from a mutual company is paid out to policyholders in accordance with the insurance policy they own, and is called a dividend. Since the IRS considers this an "excess premium" returned to the policyholder, it is not taxable. Dividends left to accumulate with the insurance company, however, earn interest, and this interest is taxable as interest income. The surplus paid out by stock companies is also called a dividend, but it is taxable as it is received.

A life insurance policy offers the following provisions which are not available by any other means:

1. Cash value accumulates, tax-free, until withdrawn.
2. A guaranteed minimum interest rate (which varies with each company) is in force for the life of the policy.
3. The cash value accumulation or death benefits may not be attached by any creditor—even in cases of bankruptcy.
4. In the event of the insured's death, the benefits are paid directly to the designated beneficiaries without going through probate. This eliminates red-tape and unwanted publicity.
5. Those insured have various options for receiving cash benefits when they wish.
6. The beneficiary has several options for receiving the death benefits.
7. If the premium payments are made regularly over the first two years, the policy may not be cancelled after the two years have elapsed—even if *fraudulent information was given at the time of application!*

This last statement merits some comment. It means that the insurance company has two years from the effective date of the policy to withdraw and then only for valid reasons. If the company cancels the policy the premiums paid must be returned to the insured. Naturally, the insurance company will make every effort to protect itself from possible fraud. A medical examination may be required unless the insured is under thirty or thirty-five years of age and the death benefits are less than $50,000 to $100,000, in which case written medical information from the insured may be all that is necessary. Medical requirements vary from company to company.

Insurance companies may also investigate the lifestyle, occupation, and even hobbies of the proposed insured. Does he or she fly a plane or scuba dive, for instance? Certain occupations present hazards: racing car drivers, high-rise window washers, and certain circus performers, for example, may have difficulty obtaining insurance. Insurance companies may ask for higher premiums, or may even refuse to issue a policy.

It should be pointed out that an insurance policy is a unilateral contract—that is, only one party to the contract is bound by it. Once a policy is issued, the insurance company is bound by its provisions as long as the premiums are paid when due, or no later than the "grace period" written into most policies. The grace period allowed is usually up to 31 days after the due date of the premium and is dependent upon the premium payment plan, which may be monthly, quarterly, semiannual, or annual. The insured can cease payments at any time and allow the policy to lapse, which also terminates the insurance company's obligation.

Basically, there are two types of life insurance policies: the "permanent" or "cash value" policy and the "term" policy. Each type offers various plans, and each is intended to meet specific purposes.

PERMANENT OR CASH VALUE POLICY

These policies, (sometimes called *straight life*) are based on a whole-life payment plan. (See Fig. 16-1, A.) The premium is payable up to the death of the insured or up to the point of "maturity"—that is, the policy reaches maturity when the insured reaches a specified age, such as 80, 85, 90, or 100. The maturity limit varies with each company or policy offered. When the insured reaches the

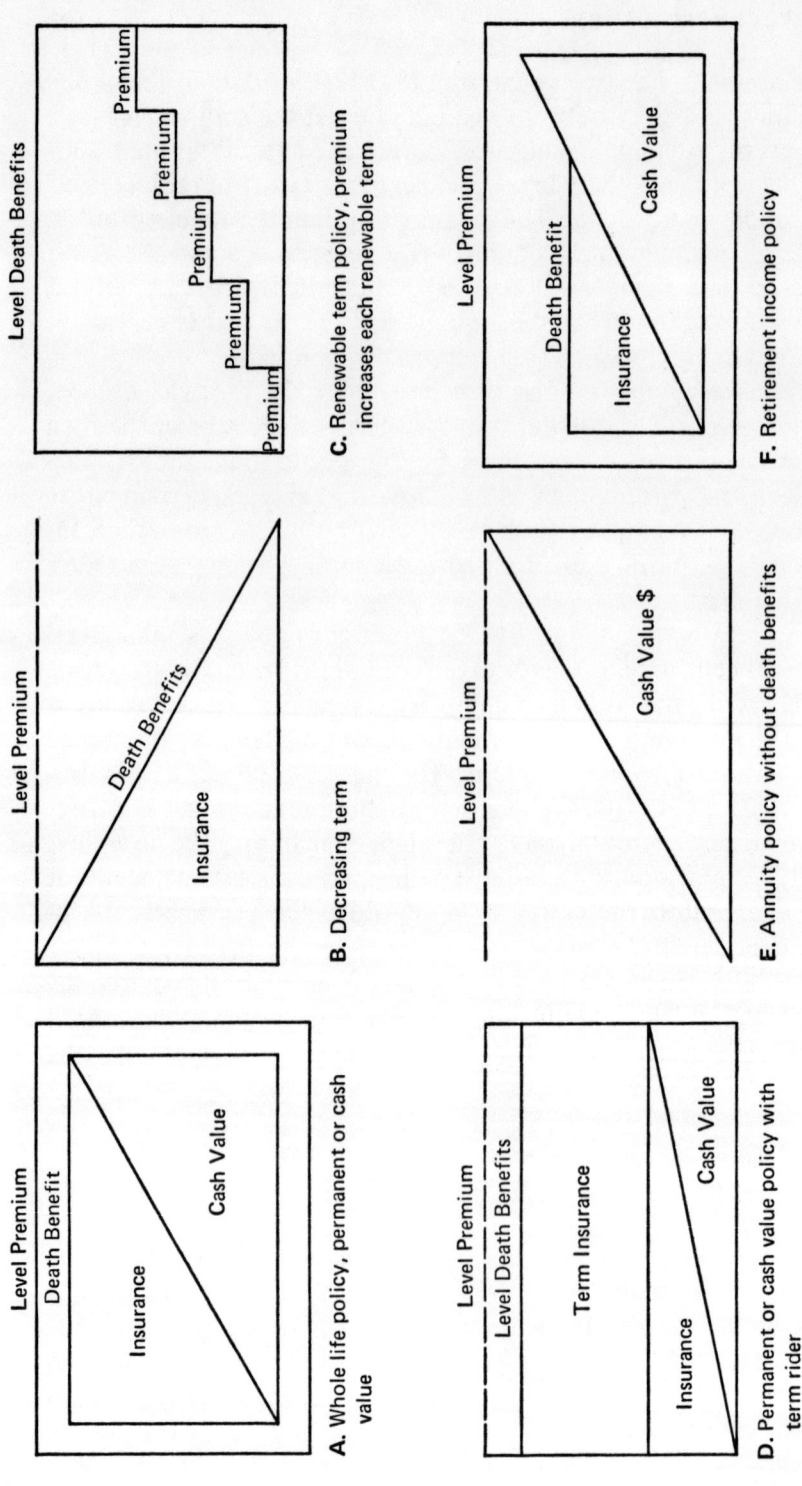

A. Whole life policy, permanent or cash value

B. Decreasing term

C. Renewable term policy, premium increases each renewable term

D. Permanent or cash value policy with term rider

E. Annuity policy without death benefits

F. Retirement income policy

Figure 16-1

maturity limit of the policy, the amount of the death benefit is paid out. The premiums paid in were established at the time the policy was issued and remain the same throughout the life of the policy. The older the insured was at the time of writing up the policy, the higher the premium.

Part of this premium is put aside to accrue as cash value. This accumulation can be considered an enforced savings for the benefit of the insured. You can borrow up to 95% of the cash value of the policy at a very low interest rate, which is generally much lower than the current commercial loan interest rate. This loan does not have to be repaid, but of course the amount of the unpaid loan will be deducted from the death benefits should the insured die in the meantime. A well-established life insurance policy is, therefore, a good source of ready cash. If you pay the insurance company the interest charged for the loan, you can deduct this interest payment from your income tax. You cannot deduct it if you do not pay it and it is simply added to the amount you owe the insurance company. At the same time, the insurance company is adding three to four percent interest, which is tax-free, to the cash value of the policy. A mutual company may also add dividends each year, but of course these are not guaranteed. Such dividends are not taxable at the time they are received.

TERM POLICIES

Term policies offer protection only, and then only for a specific time. Premiums for these kinds of policies are generally lower than for other kinds of plans. Some policies—"renewable term" policies—extend only over a one-year period, or can be bought over five- or ten-year periods, or up to age 65 or older. Terms vary with each company. Some of these policies are renewable without a medical examination, but at a premium rate determined by the "attained age" of the insured. Since the insured is older at the time of renewal, the premium is correspondingly higher. (See Fig. 16–1, C.)

Some policies have a constant or "level" premium, but their death benefits are reduced each year. These policies are often referred to as "mortgage insurance" plans, and are pegged to the mortgages insured have on their property. When the insured are young, their mortgages are likely to be large, and the purpose of this type of insurance is to protect the surviving family up to the amount of the mortgage should the insured die at an early age. The death benefit reduces at about the same rate as the debt of the mortgage—slowly in the early years of the mortgage and faster later on. These policies are also known as "decreasing term" plans. (See Fig. 16-1, B.)

Some policies that have a steadier reduction of the death benefits—such as 1/20 each year of a twenty-year policy—are most often used as income policies. The death benefits reduce as the financial needs diminish. As the insured become established in their occupations, as years of mortgage payments reduce the size of their mortgage debts, and as children approach an age when they can support themselves, the insured need less financial protection. The premiums of these kinds of policies are lower than those for permanent or cash value policies, since only protection is provided—there is no savings accumulation. Some of these policies, however, have a "conversion" privilege. They can be converted into a whole-life cash value policy with the same death benefit of the current decreased term policy without a medical examination. The advantage is obvious. Should the insured develop a terminal condition, the death benefits are locked in and cannot be reduced. The premiums will be the same as they normally would be for a person of that "attained" age.

RIDERS

A "rider" is an addition or amendment to a document. Riders can be attached to a legislative bill to make it more attractive to voters or to a contract to make it more acceptable to the signer. Thus, some term policies can be attached to permanent or cash value policies as riders. (See Fig. 16-1, D.) Another rider can be a "waiver of premium," which means that the insurance company will forgo collecting premiums after six months of a disability that prevents the insured from making premium payments. Another rider can be one that will increase death benefits of the policy at periodic intervals. There are riders which will double the death benefit (double indemnity) in case of accidental death and riders which will return the premiums paid up to the date of death. Riders attached to a life insurance policy which expand the coverage must be paid for by higher premiums.

LAPSED POLICIES

As I said earlier, an insurance policy is a unilateral contract. Only one party to it—the insurance company—is bound by its contractual obligations. The premium payer is not bound to make the payments but the insurer (the company) is bound to the contract as long as the premiums are paid. When no payments are made, the policy lapses—usually after a grace period, as explained earlier. What happens then? The death benefits terminate at the end of the grace period. The cash or non-forfeiture value can be withdrawn or left with the insurance company. If the cash value is not withdrawn, the policy can be put on a paid-up status, which means that no more payments are due. It also means that the death benefits are correspondingly reduced in proportion to the amount of money that has accumulated. An alternative is to use the cash value to buy a term policy with the same death benefits as the original policy, except that now an expiration date will be written in. All of these options are in the insurance contract and are part of the policy. As with any contract, it is worthwhile for the signer of a document to read it through carefully.

As you can see, life insurance fills many needs. It can provide financial support for dependents in the event of the death of the insured. In business and industry, life insurance is very often included in retirement and pension plans. There are even plans which will insure certain "key" people in an organization upon whom the success of the organization depends. If one of them should die the business gets sufficient financial resources to compensate it for the loss, which it can use to train or obtain a trained replacement. Partners often buy insurance on each other so that the survivor(s) can purchase the deceased's share of the business. Insurance applications are unlimited, and can even be expanded to include sufficient amounts to pay estate taxes.

Fortunately for both the insured and the insurer, not every policyholder dies immediately after obtaining a policy. It has been figured that 72% of all straight life policies issued are terminated by withdrawal of the cash value, either for other investments, emergency needs, or conversion into an annuity. Annuity provisions are outlined in every insurance policy in a section called "settlement options."

SETTLEMENT OPTIONS

These are options or "choices" an insurance company offers to its policyholders or beneficiaries for withdrawing the cash value or death benefits. The choice may be a lump sum withdrawal, a withdrawal over a fixed period of time, or a fixed amount payable at designated times until the total amount is paid out. Other choices may be in the form of a life income for the policyholder or beneficiaries, with guarantees of payment of at least five, ten, fifteen, or even twenty years. There are "joint lifetime income" options for two people, with various amounts guaranteed for both and then the one survivor. In addition to the time period these options guarantee, they also guarantee the minimum amount to be paid for *each* $1,000 accumulated. The full amount need not be put into an option elected, but once an option has been selected it cannot be changed unless the option is the one that allows the proceeds to remain "at interest." This means that the decision to select another option is delayed.

Read your insurance contract thoroughly. There is more to a policy than simply signing your name and knowing the amount of the death benefit. Most policies have enough options to meet just about any need. Your insurance representative will answer questions you may have, but you must *ask* the questions before they can be answered.

GUARANTEES

Whenever the topic of insurance comes up, so does the word "guarantee." Insurance companies have had a remarkably good record, at least this century, in meeting their obligations to their policyholders. Federal and state regulations have done much to protect the interest of the public by enacting strict laws to which insurance companies must adhere. Insurance companies have benefited by a lower mortality rate, their policyholders live longer and pay premiums longer, allowing the insurance companies to amass a large portfolio of assets. Furthermore, by making these guarantees up to the maximum lifetime of a policyholder, insurance companies projected high future expenses to cover these costs. These estimates led them to invest very conservatively, with the result that their assets have grown enormously. Some insurance companies have become so wealthy that they have opened themselves to complaints and criticism about their rate of payout as compared to their resources.

Be that as it may, insurance companies do make guarantees, and the reason that they can make these guarantees is that most of their assets are invested in debt debentures, government papers, corporate and municipal bonds, and real estate. All are conservative investments, to be sure, and all are relatively safe. In recent years they have expanded into the equity market, which is not as safe an investment, but which has a good chance for growth and appreciation.

VARIABLE LIFE INSURANCE AND MINIMUM TERM DEPOSITS

Some insurance companies have introduced two new types of policies for insurance buyers willing to assume some risks. One of these is the "variable life" policy. In this policy, the death benefits could be greater than the amount specified, but they also could be less if the financial backing of the policy is invested in a combination of equity and debt instruments. The cash value, if used for an annuity, could provide a greater return than the specified amount—or it could be less. How much more or less is the risk the policyholders or annuitants must assume if they choose a variable life insurance plan.

To reduce some of the risks, the insurance company will guarantee a minimum death benefit that it will pay out in any event. Some of the usual riders such as "waiver of premium" or "accidental death" may also be available. For the annuitant, the cash value will be converted into "units," the value of which will fluctuate with the market value of the underlying securities. The annuitant will be guaranteed an income, but the amount may vary each month.

Another new type of policy is one that involves a one-time deposit to be made during the first year of a ten-year term. These policies have several names, but the generic title is "minimum deposit term insurance." The length of time period a policy is in force—that is, the time over which it generates income for the company (the premiums the insured pay) without any payout—enhances its profitability to the insurance company. On an actuarial basis, if a policy is still in effect after ten years, an insurance company can realize a profit even by charging a minimum premium. If a policy lapses, however, the insurance company will sustain a loss. Insurance companies, therefore, need to be sure that a policy will last a minimum period of time. How can this be done? The answer the insurance companies have come up with is to require a deposit at the start of the policy, or at least within the first year of the policy's life. Should the policy terminate during that time due to the death of the insured or because of non-payment of premiums, the deposit will be forfeited. If the policy is not terminated, the deposit will be returned with interest added. Currently, the interest rate is about 7-1/4%, and twice the amount of the deposit will be returned according to the "rule of 72." (See Chapter 5.) If the policy was guaranteed renewable, another policy can be issued at the "attained age" premium with another deposit required during the first year of the policy's life.

Earlier I talked about guarantees. The insurance company's staff of statisticians (actuaries) tries to arrive at a favorable cost of insurance (premium) and also projects the costs of fulfilling the company's obligations to its policyholders. All of its financial projections must be accurate so that it can guarantee benefits. The only thing that cannot be guaranteed is the dividend.

It is important to understand that each insurance policy involves five parties: the insurance company, the insured, the premium payer, the owner of the policy, and the beneficiary. The insured can also be the premium payer. All must have insurable interest in the insured and can be a creditor, a charitable organization, the insured's estate, and so on. With so many parties involved, special care should be taken in estate settlement cases. Up-to-date information can be obtained from your insurance agent, a trust officer of a bank, a qualified lawyer, or U.S. Government Pamphlet #448, "A Guide to Federal Estate and Gift Taxation."

One of the most perplexing problems for insurance buyers is selecting a policy that will give them what they want at a competitive rate. Comparison shopping has become somewhat easier now that some states are requiring that a standard cost analysis be made available to the buyer at the time the policy is bought. This analysis is called an "interest-adjusted" index or cost.

INTEREST-ADJUSTED COST

When comparison shopping, buyers of any commodity must be certain that they are comparing like with like. In the case of insurance buying, you should compare benefits with like benefits. Apples must be compared with apples, and not with oranges. In a survey conducted in 1972 by a department that regulates insurance in Pennsylvania, the difference in cost between the lowest and highest premiums in otherwise similar policies was as high as 170%! Not only do policies differ from company to company, they can differ within one company.

Insurance agents attempt to explain to prospective buyers the "pure insurance" cost for a period of twenty years by multiplying the annual premium by that length of time and deducting its twenty-year cash value or cash value and dividends, depending upon whether the company is a stock or a mutual company. When this number is divided by twenty, the answer is the cost of the annual "pure" insurance, and this figure can be compared to the annual premium rate. Sometimes the accumulated dividends plus the cash value is more than the cost of the premiums, and the happy insurance buyers think they obtained their insurance protection free. But this is not the whole story. For one thing, this calculation ignores the interest the buyers' money would have earned if they had invested the premium cost elsewhere. For another thing, this formula does not take into account the diminished current value of dollars payable in the future.

Let us assume that the annual premium is deposited each year to compound at 4% interest, tax-free, and then the accumulated cash value of the policy is deducted from the total. The difference is the "interest-adjusted cost" of the pure insurance protection. The interest-adjusted cost, then, is equal to the amount of money that buyers would have realized if they had set the money aside to grow at 4% interest, and is the buyers' net dollar cost of the policy at the end of twenty years.

In all fairness, it should be pointed out that insurance agents have legitimate objections to interest-adjusted cost comparisons. Such comparisons assume that the policy will ultimately be surrendered, and so they don't really measure the cost of lifetime protection. Companies showing relatively high costs for one age group may have set their cash value accumulation to favor another age group, and hence it is necessary to look at the overall features of a policy to see its value. Comparing only the interest-adjusted costs fails to take into account other features of a policy such as availability and cost of policy loans, conversion privileges, and annuity options. This is what I meant by comparing apples with apples and benefit with benefit, which I cautioned earlier should be done before selecting a policy.

Table 16-1 shows comparative calculations. All values were taken from the rate books of a mutual, dividend-paying insurance company and a non-participating, non–dividend-paying stock company. If you deduct line 2 from line 3 you can see that at the end of a ten-year period the pure insurance cost for a $10,000 policy is $309 from a stock company as against $175 from a mutual company.

The accumulations from investing the annual premium of both kinds of companies at 4% compounded interest is shown in line 5. Deducting line 2 from line 5 shows that both would cost about the same (line 6). The difference in line 4 is the result of the extra cost of $51.30 each year for the mutual company. The cash value plus dividends add up to a higher accumulation, but when invested at the same rate the net difference is nil.

The stock company's agents will argue that by buying a non-participating policy the insured can invest the difference in premium costs at a higher return, so that the cash outlay will be less. The mutual company's agents will say that their policy has a built-in enforced savings plan which accumulates funds tax-free.

By comparing the values shown at 10, 20, and 30 years in Table 16-1, you can readily see the advantages of each policy. The net cost of a $10,000 policy including annual premiums for ten years, would be about the same for either type of company. In the case of the stock company policy, however, the annual outlay is $173.10, the cash value accumulation is $1,422.10, and the interest-adjusted cost is $7.39 for each $1,000 annually. In the case of the mutual company, the annual dividends are $224.40, cash value and dividends accumulation is $2,068, and the interest-adjusted cost is $7.33 per $1,000. The difference between the cash value accumulation of the two is $646, which is "enforced" savings. Could you have done better by investing $51.30 each year some other way? Would you have put aside that $51.30 each year?

I must repeat that dividends are not guaranteed, but I know of no insurance company that has paid less than that projected in Table 16-1 in the last forty years. The thirty-year value of the mutual company policy is very favorable to policyholders. If the dividends have not been withdrawn when the policyholder reaches age 65, they would represent a very nice savings of $5,897, yet on a paid-up basis

Table 16-1

Comparison Costs of a $10,000 Whole Life Policy for a 35-year Old Male, Paid Annually
Premium: $163.10 (Stock Company Policy); $224.40 (Mutual Company Policy)

	At the End of 10 Years		At the End of 20 Years		At the End of 30 Years	
	Stock Co.	*Mutual Co.*	*Stock Co.*	*Mutual Co.*	*Stock Co.*	*Mutual Co.*
1. Cash value accumulation	$1,422	$1,690	$3,800	$3,750	$ 5,650	$ 5,580
*2. Dividend accumulation	0	378	0	1,413	0	5,897
3. Premium investment	1,731	2,244	3,460	4,488	4,193	6,732
4. Insurance cost (line 3 minus line 2)	309	175	340	675	453	4,745
**5. Premium investment (4% interest)	2,161	2,801	5,360	6,949	10,096	13,088
6. Insurance cost (line 5 minus line 2)	739	733	1,560	1,786	4,446	1,611
Paid-up death benefits at age 65					7,570	7,550

(Cash value accumulation only)

Interest-Adjusted Cost Annual Average per $1,000 Life Insurance

	Stock Co.	Mutual Co.
At the end of 10 years	$7.39	$7.33
At the end of 20 years	$7.80	$8.93
At the end of 30 years	$14.82	$5.37

*Dividend accumulation projected—not guaranteed.

**Premium invested annually at 4% compound interest.

the policy has the same benefits as that from the stock company. Why not calculate the twenty-year value of your insurance policy? Use the compound interest table in the Appendix.

By comparing the interest-adjusted average annual cost per $1,000 of life insurance at the end of ten, twenty, or thirty years, you can see that there is no discernible pattern. One policy is more competitive during the first ten years, the other during the first twenty years. This variation applies to all policies offered by all insurance companies. Even policies within the same company may offer different accumulation rates. How can prospective insurance buyers be guided to choose the right policy with the right company? Determining the right policy for any situation requires research and an understanding of insurance principles. Recognizing that the accumulation is tax-deferred, making a few simple calculations, and sound budgeting can help your choice.

We know that we need insurance protection, but which form of insurance is best? Would term insurance be the better choice if the difference in cost is invested, or is a cash value policy better? An experienced agent can be of great service if you know what questions to ask and if you understand the answers you get.

Insurance is the only way to buy a fixed guaranteed future return, and there are many plans and options available for meeting this goal. There is no guaranteed substitute for insurance in carrying out obligations which are interrupted by death. Although no one wants to face that eventuality, it cannot be avoided.

PROPERTY INSURANCE

Life insurance is protection against financial loss precipitated by death. Property insurance is protection against financial loss of property. The loss might be anything from total destruction to some less substantial damage that interferes with use of the property. The purpose of insurance is to indemnify those who have an insurable interest in property against such loss. Normal depreciation and wear and tear on property are not insurable. To "indemnify" means to restore the property to the same condition it was in prior to the loss or damage. Naturally, a value has to be placed on the property before it can be insured. Considering the current inflation rate and the appreciation of real property, investors should make periodic reviews of their insurance policies and have their property reappraised regularly. Since land cannot be destroyed it cannot be insured, so its value should not be included in any insurance appraisal. If the insured value is below 80% of the current market value, a coinsurance provision will automatically go into effect. This means that the policyholder assumes a portion of the risk. For example, if a property valued at $100,000 suffers a loss of $75,000 and the maximum insurance coverage is $80,000, the insurance company will pay the full $75,000. If the owner of the property had insurance for only $75,000 and the loss was $70,000, the owner's indemnity would be computed as follows:

Insurance coverage $75,000

Insurance Maximum $80,000

$$\frac{\$75,000}{\$80,000} \times \$70,000 = \$65,625$$

Many people misunderstand insurance policies because they simply do not take the time and trouble to read them through carefully. The various clauses are in fine print and are written in unfamiliar terminology. These "legalese"—or, more properly, "insurancese"—terms are the end-products of various court interpretations of insurance company obligations and exclusions. Since about 1975, however, many insurance contracts are written in an easily understandable form which, although still boring to read, explains what is and is not covered in terms that the average person should have no difficulty interpreting.

Before an insurance company can sell insurance policies in any state, it must be authorized by that state's superintendent of insurance. The insurance company must appoint an agent for the state who must pass an examination before the state will license him or her. The agent, in turn, may employ salespeople, called "solicitors," who must also pass a test before they can be licensed. All of this is intended to insure that knowledgeable and responsible people are hired to offer proper protection for the citizens of the state.

Some insurance companies employ agents and solicitors to sell exclusively for them. Others offer their policies through independent agents who may also employ solicitors to work for them. Still other insurance companies sell policies by mail. Each insurance company (also called a "carrier") must be licensed specifically for each type of insurance—such as fire, casualty, sickness and accident, and so on. Each policy and its premium rate must be approved by the state before it can be offered. Among all the insurance companies conducting business in the United States today, there is very little variation in the policies offered. The only "deviations" will be in the price of the coverage and the service provided for each policyholder.

All policyholders should know exactly what their policy covers, and should fully understand exactly what it does *not* cover. You should not hesitate to ask your insurance representative questions about any aspect of the policy that you do not understand. All too often, policyholders take matters for granted when they should not. You must understand that, by accepting your premiums, insurance companies obligate themselves to meet and fulfill the provisions in the policy, but only as they are specified.

When a property loss occurs, an insurance adjuster will inspect the damage and appraise the cost. Some insurance companies have their own adjusters, while others use adjusters who work for companies that appraise for several carriers. It is common practice to get three appraisals from companies who are in the business of making the particular kinds of repairs called for. Adjusters will examine the appraisals for the repairs to be made and, if they approve them, the insurance company will issue a check for the amount of the loss, either to the insured or to the company selected to do the work.

Reading your Policy

Wrapped around all the papers making up the policy itself is the jacket which shows the name and address of the insurance company. The first inside sheet is the Declaration, which gives the name and address of the insured and the period which the policy covers. The period of time specified will be from six months to three years, and during this time the premium rate may not change. The premium may be paid annually or semiannually.

Get out your own property insurance policy and follow it as you read the following description.

A line or column in Section I of the policy will give the dollar amount and the dollar limits of liability.

Section II will show the amount of personal liability and medical payments to others should an accident occur on your property.

One column will show the premium cost of each section.

The next item shown will probably be the deductible amount for each section. "Deductible" means the amount the insured will have to pay, with the insurance company paying the balance above the deductible to the limit of the policy.

There will be a line or column which shows the designation numbers of the various plans selected and the specific endorsements. These are shown as HO 1, 2, 3, 4, 5, or 6. HO stands for homeowner. A comparison of these plans is shown on page 183.

The Declaration page will also show the amount of the mortgage on the property and the name and address of the bank or institution that provided the mortgage money. In case of loss, the mortgagee has first claim on the insurance proceeds to the amount still owed to it. Underneath all of this will be the signature of the authorized insurance representative.

How are insurance premiums arrived at? It all depends on the risk and peril involved. "Risk" is the uncertainty of loss and "peril" is the cause of loss. A wooden structure far away from an adequate water supply in an arid area represents a greater risk than a home built of bricks a thousand feet from a fire hydrant located in an area of frequent rainfall. A state will be divided into territories and subdivided into sections as small as neighborhoods. For insurance purposes, all are rated according to perils and prevailing risks.

An average premium can be computed by analyzing a risk of exposure to various perils. An insurance company can limit its exposure to risks by being selective in picking its policyholders as well as its territory, and can thus be more profitable and thereby charge a lower than average premium. An insurance company is not in business to *lose* money. Adverse claim experiences and too many claim payouts force companies to raise premiums or to decline to renew policies with high past losses. They may even pull out of some territories or states entirely.

Some areas of the country are exposed to risks that are not covered by insurance because these risks are beyond the control of individuals. Areas of frequent forest fires, floods, or high crime, for example, are all at risk. Some states have asked all insurance companies admitted by them to assume a "collective risk" in areas where single companies cannot operate profitably but where insurance protection is still necessary. These plans offer a minimum protection at an affordable price providing that property owners have met all building codes and other requirements to minimize the risk to themselves and to the insurance company.

The National Flood Insurance Act of 1968, a part of the Housing Urban Development Act of the same year, provides a federally subsidized insurance for land usage in areas which have taken flood control measures. The National Flood Insurers Association was formed to administer this program. In this way, inhabitants of flood-prone localities are able to get protection and individual insurance companies are not exposed to repeated mammoth losses.

The Housing and Urban Development Act of 1970 authorized the federal government to offer the Federal Crime Insurance Program. The federal government, as an insurer, offers protection against burglaries and robberies through servicing agents in areas where such crimes are frequent. This program is not as popular as it should be. Surprisingly few people have applied for such insurance, perhaps because potential buyers decided it made more sense to move than to pay the premiums for protection.

What follows is a comparison of the various coverages under different homeowners' programs and the endorsement designations for additional insurance that can be attached to homeowner policies. These forms are accepted and approved throughout the country for most homeowner programs.

Comparison of Coverages Under Homeowners Program

	Basic HO-1	Broad HO-2	Special HO-3	Tenant Policy HO-4	Comprehensive HO-5	Condominium HO-6
1. Fire, lightning, windstorm, hail, riot, civil commotion, aircraft	Yes	Yes	Yes	Yes	Yes	Yes
2. Explosion, other than steam boiler.	Yes	Yes	Yes	Yes	Yes	Yes
3. Explosion of steam boiler.	No	Yes	Yes	Yes	Yes	Yes
4. Bursting of Steam or hot water appliances and heating systems.	No	Yes	Yes	Yes	Yes	Yes
5. Damage by vehicles: (a) Building	Yes, except by occupant of premises	Yes	Yes	Yes	Yes	NA*
(b) Fences	No	Yes, except by vehicle owned or operated by occupant of premises	Yes	Yes	Yes	NA
(c) Driveways	No		Yes	Yes	Yes	NA
(d) Walks	No		Yes	Yes	Yes	NA
(e) Lawns	Yes, except by vehicle owned or operated by occupant of premises					
(f) Trees, shrubs, plants						

*Not Applicable.

183

	HO-1	HO-2	HO-3	HO-4	HO-5	HO-6
6. Smoke						
(a) From fireplaces	No	Yes	Yes	Yes	Yes	Yes
(b) Heating or cooking unit	Yes, on premises	Yes	Yes	Yes	Yes	Yes
(c) Industrial operations	No	No	No	No	No	No
7. Vandalism and Malicious Mischief	Yes, except vacant over 30 days	Yes, except vacant over 30 days	Yes, except building loss when vacant over 30 days	Yes	Yes, except building loss when vacant over 30 days	Yes
8. Water:						
(a) Surface water or flood *Suggestion: Ask your agent about the Nat'l Flood Ins. Program	No	No	No	No	No, except personal property off premises	NA
(b) Back up of sewers or drains	No	No	No	No	No, except personal property off premises	NA
(c) Leaking from plumbing, heating or air-conditioning systems	No	Yes, excluding repair to involved system. *Repeated leakage causing loss is excluded.*	Yes, excluding repair to involved system. *Repeated leakage causing loss is excluded.*	Yes, excluding repair to involved system. *Repeated leakage causing loss is excluded.*	Yes, excluding repair to involved system. *Repeated leakage causing loss is excluded.*	Yes, excluding repair to involved system. *Repeated leakage causing loss is excluded.*
(d) Rain through faulty roof, windows or doors	No	No	Building only	No	Yes	No
(e) Freezing of plumbing or heating systems	No	Yes, except while vacant or unoccupied and proper heat not maintained or system drained	Yes, except while vacant or unoccupied and proper heat not maintained or system drained	Yes, except while vacant or unoccupied and proper heat not maintained or system drained	Yes, except while vacant or unoccupied and proper heat not maintained or system drained	Yes, except while vacant or unoccupied and proper heat not maintained or system drained

	HO-1	HO-2	HO-3	HO-4	HO-5	HO-6
9. Sonic boom	No, except $50 on glass	Yes	Yes	Yes	Yes	Yes
10. Falling objects, including trees	No, except objects from aircraft	Yes	Yes	Yes	Yes	Yes
11. Weight of ice, snow, sleet	No	Yes	Yes	Yes	Yes	Yes
12. Wind damage to trees and their removal	No	No	No	No	No	No
13. Collapse of building	No	Yes	Yes	Yes	Yes	Yes
14. Landslide – Mudslide *Suggestion: Ask your agent about the National Flood Insurance Program.*	No	No	No	No	Personal Property only	No
15. Earthquake	No, except by endorsement				Personal Property only; dwelling by endorsement	No, except by endorsment
16. Damage by pets to personal property	No	No	No	No	No	No
17. Glass breakage	Yes, to $50 except if vacant over 30 days	Yes, except if vacant over 30 days		NA	Yes, except if vacant over 30 days	NA

	HO-1	HO-2	HO-3	HO-4	HO-5	HO-6
18. Sudden, accidental injury to electrical appliances	No	Yes	Yes	Yes	Yes	Yes
19. Theft:						
(a) Building materials	Yes, except when dwelling is under construction and prior to occupancy					
(b) Personal property	Yes	Yes	Yes	Yes	Yes	Yes
(c) Unscheduled jewelry and furs	Yes, subject to aggregate limit of $500 per occurrence					
(d) From unattended auto off premises	No, unless forced entry. Available by endorsement HO-2-3-4 and 6				Yes	No, except by endorsement
(e) *Mysterious disappearance*	No	Not as a named peril; however, coverage does not apply to loss of property from known place when probability of theft exists			Yes	Same as HO-2-3-4 and 6
20. Consequential loss to personal property (Spoilage)	Yes, when temperature change is due to damage by insured peril to power, cooling or heating equipment *on premises*					
21. Loss deductibles	Yes. Flat deductible of $100 now standard in basic forms, applying to all losses. Can be modified by endorsement					
22. Bodily injury and property damage claims on occurrence basis	Yes, $25,000 coverage in basic form. Can be increased by endorsement					
23. Liability coverage off premises for owned recreational motor vehicles	No, except a golf cart, *while being used for golfing purposes*					

	HO-1	HO-2	HO-3	HO-4	HO-5	HO-6
24. Fire legal liability	Yes	Yes	Yes	Yes	Yes	Yes
25. Medical payments	Yes, limits of $500/$25,000 in basic policy can be increased					
26. Damage to property of others	Yes, limit of $250 in any one occurrence. Exclusion for damage caused intentionally by any insured "who has attained age 13"					

NOTE: This chart is not intended to provide complete policy information in any given situation, but rather to highlight basic comparisons.

Significant Coverages of the Homeowners Program

Property Coverage—Section I

	HO-1	HO-2	HO-3	HO-4	HO-5	HO-6
COVERAGE A DWELLING — Covers the described dwelling building, occupied principally as a private residence. Also covers building equipment, fixtures and outdoor equipment (not otherwise covered) which pertains to the service of the premises and while located thereon or temporarily elsewhere; and materials and supplies on premises or adjacent thereto, for use in construction, alteration or repair of such dwelling.	✓	✓	✓	NA	✓	NA

	HO-1	HO-2	HO-3	HO-4	HO-5	HO-6
COVERAGE B APPURTENANT STRUCTURES — Covers structures (other than described dwelling building) appertaining to the premises and located thereon. Excludes any structure rented in whole or in part to other than a tenant of described dwelling, except for private garage purposes.	✓	✓	✓	NA	✓	NA
COVERAGE C UNSCHEDULED PERSONAL PROPERTY — Covers unscheduled personal property usual or incidental to the occupancy of the premises as a dwelling. Automatically written for 50% of Coverage A – Dwelling, or can be reduced to 40%. Can also be increased for additional premium.	✓	✓	✓	$4,000 min.	✓	$4,000 min.
Automatic coverage for 30 days at new location, on Pro-rata basis.	✓	✓	✓	✓	✓	✓
COVERAGE D ADDITIONAL LIVING EXPENSE — If loss covered by policy renders premises "untenantable", policy covers necessary increase in living expense incurred to continue as nearly as practicable the normal standard of living of named insured's household for the time required to (1) repair or replace damaged property as soon as possible or (2) for insured's household to become settled in permanent quarters; whichever is less.	✓	✓	✓	✓	✓	✓

THEFT PROVISIONS	HO-1	HO-2	HO-3	HO-4	HO-5	HO-6
Covers theft of property from "known place when probability of theft exists".	No	✓	✓	✓	All Risk	✓
Property unattended in motor vehicle covered if insured required to surrender keys to a bailee. (Off Premises)	✓	✓	✓	✓	All Risk	✓
No Coverage for property off-premises, unattended in or on private watercraft, unless evidence of forced entry. Watercraft and equipment off-premises not covered. All trailers off premises not covered.	✓	✓	✓	✓	✓	✓
Aggregate limit of $500 for any one loss by theft to jewelry and furs.	✓	✓	✓	✓	✓	✓

Liability Coverage—Section II

THIS SECTION OF THE POLICY IS IDENTICAL
UNDER ALL FORMS HO-1, HO-2, HO-3, HO-4 AND HO-5

COVERAGE E
PERSONAL
LIABILITY

Company agrees to pay on behalf of the insured all sums which the insured shall become legally obligated to pay as damages because of bodily injury or property damage, to which the insurance applies, caused by an *occurrence.* "Occurrence" is defined to mean an accident, including injurious exposure to conditions, which results, during the policy term, in bodily injury or property damage.

DEFENSE: Company shall not be obligated to pay any claim or judgment or to defend any suit after the applicable limit of the company's liability has been exhausted by payment of judgments or settlements.

COVERAGE F
MEDICAL
PAYMENTS
TO OTHERS

Company agrees to pay all reasonable medical expenses, incurred within one year from the date of the accident, to or for each person who sustains bodily injury to which the insurance applies, caused by an accident, while such person is:

1. on an insured premises with the permission of any insured, or

2. elsewhere if bodily injury

   (a) arises out of a condition in the insured premises or the ways immediately adjoining

   (b) is caused by the activities of any insured, or resident employee in the course of his employment by any insured

   (c) is caused by an animal owned by or in the care of any insured, or

   (d) is sustained by any resident employee and arises out of and in the course of his employment by any insured.

SOME IMPORTANT EXCLUSIONS UNDER COVERAGES E AND F

Policy does not apply:

a. to bodily injury or property damage arising out of the ownership, maintenance, operation, use, loading or unloading of:

Aircraft

(1) any aircraft; or

Motor Vehicles

(2) any motor vehicle owned or operated by, or rented or loaned to any insured *except* for bodily injury or property damage occurring on the residence premises if the motor vehicle is not subject to motor vehicle registration because of its *exclusive* use on the premises or kept in dead storage on premises; or

Recreational Motor Vehicles

(3) any recreational motor vehicle owned by any insured, if bodily injury or property damage occurs away from premises *except* in the case of golf carts *while used for golfing purposes* . . . The policy defines "recreational motor vehicle" to mean (a) a golf cart or snowmobile, or (b) if not subject to motor vehicle registration, *any other land motor vehicle designed for recreational use off public roads.*

Watercraft

b. to bodily injury or property damage occurring away from the residence premises, arising out of the ownership, maintenance, operation, use, loading or unloading of any watercraft:

(1) owned by or rented to any insured if watercraft has inboard or inboard/outboard motor power more than 50 h.p. or is a sailing vessel more than 26 feet in overall length

(2) powered by any outboard motor(s) more than 25 total h.p., if such outboard motor(s) is *owned* by any insured.

Professional Liability

c. to bodily injury or property damage arising out of the rendering of or failing to render professional services.

Business Pursuits

d. to bodily injury or property damage arising out of business pursuits of any insured *except* activities therein which are *ordinarily incident to non-business pursuits.*

Premises Liability

e. to bodily injury or property damage arising out of any premises, *other than an "insured premises",* owned, rented or controlled by any insured.

Intentional Injury

f. to bodily injury or property damage which is either expected or intended from the standpoint of the insured.

Supplementary Coverages

1. DAMAGE TO PROPERTY OF OTHERS:

This coverage appeared as "Coverage G – Physical Damage to Property of Others" on earlier homeowners policies. The coverage does not depend on legal liability, being referred to sometimes as the "good neighbor" endorsement. Coverage is limited to $250 in any one occurrence. Property owned by or rented to any insured, tenant or resident of insured's household is not covered and any damage caused intentionally by any insured who has reached age 13, is excluded.

2. PERSONAL LIABILITY CLAIM EXPENSES:

Company agrees to pay all expenses incurred by the company (such as investigation and adjustment costs) and costs taxed against the insured in any suit *defended* by the company. Further costs include the premiums charged on appeal bonds and bail bonds up to $250 *(for which coverage applies under the policy)* and the reasonable expenses incurred by the insured at the company's request, including loss of earnings not to exceed $25 per day, because of his attendance at hearings or trials.

Any expenses incurred by the company under this provision do not reduce the applicable limit of liability.

3. FIRST AID EXPENSES:

In addition to the company's limit of liability, the company will pay expenses incurred by the insured for first aid *to others* at the time of an accident, for bodily injury *to which the insurance applies.*

4. PROPERTY IN CONTROL OF THE INSURED:

This coverage is recognized as what is often termed Fire Legal Liability Insurance. This provides protection to the insured for his legal liability for property damage to any insured premises and to house furnishings therein, if such damage arises out of *fire, explosion, or smoke or smudge caused by sudden, unusual and faulty operation of any heating or cooking unit.*

Endorsements Frequently Used with the Homeowners Program

HO-40	Appurtenant Structures—Rented to Others		**HO-43**	Office, Professional, Private School or Studio Occupancy. Additional Residence Premises (Section II only)
HO-41	Additional Insured—Designated Premises only			
HO-42	Office, Professional, Private School or Studio Occupancy. Described Residence Premises only		**HO-45**	Change Endorsement

HO-46 Theft Coverage Extension (Form HO-2, HO-3 or HO-4 only—Section I)

HO-47 Inflation Guard Endorsement

HO-48 Appurtenant Structures (Section I only)

HO-49 Secondary Residence Premises, Building Additions and Alterations. Increased Limit of Liability (Form HO-5 only—Section I)

HO-50 Additional Amount on Unscheduled Personal Property. In Secondary Residence. (Form HO-5 only—Section I)

HO-53 Credit Card Forgery and Depositors Forgery Coverage Endorsement (Section I only)

HO-54 / **HO-54A** / **HO-54C** Earthquake Damage Assumption Endorsements (Form HO-1, HO-2, HO-3 or HO-4 only—Section I—variable in coverage for earthquake and/or volcanic eruption and deductibles)

HO-55 / **HO-55A** / **HO-55C** Earthquake Damage Assumption Endorsements (Form HO-5 only—Section I—variable in coverage for earthquake and/or volcanic eruption and deductibles)

HO-56 $100 Special Loss Deductible Clause (Form HO-1, HO-2, HO-3 or HO-4 only—Section I)

HO-57 $50 Loss Deductible Clause (Form HO-5 only—Section I)

HO-58 $250 Special Loss Deductible Clause (Section I only)

HO-59 $500 Special Loss Deductible Clause (Section I only)

HO-61 Scheduled Personal Property Endorsement

HO-65 Increased Limits on Money and Securities (Section I only)

HO-66 Additional Amount on Unscheduled Personal Property—Away from Premises (Form HO-1, HO-2, HO-3 or HO-4 only—Section I)

HO-67 Secondary Residence Premises Endorsement

HO-68 Scheduled Glass Endorsement (Section I only)

HO-69 Physicians, Surgeons, Dentists and Veterinarians—Away from Premises Endorsement (Form HO-2, HO-3 or HO-4 only—Section I)

HO-70 Additional Residence Premises—Rented to Others (1 or 2 families—Section II only)

HO-71 Business Pursuits Endorsement (Section II only)

HO-72 Farmers Comprehensive Personal Liability Endorsement

HO-75 Watercraft Endorsement (Section II only)

HO-114 $50 Loss Deductible Clause No. 1 and No. 2 (Form HO-5 only—Section I)

HO-122 Loss Deductible Clause No. 1—Windstorm or Hail (Form HO-1, HO-2, HO-3 or HO-4 only—Section I)

HO-148 $50 Modified Loss Deductible Clause No. 2 (Form HO-2, HO-3 or HO-4 only—Section I)

HO-162 Credit for Existing Insurance Endorsement (for those states where permitted)

HO-164 Snowmobile Endorsement (Section II)

HO-171	Unscheduled Jewelry, Watches and Furs Increased Limits of Liability (Form HO-1, HO-2, HO-3 or HO-4 only—Section I)	**HO-174**	$100 Loss Deductible Clause (Form HO-1, HO-2, HO-3 or HO-4 only—Section I)
HO-172	Unscheduled Jewelry, Watches and Furs Increased Limits of Liability (Form HO-5 only—Section I)	**HO-175**	$100 Loss Deductible Clause No. 1—Windstorm or Hail (Form HO-1, HO-2, HO-3 or HO-4 only—Section I)
		HO-192	Condominium Unit—Owner's Endorsement (Form HO-4 only—Section I)

Some General Provisions

1. Owner-Occupant

Policy can be written in the name of the owner-occupant on a dwelling in course of construction.

2. Endorsement HO-40

Provides coverage for appurtenant structures on premises rented or held for rental to others, for residential purposes.

3. Fire Department Service Charge

Automatic limit of $250 can be increased by endorsement.

4. Endorsement HO-43

Used to provide liability coverage for office occupancy at residence premises other than described premises (Section II only).

5. Endorsement HO-46

Theft Coverage Extension. Extends theft coverage to unattended property in unlocked motor vehicle or watercraft (Section I only).

6. Deductibles

Policies can be endorsed to provide for flat deductible of $250 or $500 under all forms, for premium credit.

7. Endorsement HO-66

Used to increase basic off-premises limit for personal property.

8. Replacement Cost

Replacement Cost appears as a *Condition* of coverage, due to the conditional nature of the provision requiring insurance to 80% of replacement cost and the fact that coverage is optional for an insured. The term "cloth awnings" is changed to read "awnings." Therefore, all types of awnings are subject to actual cash value coverage, along with outdoor radio and TV antennas, carpeting, domestic appliances and outdoor equipment.

9. Additional Conditions

The following provision is added to all Homeowners policies to clarify that the HO policy is not intended to cover a dwelling associated with or located on farm premises.

Occupancy Clause: It is a condition of this policy that if the described dwelling is associated with and in proximity to farming operations, (1) the agricultural products produced on the land are incidental to the occupancy of the dwelling and are principally for home consumption, or (2) that the occupants of the dwelling and building appurtenant thereto are not engaged in the operation of the farm and said buildings are in addition to a complete set of farm buildings on the farm and are not exposed within 200 feet by any farm building.

10. Automotive Stereo Equipment and Tapes

Since their introduction into the market, Automotive Stereo Equipment and Tapes has been a most controversial issue between insurance carriers. Coverage is now available by endorsement under Automobile Policies.

All Homeowner Policies now exclude such equipment with the addition of the following exclusions under Coverage C-Unscheduled Personal Property:

This coverage excludes:

8. Any device or instrument for the recording, reproduction or recording and reproduction of sound, which may be operated by power from the electrical system of a motor vehicle, or any tape, wire, record disc or other medium for use with any such device or instrument while any of said property is in or upon a motor vehicle.

11. Personal Property Rented to Others

It was felt that exclusion No. 6 under Coverage C-Unscheduled Personal Property, did not properly reflect the intent to cover household furnishings belonging to the insured while he temporarily rents the portion of the described dwelling customarily occupied exclusively by the insured. The exclusion now reads as follows, in all forms:

This coverage excludes:

6. Property rented or held for rental to others by the Insured, except property contained in that portion of the described premises customarily occupied exclusively by the Insured and occasionally rented to others or property of the Insured in that portion of the described dwelling occupied by roomers or boarders.

12. Theft Peril Exclusions

1. Credit Cards, etc.: All forms contain an exclusion concerning theft of credit cards, checks, etc. Theft losses to these properties create misunderstanding since the policy affords coverage for securities. Exclusion is reworded as follows, in all forms:

"arising out of or resulting from the theft of any credit card or loss by forgery or alterations of any check, draft, promissory note, bill of exchange, or similar written promise, order or direction to pay a sum certain in money."

2. Property Away from Premises: Under original 1968 Forms, exclusion C under the Theft Peril provided no coverage for "loss away from the described premises of property at any location owned, rented or occupied by an insured except while he is temporarily residing thereat."

Exclusion is reworded as follows:

This policy does not apply to loss away from the described premises:

(1) property while in any dwelling or premises thereof, owned, rented or occupied by an Insured, except while an Insured is temporarily residing therein.

13. Water Damage

Form HO-2, Peril 16 is revised as follows:

16. Accidental discharge or overflow of water or steam from within a plumbing, heating or air conditioning system or from within a domestic appliance, including the cost of tearing out and replacing any part of the building covered necessary to effect repairs to the system or appliance from which the water or steam escapes, but excluding loss:

a. to the building caused by continuous or repeated seepage or leakage over a period of weeks, months or years.

b. if the building covered had been vacant beyond a period of 30 consecutive days immediately preceding the loss;

c. to the system or appliance from which the water or steam escapes; or

d. caused by or resulting from freezing.

Forms HO-3 and HO-5 have the following added to Additional Exclusions:

Loss caused by continuous or repeated seepage or leakage of water or steam from within a plumbing, heating or air conditioning system or from within a domestic appliance which occurs over a period of weeks, months or years.

14. Collapse Peril

The Collapse Peril is reworded in Form HO-2 to exclude loss to cesspools and septic tanks since these are felt to be, for the most part, maintenance expenses. Look for this new wordage:

"Collapse of buildings or any part thereof but excluding loss to outdoor equipment, awnings, fences, pavements, patios, swimming pools, underground pipes, flues, drains, cesspools and septic tanks, foundations, retaining walls, bulkheads, piers, wharves or docks, all except as the direct result of the collapse of a building. Collapse does not include settling, cracking, shrinkage, bulging or expansion."

Forms HO-3 and HO-5 are not changed in this regard since they presently exclude loss due to "wear and tear" and "deterioration."

15. Endorsements

1. HO-53—Credit Card Endorsement

The original endorsement provides coverage for forgery. Many credit cards that may be lost or stolen do not require the signature of the Insured in order to effect a purchase. New wordage in this coverage provides for any loss suffered by an Insured arising out of the "unauthorized use" of a credit card, thereby enlarging the scope of coverage.

2. HO-164—Snowmobile Endorsement (Section II)

This endorsement is used to provide liability coverage for operation of snowmobiles away from the premises. Some forms of the endorsement also provide coverage for scheduled snowmobiles caused by fire, lightning or theft while located on the described residence premises.

3. HO-192—Condominium Unit—Owner's Endorsement (Form HO-4 only—Section I)

This endorsement provides an owner of a condominium unit coverage for building additions or alterations which he installs in his unit. Coverage limited to 10% of the limit of liability applicable to Coverage C—Unscheduled Personal Property without charge. The amount may be increased for an additional premium.

NOTE: Most states have approved these provisions at the time of our printing. Obviously, individual policies must be reviewed to properly determine coverage in any specific case.

Courtesy of GAB Business Services Inc.

TAX SHELTERS

Oil and Gas • *Cattle Feeding and Breeding* • *Real Estate* •
Equipment Leasing

The United States is probably the only country in the world that is not in competition with free enterprises within its own borders. Other governments either completely control various enterprises or are their major stockholders. Communications (telephone, postal services, etc.) are subsidized in many countries, as are high-risk ventures such as the aircraft industry, railroads, and oil and gas production.

The United States government prefers to shelter the investment against the liability of paying taxes rather than to own it outright. The amount "at risk" is deducted from the gross income of the investor. In this way, the government stays out of high-risk ventures, preferring that the investor assume such risks. The tax shelter is the inducement to the private investor to take on the risk. Those in the 50% tax bracket are obviously in a better position to bear the risks than those in a lower percentage tax bracket, and their out-of-pocket risk is proportionately less. Unfortunately, all too often someone invests in a venture because it *is* a tax shelter without considering the merits of the actual investment.

Among salesmen there is an expression: "Don't sell the steak; sell the sizzle of the steak." A steak's aroma, appearance and "sizzle" may be mouth-watering, but it is the steak itself that should be the actual reason for eating. The same analogy could be applied to tax shelters. At no time should the tax shelter provision be the only reason for investing. A tax-sheltered investment is first and foremost an investment, and should be investigated as closely as any other investment, regardless of its tax-sheltered advantages.

OIL AND GAS

The demand for energy is constantly increasing, and at our present stage of technological development oil and gas provide the major source. Fossil energy is non-renewable and the world's known deposits are limited. The cost of this energy has accelerated at an unprecedented rate and makes additional exploration and development more profitable. In other words, it is economically well worth the risk to look for more oil and gas. Exploration is the search for oil and gas by drilling in areas that geologically and geophysically warrant such exploration. Development is drilling additional wells in an area where gas and oil have been found before.

Obviously, exploration represents a greater risk than development, although exploration may bring the higher return. By selecting a program which combines exploration and development, investors can reduce the risk of not getting a full return of their money by about 40 to 50%. Because of the increased need, wells are sunk deeper today than the 15,000 feet depth that was common in the past. Deeper wells were not profitable when energy was cheap, but they are now. Depending upon the reservoir, a well can be productive for up to about fifteen years, and the longer a well is productive the greater the return on the investment.

It costs a great deal of money to conduct an oil or gas exploration; only a consortium of people can undertake such a venture. The consortium will include a general partner and limited partners. The general partner will provide the expertise, and the limited partners the financial resources. The liability of the limited partners is limited to the amount of their investment. Because of the high risk involved, the law requires limited partners to be in at least the 50% tax bracket and to have assets, not counting their residence, of at least $100,000.

The intangible drilling and development costs of a productive well may be considered a tax deduction for the limited partners in the year in which these costs are incurred. This could be as high as 60 to 80% of the investment in the first year. The balance of 20 to 40% may be deducted the following years. If all goes well, the limited partners can begin to look for some return on their investment after the second year.

In some programs, the general partner may get a loan from a bank to do additional drilling. Although the assets of the program may be used as collateral, the limited partners may also be asked to sign a note for the amount, or even asked to put up more money. This increases their liability (risk), but also increases their tax deduction. This kind of program is referred to as "assessable."

Since removal of oil or gas will deplete the well reservoir, the limited partners are entitled to a "depletion allowance," which is a partial tax exemption from the income. This allowance has been set at 22% for 1980, 20% in 1981, 18% in 1982, 16% in 1983, and 15% each year thereafter, and is computed from the gross income of the well for each given year. Gross income is income before operating and management expenses are deducted. The tax saving could be up to 33% of the actual income received by the limited partners, and as a result of the tax shelter the return may be as much as two and a half times the investment over the life of the program—if the program succeeds, of course.

Brokerage houses sell limited partnerships in gas and oil programs. Reputable firms go to great lengths to investigate the background and past success ratio of the general partner. It is important for investors to know the percentages of their investment that will go into marketing, managing, and actual drilling.

There is no public market for the limited partners' shares (called "units"). When the general partner has spent all investments available, he or she can usually project the results of the program after it is appraised by a qualified third party. The general partner may offer to buy back any units offered at a discounted price. Once the value has been established, it may be advantageous to transfer any units at that price to any members of the limited partners' families as a gift. This may be within the IRS gift allowance, and the return is taxed as property of the recipient. Before investing in any gas and oil tax shelter (or in any tax-sheltered investment) you should consult an accountant.

CATTLE FEEDING AND BREEDING

Cattle can be bought to be fattened up prior to slaughter or for breeding purposes. The two industries combined have in the past been subject to a nine to eleven-year cycle, and an investment in feeding and breeding is principally a seven to nine-year tax deferral.

There are two programs which, if successfully combined, reduce the risk and lower the tax on the profit. If you invest in a feeding program, the initial cash outlay is spent on purchasing the herd and a two-year supply of feed, and this could result in a total tax write-off of the initial investment. The cattle purchased should weigh about 400 pounds each and be grain-fed until they reach a weight of 1000 to 2000 pounds. The profit, minus expenses, is considered ordinary income. If breeding and feeding programs are run simultaneously, however, the profit is invested in breeding cattle. The calves are raised to the feeding stage of about 400 pounds and then sold. When the calves are sold, hopefully at a profit, the profit is then a capital gain.

REAL ESTATE

Although the reason for investing in real estate may be a tax deduction, the ultimate objective for the general partner is to offer the limited partners a tax deferral, with the profit being taxed ten to twelve years hence as a capital gain. The real estate will most likely be rental property under a long-term lease to a quality tenant. Again, the general partner will provide the know-how: the ability to acquire the right property at a favorable price, along with good financial and management skills. The limited partners' contribution is, as before, cash sufficient to qualify for a favorable mortgage rate. As explained in chapters 11 and 19, management fees, maintenance, taxes, insurance, mortgage interest, and depreciation provide a paper loss which will give either tax-free income or a tax write-off in case of actual loss. As time goes on, the mortgage loan will decrease, as will the tax-deductible interest, and the property will produce taxable income. If the property is then sold, the appreciation of the real estate value and the greater equity in the property results in a capital gain profit. The proceeds can be reinvested in other property, which in turn provides another tax shelter.

EQUIPMENT LEASING

Computers, airplanes, rail cars, ships, large machinery, or anything that can be provided to a user on a rental basis can be a tax shelter. The tax benefit is the result of accelerated depreciation and short-term financing. The profit is the residual value of the leased equipment at the termination of the rental agreement. If and when it is sold, any gain is a capital gain for tax purposes.

There are other potential tax shelters. Coal mining, tree crops, and others that probably haven't even been thought of yet can qualify as tax shelters provided they meet IRS approval. Any tax shelter should be cleared with the IRS *before* any money is invested.

Public offerings have to pass certain Securities and Exchange Commission disclosure requirements, and these do not constitute a recommendation to invest. Offers to participate must be accompanied by a prospectus which will give potential investors the opportunity to evaluate the financing procedure, the investment to be made, and the objective to be met, as well as a history of the experience and past performance of the general partner. The risk can be reduced to an affordable level with the assistance of an accountant, lawyer, and your stockbroker.

Private offerings are made to fewer investors and require larger financial participation. In a private offering, the maximum number of investors is at present 45, with a minimum investment of $150,000 each. Because private offerings do not have to be submitted to the Securities and Exchange Commission, they demand closer scrutiny by the investors and their advisors.

In conclusion, I should point out that tax shelters are not for everyone. Only people in high income tax brackets will be invited to participate—or should participate. A gas or oil well may prove to be a dry hole; the resale of cattle may be below cost; real estate may not rent; and equipment become obsolete faster than anticipated. These are real risks. Furthermore, tax shelters provide very little liquidity before maturity.

Money invested in tax shelters should always be surplus money, and I cannot emphasize enough that a careful investigation of the merit of the investment is essential. Know where your money is going!

INVESTMENT STRATEGIES:
STOCKS AND BONDS

Predicting the Unpredictable • *Stocks* • *Bonds* • *Convertible Bonds and Preferred Stocks* • *How to Read the Stock Pages in Your Newspaper* • *How New Issues are Introduced to the Market*

PREDICTING THE UNPREDICTABLE

There are as many ways to get rich (or to lose your shirt) in the stock market as there are investors. A knowledge of the market, sound judgment, and strategic moves are essential when managing a stock portfolio. Even then, things can go wrong. The investor either should have sold instead of holding on, or should have bought more or sold some securities. Trading stocks and bonds offers everyone a chance to make money. You can do this in a rising as well as a declining market if you use common sense.

In this chapter I will discuss common and preferred stocks, bonds (corporate and municipal), and convertibles, and the strategies that can be used to achieve maximum return. Stockbrokers could not begin to count the times they have been asked: "What's the market going to do? Will it go up or down?" No matter what they answer, they will have a 50–50 chance of being right.

What the inquirer wants to know is how the stocks are performing on the investment scene. The overall change is measured by what is popularly known as the "Dow Jones Industrial Averages," but this only gives an overview and generalization of the market performance of certain stocks—not the market value of specific stocks. Dow Jones and Company devised this method of analyzing the stock market in 1928 as a method for determining market trends by averaging certain representative stocks. In the beginning, Dow Jones included mostly railroad stock but now it indexes 30 industrial common stocks, 20 transportation stocks, 15 utility common stocks, and a composite average of all 65 issues.

The New York Stock Exchange and the American Stock Exchange also compile an index and publish averages based on actual securities traded. All of these "average" changes reflect only past performance, and cannot be used to safely predict future action. Decisions based on past performance are informed decisions, but past behavior obviously will not guarantee future performance.

A company's balance sheet and profit and loss statements can tell potential investors a great deal about it. These are issued annually or, in the case of interim reports, quarterly. It must be remembered, however, that these are a reflection of the *past,* not a prediction of the future. Their value lies in the insight they can give investors about how a company has performed. Investors can compare them with the balance sheets of other companies or with balance sheets for several years running of the same company. Trends may emerge which will help investors decide whether or not to buy into the company. There is nothing mysterious about balance sheets or profit and loss statements, but you must learn how to read them.

The prices of individual stocks change with the demand and the supply. Investors may feel that the world's condition, business opportunities, a change in management, and so on, will adversely influence the profitability of the company the stock represents. If they feel that the value of their stock will no longer appreciate, they will sell their holdings in order to protect their investment. In order for investors to be able to sell, there must be buyers whose analysis of the situation causes them to feel differently. Imbalance of buyer and seller, however small, will influence the market. Factors prompting differences of opinion can include national or world news, labor or management action, rumors—anything and everything, true or false.

Something that affects one company adversely may be to the advantage of another company. For instance, the building of superhighways sounded the death knell for manufacturers of streetcars, railway equipment, and railroad companies but was a boon to road-building equipment manufacturers and the trucking industry.

STOCKS

There are three ways in which investors can own securities. One is to own the stock outright by paying for it in full. The second is to buy the stock by paying only a part of its cost and borrowing the balance from the broker. In this case the stock is said to have been bought "on margin." The third way is to borrow the stock certificate from a broker and then sell it. This is referred to as "selling short."

The first method is simple and self-explanatory.

Buying on Margin

When buying on margin, the investor controls a greater portion of ownership with a smaller investment. The unpaid balance can be borrowed from the broker by using the stock itself as collateral. Not all stocks are marginable or can be used as collateral. The Federal Reserve Board establishes the type of stock that can be used and the down payment necessary. The interest rate charged to borrow the balance is about 1-1/2 to 2% above the prime rate, and is payable monthly to the brokerage house. If the market value of the margined stock drops and the collateral value is below 25% of the loan, the borrower has to increase the downpayment up to 25% of the loan. Investors are sent official notices known as "federal margin calls." The brokerage house may require a 30% minimum, which is called a "house call." On the other hand, if the stock increases in value, the investors will realize a greater profit (minus interest and commission paid) on their investment when they sell the margined stock.

Buying on margin has its advantages and disadvantages, and your broker can assist you in weighing the pros and cons. Older investors will remember the panic that buying stocks on margin created during the Great Depression. Since that time, certain controls have been devised to protect both investors and brokers, but buying on margin still represents considerable risk and is only for the sophisticated investor.

Selling Short

Selling short is the method used by investors who believe that a certain stock will decrease in value. Investors borrow the stock certificate from their broker and sell it. The money stays in the investor's account as collateral. If all goes well and the stock "goes down," the investor can buy it back on the open market, replace the certificate, and realize a profit. The risk, of course, is that the value of the stock may "go up" and when it has to be replaced, it must be bought back at a higher price. The result is a loss in addition to the commission plus any dividends paid.

Stock Analysts

Different people feel comfortable with different securities. Some buy stocks because of their dividends, others for appreciation. Speculators try to take advantage of the up and down movements of stock values—buying when they are down and selling when they are up.

In general, brokers divide their recommendations into categories: preservation of capital with high current income and moderate growth; moderate income with long-term appreciation; and some current income (or none) with aggressive growth. The choices depend on what the investor's investment objectives are. To arrive at these recommendations, brokerage houses rely on their staff of "fundamental analysts" and "technical analysts."

Fundamental Analysts. Fundamental analysts will examine operations and managements of various industries, the position of a particular company within its own industry, and make judgments about the possible future performance of these companies. They will compare the balance sheet of a particular company with the balance sheets of similar companies, compare their efficiency and production, trends in earnings and dividend payments, and analyze their current and future shares of their market. They will take into consideration world, national, and local conditions, or any other circumstances that may affect the future of the company. They will be as familiar with the company as any outsiders can be expected to be. Although their projections cannot be guaranteed, they will be based on hard data and as accurate as possible. The fundamental analyst's greatest strength, however, is his ability to interpret profit and loss statements and balance sheets.

Every company that maintains a large inventory has to have an accounting method for evaluating and re-evaluating it. An inventory is an asset, but it can also be a liability if it takes up valuable storage space and remains unsold over a long period of time. The inventory can consist of raw materials or finished goods, and may be maintained for a short period or for seasonal delivery or over a period of a year.

Raw material is continuously being received (at rising prices) and sold some months later as a finished product (at inflated values). The raw material has to be replaced, of course, to keep the cycle going. In inflationary times, the cost of replacement inventory keeps rising dramatically. At what price does a company carry its inventory on its books at the time of inventory evaluation? If the raw material that was received first is made into a product and sold first,* the manufacturer will show a high profit margin and a close-to-current inventory evaluation. If the material bought last is sold first,† the profit margin is only out of balance to the time-lag increase in sales price— but the inventory is carried on the books at a low value.

All this serves to show an imbalance on the company's balance sheet, and will have a bearing on the taxes paid and the profit earned.

Technical Analysts. Technical analysts chart the performance of the overall stock market, concentrating on the activities of particular companies. Although it is impossible to predict any period of the future with certainty, it is possible to chart the performance of a particular company and compare it with the overall performance of the market to arrive at a projection.

One research organization, Value-Line Investment Survey, has used what they call their "Beta co-efficient" as a measure of a stock's sensitivity to the fluctuation of about 1700 selected stocks in their averages. For example, a Beta factor of 1.5 would indicate a variation of 15% above or below a 10% change in their overall market value, and a Beta factor of less than 1 would indicate a change of less than 10%. (For instance, .7 is 7% change.) How they arrive at their Beta co-efficients need not concern us here. What is important is that their analyses hit the mark as often as any other method.

Accounting abbreviations: *LIFO †FIFO

Logic dictates that a large staff of qualified and experienced securities analysts is a great expense to a brokerage house. The expenses to maintain such a staff must be paid out of the commission charged for each trade. Commission rates are not set by law, and exchanges are no longer allowed to set the commission rates their members must charge. Some brokerage houses, such as "discount" houses, do not employ analysts and offer no investment service other than trading, so their commission charge is less. You get what you pay for.

BONDS

Bond buyers also employ strategies to maximize their income and gain. The interest payments on the bond (income to the bond-holder) are assured by the quality of the bond (see Chapter 20). Although the current interest rate fluctuates, bond interest payments do not. The market price of a bond will change inversely with the current interest rate—that is, as the current interest rate rises above the bond yield, the market price of the bond goes down. If the current interest rate is below the coupon yield of the bond, the market price goes up. Sometimes, bondholders want to get the profit when the interest rate declines by selling their bonds. Other bondholders use the decline of bond market value to take advantage of a "bond swap." This means exchanging bonds with a coupon yield lower than the current yield (see Chapter 8 to find out how to figure current yield) for bonds with a coupon yield equal to or higher than the current yield, when both produce the same amount in monthly interest payments. This is similar to exchanging discount bonds for bonds at par value or higher. The income would be the same, but the new bond would have a higher maturity value. A current "paper loss" would be realized which would be balanced against future gain.

Bonds offer opportunities to speculate. A speculator can buy a "deep discount" bond issued by a company or municipality with a lower than BBB rating (see Chapter 20). The market price may be so low that the interest payments may be as much as 15 to 20% of the cost. Should the rating of the issuer be raised, the market value of the bond will rise or the bond issuer will pay off the bond at par at maturity, and the speculator will realize a handsome profit. If the current yield of the bond is 20%, income from the bond will pay for the bond in about five years. After that, any increase in the market value would be a clear profit. Speculating in bonds is not for the unsophisticated—the return may be high, but so is the risk.

CONVERTIBLE BONDS AND
PREFERRED STOCKS

Convertible corporate bonds are attractive to those who are looking for a higher current yield, but who also like to play the stock market because common stocks offer greater capital appreciation than convertible bonds. If capital appreciation is your objective, convertible bonds which can be exchanged for common stocks are for you.

Convertible bonds have a fixed maturity date, and will retire at par or can be converted into common stocks at maturity. Conversion privileges are usually adjusted for any stock splits or dividends. Convertible bonds generally decline at a lower percentage rate than common stocks.

Convertible preferred stocks have many of the same characteristics as convertible bonds. Convertible preferred stocks, however, are not as safe as convertible bonds. The investor's strategy should be to compare the preferred stock of one company to the convertible bonds of another—one company's stocks may be safer than another company's bonds. Convertible preferred stocks do not have maturity dates and are usually subject to redemption.

Strategies in anything—love, war, or investing—depend upon present and future circumstances. In the case of investments, strategy depends upon the market, which itself is dependent upon many factors. The question: "What is the market going to do?" can best be answered: "It will go up or down—but not necessarily in that order." In the long run, however, there has been a steady increase in the value of most stock. For instance, in 1928 the Dow Jones average was 300. A few years ago the Dow Jones broke 1000, and it has hovered around 800–900 for the past few years. The moral of the story is: buy good quality and you will be ahead in the long run. Diversify and you preserve; specialize and you speculate. Investors who are armed with as much information as they can muster can plan the best investment strategy.

HOW TO READ THE STOCK PAGES
IN YOUR NEWSPAPER

Many people who are considering investing approach the stock market pages in the financial sections of their newspaper with fear and trembling. All that small print and all those numbers are intimidating, but there is nothing mysterious about these figures if you know how to read them.

The best explanation of how to begin reading these pages that I have found comes from a newspaper itself, and it appears in Fig. 18-1.

Most newspapers will periodically reprint some such guide to their stock pages.

What follows in Fig. 18-2 are some samples of the various securities and different exchanges as listed in newspapers. If you read the directions and glance at the samples, you will no longer be timid about opening your newspaper to the financial section and following the progress of securities you own or are thinking of buying.

HOW NEW ISSUES ARE INTRODUCED
TO THE MARKET

Have you ever wondered how new securities (stocks and bonds) are introduced to the market?

According to the regulations of the Securities and Exchange Commission, a complete disclosure must be made to the SEC showing assets of the corporation, its management, names of the members of the Board of Trustees, and names of major stockholders and the number of shares they own. In addition, the Department of Commerce, Division of Securities in each state must also approve before the securities can be offered to the public within the boundaries of the state. Approval by the state or federal government does not constitute a "recommendation for the public to buy," and this disclaimer is clearly noted on the face of the prospectus. The prospectus is an abbreviated form of the statement filed with the SEC. The first time an issue is offered to the public it must be accompanied by a prospectus.

When approval to make the offering has been obtained, the

Composite trading quotations on New York Stock Exchange and American Stock Exchange include trading in those stocks on the Pacific, Midwest, PBW, Boston and Cincinnati Stock Exchanges as well as trades reported by NASDAQ and the instinet system. Prices and volume are as of 5:30 p.m. EST.

Over-the-counter quotations are of stocks trading on the National Association of Securities Dealers' (NASDAQ) national list which are not traded on the New York or American Stock Exchanges.

Q-T-C quotations are supplied through NASDAQ as of 4 p.m. EST. Quotes do not include retail markup, markdown or commissions. Bid and ask are the most recent prices offered or sought by buyers and sellers in the dealer market exchange.

Reading the tables

From left to right, the tables start with **high** and **low** prices for the most recent 12 months. The company's name (abbreviated) is followed by the annual **dividend** rate paid on each share of stock. The dividend rate is based on the last quarterly or semiannual declaration, unless otherwise noted.

Sls.Hds. means volume of shares traded during the week, expressed in hundreds. 15 means 1,500 shares traded. **Yield** in percent is the total dividends paid on the stock during the past 12 months divided into the market price to express the return received as a percent.

PE means price/earnings ratio, the ratio of the stock's market price when it is divided by annual earnings per share of stock. **Last** is the closing price of the stock for the last trading day of the previous week. Net change is the accumulative change in the price of the stock during the preceding week. If no change, the space is occupied by a dotted line. Changes are reflected in dollars and eighths, an eighth being 12.5 cents.

1/2 — .50
1/4 — .25
1/8 — .125
1/16 — .0625
1/32 — .03125
1/64 — .015625

Fraction decimal values as used in stock and bond trading.

Common symbols and footnotes

pf — indicates preferred shares.
wt — indicates a warrant, the right to buy at a specified price by a specified date.
h — (Over-the-counter only) stock does not meet NASDAQ qualifications. This designation usually is temporary.
n — new issue since Jan. 1.
z — (after sales figure) — fewer than 100 shares were traded and reported figure represents sales in full.
cld — called (on preferred shares).
nd — next day delivery.
vl — in bankruptcy or receivership or being reorganized under the bankruptcy act or securities assumed by such companies.

Footnotes on Dividends

a — includes extra dividend(s).
b — annual rate plus stock dividend.
c — liquidating dividends.
e — no dividend presently announced, dividend shown was paid in preceding 12 months.
g — dividend or earnings in Canadian funds, no PE given unless stated in U.S. funds.
l — dividend declared or paid after stock dividend or split.
k — declared or paid this year on cumulative issues with dividends in arrears.
p — paid this year, dividend omitted, deferred or not action taken at last dividend meeting.
r — declared or paid in the preceding 12 months in addition to stock dividend.
t — paid in stock in stock in preceding 12 months, estimated cash value on ex-dividend or ex-distribution date.
x — ex-dividend, meaning any dividend payable on the stock is payable to the seller, not the buyer.
y — ex-dividend and sales in full.
x-dis — ex-distribution.
xr — ex rights.
xw — ex warrants.
ww — with warrants.
wd — when distributed.
wl — when issued.

Figure 18-1

Coupon yield

Maturity (1995)

CORPORATION BONDS
Volume, $24,110,000

Bonds	Cur Yld	Vol	High	Low	Close	Net Chg.
AMInt 9⅜95	13.	15	72	72	72	+2⅛
APL 10¾97	14.	7	75½	73	75½	+2½
ATO 4⅜s87	cv	30	62	62	62	−1
ATO 10⅜98	13.	4	81	81	81	+ ⅛
AbbtL 7⅝96	8.5	10	89¾	89⅝	89¾	.....
AetnCr 8¾83	9.7	10	90	90	90	.....
AetnLf 8⅛07	11.	10	73⅞	72¼	72¼	−1⅝
AlaP 9s2000	12.	12	76	75½	76	+2
AlaP 8½s01	12.	16	69½	69½	69½	+2½
AlaP 8⅞s03	12.	10	71½	71½	71½	+ ¾
AlaP 9¾s04	12.	10	79	79	79	.....
AlaP 10⅞05	13.	10	86	86	86	.....
AlaP 10½05	13.	3	84	84	84	.....
AlaP 8⅞06	12.	3	72½	72½	72½	.....
AlaP 8¾07	13.	16	70	68⅜	70	.....
AlaP 8⅝87	11.	16	81⅞	80	81⅞	+2⅞
AlaP 9¼07	13.	2	71⅛	71⅛	71⅛	−1⅞
AlaP 9½08	13.	5	76	74½	74½	−1½
AlaP 9⅝08	12.	68	78	75½	78	+1½

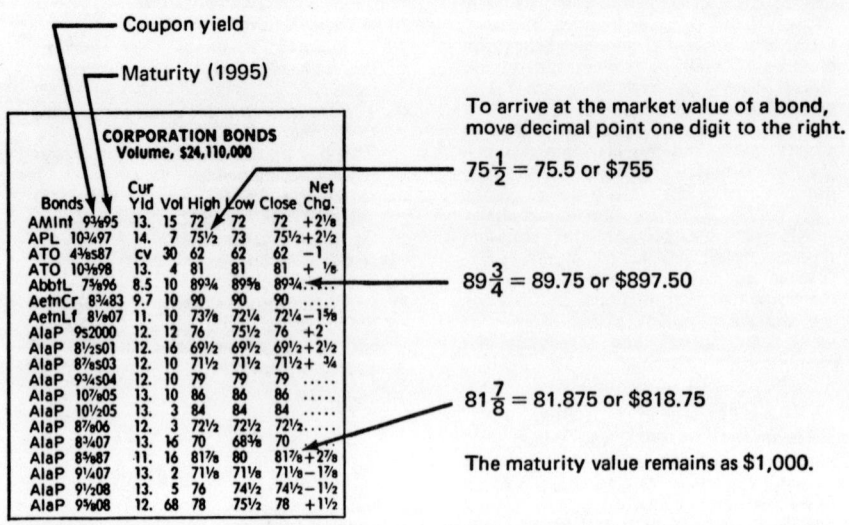

To arrive at the market value of a bond, move decimal point one digit to the right.

$75\frac{1}{2} = 75.5$ or $755

$89\frac{3}{4} = 89.75$ or $897.50

$81\frac{7}{8} = 81.875$ or $818.75

The maturity value remains as $1,000.

Treasury Issues

* * *

Bonds, Notes & Bills

Monday, May 5, 1980

Over-the-Counter quotations; sources on request.

Decimals in bid-and-asked and bid changes represent 32nds; 101.1 means 101 1/32. a-Plus 1/64. b-Yield to call date. d-Minus 1/64. n-Treasury notes.

Treasury Bonds and Notes

Rate	Mat.	Date	Bid	Asked	Bid Chg.	Yld.
6⅞s,	1980	May n.............	99.28	100	+ .1	9.41
8s,	1980	May n.............	99.24	99.28	.....	9.59
7⅝s,	1980	Jun n.............	99.17	99.21	+ .1	9.71
8¼s,	1980	Jun n.............	99.19	99.23	+ .1	9.89
8½s,	1980	Jul n.............	99.16	99.20	+ .4	9.92
6¾s,	1980	Aug n.............	99	99.4	+ .5	9.86
9s,	1980	Aug n.............	99.16	99.24	+ .4	9.73
8⅜s,	1980	Aug n.............	99.9	99.13	+ .5	10.16
6⅞s,	1980	Sep n.............	98.20	98.24	+ .6	10.06
8⅝s,	1980	Sep n.............	99.10	99.14	+ .6	10.01
8⅞s,	1980	Oct n.............	99.10	99.18	+ .7	9.81
3½s,	1980	Nov...............	96.20	96.28	+ .8	9.78
7⅛s,	1980	Nov n.............	98.11	98.15	+ .8	10.21
9¼s,	1980	Nov n.............	99.13	99.17	+ .7	10.12
5⅞s,	1980	Dec n.............	97.8	97.12	+ .10	10.85
9⅞s,	1980	Dec n.............	99.26	99.30	+ .12	9.98
9¾s,	1981	Jan n.............	99.21	99.25	+ .9	10.06
7s,	1981	Feb n.............	97.24	97.28	+ .20	9.89

Figure 18-2

Composite trading NYSE

Quotations include trading on the New York, Pacific, Midwest, PBW, Boston, Detroit and Cincinnati stock exchanges, and over-the-counter trades in listed stocks as reported by NASDAQ and Instinet. Prices and volume as of 5:30 p.m. Eastern time.

Stock	Div.	P. E.	Sls. Hds.	Close	Net Chg.
A					
ACF	2.50	6	257	33	+ ½
AMF	1.24	6	318	14⅞	— ⅛
AM Intl	.28	108	123	17¼	— ¼
APL	.50i	33	12	9⅛	....
ARA	1.82	6	484	30⅝	+ ¾
ASA	3	....	1341	45¼	— ½
ATO	.60	4	48	11	+ ⅛
AVX s	.32	12	276	26⅞	— ⅛
AbbtLb	1.20	14	982	42½	— ⅜
AcmeC	1.40	5	39	23⅝	+ ⅛
AmInvt	.40a	9	94	11	....
AMI s	.80	12	741	u39⅛	+ 2¼
AmMotrs	.30	4	863	5	— ⅛
ANatR	3.44	8	383	42¾	+ 1⅛
AmSLFla	.80b	4	21	21	— ¼
AShip	.80	11	49	13⅝	— ⅜
AStand	4	6	269	57	— ⅝
ASterll	.32	8	159	7⅞	+ ⅛
AmStr	.80	6	47	26⅛	+ ⅝
AmStr pf	5.51	....	9	45⅜	+ 1⅛
ATT	5	7	3834	52⅝	+ ¼
ATT pf	4	....	18	56⅛	+ ¼
AWatWk	.96	5	113	11⅝	+ ⅛
AWat pf	1.25	....	z400	10⅛	— ⅝

Composite trading AMEX

Quotations include trading on the American, Midwest, PBW, Boston, Detroit, Cincinnati and Pacific stock exchanges, and OTC trades reported by NASDAQ and Instinet. Prices and volume as of 5:30 p.m. Eastern time.

Stock	Div.	P. E.	Sls. Hds.	Close	Net Chg.
A					
AAR s	.40	6	29	9⅞	....
AAV	.20	5	3	3⅞	+ ⅛
AIC Ph n	.12	3	26	4¼	+ ⅛
APS	.48	5	22	7¼	....
ATI		23	7	1⅝	....
AVC		9	26	5½	+ ⅛
CastlAM	1b	4	5	14½	+ ⅛
CasFd	1.60a	....	2	20	....
Cavitrn	.12e	23	70	16⅛	+ ¼
CentSe	.70e	....	13	7½	....
CenS pf	1.25	....	z100	24½	....
CtryFa	.10e	5	2	6⅜	+ ⅛
Cenvill	1.40	6	16	25¼	....
Cetec	.12	7	45	5½	— ⅛
ChedMl	.60	5	5	6¾	+ ¼
ChamaHo		....	2207	1⅛	....

EXPLANATORY NOTES

(For New York and American Exchange listed issues)

Sales figures are unofficial.

The 52-Week High and Low columns show the highest and the lowest price of the stock in consolidated trading during the preceding 52 weeks plus the current week, but not the current trading day.

u–Indicates a new 52-week high. d–Indicates a new 52-week low.

s–Split or stock dividend of 25 per cent or more in the past 52 weeks. The high-low range and dividend begin with the date of split or stock dividend, and do not cover the entire 52-week period.

n–New issue in the past 52 weeks. The high-low range begins with the start of trading in the new issue and does not cover the entire 52-week period.

g–Dividend or earnings in Canadian money. Stock trades in U.S. dollars. No yield or PE shown unless stated in U.S. money.

Unless otherwise noted, rates of dividends in the foregoing table are annual disbursements based on the last quarterly or semi-annual declaration. Special or extra dividends or payments not designated as regular are identified in the following footnotes.

a–Also extra or extras. b–Annual rate plus stock dividend. c–Liquidating dividend. e–Declared or paid in preceding 12 months. i–Declared or paid after stock dividend or split up. j-Paid this year, dividend omitted, deferred or no action taken at last dividend meeting. k–Declared or paid this year, an accumulative issue with dividends in arrears. r–Declared or paid in preceding 12 months plus stock dividend. t–Paid in stock in preceding 12 months, estimated cash value on ex-dividend or ex-distribution date.

x–Ex-dividend or ex-rights. y–Ex-dividend and sales in full. z–Sales in full.

wd–When distributed. wi–When issued. ww–With warrants. xw–Without warrants.

vj–In bankruptcy or receivership or being reorganized under the Bankruptcy Act, or securities assumed by such companies.

Mutual Funds

	Sell Bid	Buy Ask
Acorn F	23.10	NL
ADV	12.92	NL
Afuture	13.79	NL
AIM Funds:		
CvYld	12.14	12.98
Edson	11.14	11.91
HiYld	10.23	10.94
Alpha F	14.41	NL
A BirthT	12.15	13.28
American Funds:		
Delta	7.11	7.77
Csh Rs	10.00	NL
Dir Cap	2.25	NL
DodCx Bl	22.86	NL
DodCx St	18.25	NL
Drex Bur	12.79	NL
Dreyfus Grp:		
Dreyf	13.85	15.14
Levge	21.05	23.01
Liq As	1.00	NL

Over-the-Counter

	Sales (hds)	Bid	Asked
A			
AEL Ind	196	8	8½
AEST	33	3¼	4¼
AcadIns	106	4¼	4½
Accelrtn	26	4¾	5¾
Accuray	86	7⅜	7⅞
AcmeEl	3	6½	7¼
AcmeGn	....	7	7¾
AdacLb	75	9¼	10
AddisnW	36	8	8¾
	138	5⅜	5¾
		[illegible]	6
AMS	8	21½	23
AMicros	564	17⅜	17⅞
AMonitr	5	21¾	22¾
ANatIns	402	13¾	14⅛
AmNucl	187	11⅛	11⅝
APacInt	187	2⅜	2⅝
AQuasar	298	29⅜	29⅞
AResMg	568	49	50
ASecCp	126	27¾	28½
AUndrwt	....	7⅞	8⅜
AmVisn	74	1⅛	1⅝
AWeldng	37	36½	37½
Amrtrst	48	30¾	31¾
Amoskg	1	48	53
Amterr	3	3¼	3½

Chicago Grain

	Open	High	Low	Close	Chg
WHEAT					
Jul	4.02	4.04	3.97	3.97½	—.03¾
Sep	4.14½	4.16	4.09½	4.09¾	—.03½
Dec	4.32½	4.34	4.26½	4.27½	—.03¼
Mar	4.47	4.48	4.41	4.43	—.02½
May	4.51½	4.54	4.48	4.49¼	—.03
Jul	4.56	4.58	4.51	4.54	—.02

Sales Wed. 15,021.

Total open interest Wed. 44,873, up 560 from Tues.

	Open	High	Low	Close	Chg
CORN					
Jul	2.75	2.75¾	2.73½	2.73¾	—.01¾
	2.84½	2.85	2.82¾	2.83	—.01¾
	2.91¾	2.93¼	2.90½	2.90¾	—.01½
	[illegible]03½	3.05¼	3.02½	3.02½	—.01¼
		3.12¾	3.10⅛	3.10½	—.00½
		[illegible]18½	3.16	3.16	+.00¼

[illegible]. 155,770, off 564

Figure 18-2–*Cont.*

securities are then sold to the public by a "syndicate." The syndicate is a group of investment bankers and/or brokerage houses which buys these securities from the issuer at a discount by paying a lump sum. The price may have been arrived at by negotiation between the syndicate and the issuer or by bidding against other syndicates.

The securities are now advertised and the advertisement will, once again, stress that it is not an offer to sell but that it is simply a notice that such securities have followed proper procedure, under law, and are entering the market. The members of the syndicate are named in the ad, with the manager(s) in large type or prominently shown and all other participants in smaller type. The participants are listed in order according to the number of shares they have committed themselves to market. Those listed first will distribute the larger quantity. Since all selling expenses are included in establishing the discount, no commission will be charged to the buyer.

Interested investors can send away for the prospectus or obtain one from their broker.

REAL ESTATE FINANCING
AND SELLING

Why Borrow? ● *Real Estate Financing* ● *Buying and Selling Property* ● *Types of Mortgages* ● *How to Sell Your Real Estate*

WHY BORROW?

There are two reasons for borrowing: to enjoy something that you can't pay for at the moment; and to use money to greater advantage.

Borrowing for Purchases

For most people, borrowing money takes the form of short-term loans to purchase major appliances, automobiles, furniture, and so on, or to finance something such as a vacation or home remodeling project. Long-term borrowing is generally in the form of a house mortgage. In the case of homeownership, prospective owners put down a relatively small payment and borrow the rest. Over a period of time, they return the amount borrowed plus a charge for the use of the money. The question is, what is the ultimate cost of the home?

A house bought for $100,000 with a $25,000 down payment, and a 30-year mortgage at 10% annual interest will cost the buyer $261,944.80:

Monthly mortgage and interest payment	$ 658.18
$658.18 X 12 months X 30 years	$236,944.80
Plus the down payment	$ 25,000.00
	$261,944.80

A mortgage is computed on a simple interest basis: you pay interest only on what you owe each month. This interest is, of course, tax deductible.

Regular installment loans, on the other hand, are not computed this way. For instance, suppose you want to borrow $1,000 for one year at 10% with monthly installment payments:

	Monthly Payment	Total
Simple interest: $1,000 at 10%	$87.92	$1,055.04
Add-on interest: $1,000 plus $100 = $1,100 ÷ 12	$91.67	$1,100.00
Discount: $1,000 minus $100 = $900 = ($1,000 ÷ 12)	$83.34	$1,000.00

Let's analyze this. Simple interest means that you borrowed $1,000 and paid back $1,055.04, for an annual rate of 5.5% interest. Add-on interest means you borrowed $1,100, received $1,000 and paid back the $1,100 at an annual rate of 10% interest. Discount means that you borrowed $1,000 but received only $900. You paid back the $1,000 at an 11.11% annual rate.

Truth in lending laws require that the annual interest rates be shown on whatever document you signed with a lending institution. It should then be easy for you to figure how much the money you are borrowing will actually cost you.

Simple interest loans can only be had with mortgages, and then only for a minimum of five to ten years. Add-ons and discount plans are used for other kinds of loans. If you have a good credit rating, lending institutions are happy to make you a loan. After all, they exist on the interest they earn on the money they put out to work for them. It is to the prospective borrower's best interests to shop around for the best rate.

Almost all homeowners will at one time or another have paid their real estate taxes through their banks. When you first buy a home, enough money is left in your tax escrow account to pay the real estate tax when it is due. From then on, you will put one-half of the annual or one-sixth of the semiannual tax into the tax account each month, along with the actual mortgage payment. The bank will use this money until the tax is due without paying any interest on it. Homeowners are entitled to the interest this money earns, however, and you can complain to the bank about it if you don't receive it. Banks do not pay this interest as a matter of course.

Suppose you pay your homeowner's insurance, mortgage insurance, and car insurance through your bank. The bank will add the first annual premium to your loan and you will pay it at the same rate as your loan. For example, if you have a 30-year loan, you will pay on it for 30 years. The bank adds 1/12 of the annual premium to your monthly mortgage payments. This insurance premium is accumulated in your insurance escrow account until the insurance payment is due. The bank uses this money without paying you for its use.

The question is then: is this service worth it to you? Wouldn't you be better off accumulating the premium in a savings account and benefiting from the interest it will earn for you?

Borrowing for Financial Advantage

Thus far, we have talked about borrowing to buy something you need but cannot pay for at the moment. Let us now discuss borrowing for a financial advantage.

Suppose that an investment opportunity has been presented to you. You need $20,000 for a possible return of 15%. You only have $10,000, and must borrow the balance at 10% for one year. If you had the $20,000, your projected return would be $3,000. If you use $10,000 of your own money and borrow $10,000, the return is still $3,000.

	$3,000
You pay 10% for the use of $10,000 (deduct)	$1,000
The return on your own $10,000 is then 20%	$2,000

What you have done is increase your own return by using the bank's money to your own advantage. Any debt instrument can be used: bonds, buying on margin, etc., to borrow money to your advantage. Furthermore, the interest payments on the loan are tax deductible. Sounds great, but what are the risks?

Suppose the investment opportunity did not pan out as you thought it would, and you lose $5,000. You have lost your own money *and* you are still responsible for the $10,000 you borrowed from the bank.

Banking is a business; the banker's job is to produce a profit and the depositors' money is the inventory and the commodity the banker is using to produce that profit. The borrower uses the bank's merchandise—money. The bank's profit, disregarding its expenses of doing business, is the difference of what the bank pays as interest on its customers' deposits and what the bank charges for the use of its money. Ultimately, the bank gets paid for finding someone (the borrower) who has better use for your (depositor) money than you do. The bank assumes the risk that you, the depositior, will get your money back when you need it.

REAL ESTATE FINANCING

When it comes to buying real estate, very few people have a lot of experience and what experience they do have involves the purchase of a home. Most prospective buyers are very choosy when selecting a house in which to live, but then leave the most important part of home buying—the financing—to the first lender who offers to provide the mortgage money. By signing the mortgage agreement, homebuyers oblige themselves to pay as much as one quarter of their monthly income, at least in the beginning, for as long as up to thirty years. It is to your advantage, therefore, to shop around for the best possible deal when it comes to borrowing money. A conscientious real estate agent can be a big help, of course, but those looking for mortgage money should investigate sources themselves.

What Is a Mortgage?

A mortgage is a contract to repay a debt that is secured by the real property put up as collateral. It is registered in county records and becomes a lien against the property. "Lien" means "prior claim." In the case of a mortgage, the recording date establishes priority for satisfying each lien. The mortgage instrument is a contract which specifically states, among many provisions, that the monthly payments must be made by a specific day of the month, and that if payment is not made within a definite time from the due date the interest rate may be increased or the unpaid balance of the mortgage may be called on demand. If the payment is still not made, the real estate itself (which is the collateral for the mortgage loan) reverts to the lending institution. After taking certain legal steps, this institution can take ownership of the real estate and can sell it to recover its investment. The mortgage instrument also states that all taxes must be paid when due, and that sufficient insurance coverage be carried to protect the lending institution's investment.

The mortgage instrument may also include a clause which specifies that if the mortgage is paid off before a specified date, a penalty may be imposed. Another clause may state that the mortgagee may terminate or automatically renew the mortgage every fixed number of years. The penalty clause is for the benefit of the lender, and its purpose is to ensure that the expenses of issuing the mortgage will be recovered. The termination and renewal clause gives the lender the privilege of increasing or decreasing the interest rate if it is to the lender's benefit to do so. (It can be safely stated that the privilege is more likely to be exercised when the interest rate is to be raised.) If there is a *roll-over* provision in the mortgage instrument, the mortgagee must, upon the mortgagor's demand, refinance the mortgage at a lower interest rate if the prevailing interest rate has dropped without the mortgagor incurring closing costs again.

Other provisions written into the mortgage instrument are intended to maintain the market value of the property. Maintenance of property is to the advantage of both lenders and mortgagors—for lenders because the property is collateral for the loan, and for owners because each mortgage payment increases their equity, or ownership, and it is to their benefit to build equity in property which maintains or increases in value. Neglected property is a loss for everybody.

Mortgage liens. Earlier I mentioned liens against property. A lien may be placed for unpaid debts for repairs or improvements to the property, or (in the case of building a new home) may be filed by the contractor or subcontractors if they have not been paid. These are called "mechanics liens." There may also be a second mortgage on the property. Whatever the lien, it can only be removed by payment of the debt represented by the lien. Only then can a "warranty deed" be issued to convey ownership of real property. By granting a warranty deed, the seller guarantees that there are no liens currently on the property. Title companies research deeds and issue insurance policies to guarantee their findings.

In contrast to a warranty deed, a "quit claim deed" conveys the ownership of the property without any other guarantees. Liens, if there are any, are then the responsibility of the buyer and do not have to be satisfied by the seller.

Mortgage Money: Where Does It Come From?

Satisfied ownership is a combination of finding the right home and a cooperative lender. You and the lender will have close ties for a long, long time and you should realize that the lender also looks forward to a trouble-free, happy relationship. The lender has entrusted you with a tidy sum of money backed by collateral (the house) which he or she hopes you will maintain with a pride of ownership, and expects that you will pay your monthly mortgage payment as agreed.

The lender will look upon this transaction as a risk he or she has assumed until the mortgage is paid off. The lender has investigated your background and has come to some conclusions about the future of the neighborhood in which the house is located. Lenders spread their risk over many kinds of borrowers in as many neighborhoods as possible, and for this reason will be more or less favorable to certain mortgage applications at various times.

The largest number of mortgages are financed by savings and loan banks. By law they are limited to making loans strictly on residential real estate—homes or apartments. Commercial banks, on the other hand, will lend on any kind of real estate. But there are also other sources of mortgage money: insurance companies, credit unions, mortgage bankers, and individuals who will also lend either directly to the prospective homeowner or through mortgage bankers (also called "correspondents"). If your down payment is high—and what constitutes "high" depends on the nation's economic condition at the time—you are in a favorable buyer's position, and can shop around for the lowest interest rate. If your down payment is low, you may have to do business through mortgage bankers and, of course, you will have to pay for the increased risk you and your property represent by paying a higher interest rate.

In order to make homeownership possible for more people, especially special interest groups such as war veterans, the federal government has undertaken to insure the risks lending institutions must accept when issuing mortgages to such people. These mortgages are guaranteed by the Veterans Administration, the Federal Housing Administration (FHA), and other government assistance programs in case of default. When making such federally guaranteed loans, lending institutions charge a fixed maximum interest rate which is usually lower than the current rate. They are then allowed to charge up to 1% (or one point) of the mortgage to cover their additional expenses in making the loan. At times when the interest rate currently charged by the banks and the rate permitted by VA and FHA is higher, lending institutions charge additional points to compensate themselves for the lower income derived from such transactions. Since the buyer may only be charged one point, the seller will have to pay the additional points or the lender will refuse the loan application.

Points in real estate financing can be very confusing to the neophyte buyer unless the reasons for it are clearly understood. The purpose of charging points is to allow lenders to earn an additional return on their money by circumventing certain restrictions, such as the usury law limits or the maximum interest rate set by the VA or FHA. The main thing to remember about points is that one point is the equivalent of 1% of the mortgage. During the 1950s and early 1960s, when the average mortgage life was about seven years, 1% of the mortgage was the equivalent of about 1/4% interest. The average life of a mortgage today is about twelve to fifteen years.

In many states the usury law limits have been raised in recent years, and so have the maximum VA and FHA interest rates. With the regular mortgage rate as high as it is now, some lenders give the mortgagor the choice of paying the higher rates or taking advantage of points to reduce the rate. The point charge is an advantage to lenders. They will receive the point equivalent when the mortgage is initiated, so the amount they lend is the mortgage amount minus the point payment. These point charges raise mortgagor's costs. Since the points are paid at the start, the point payment is not a tax deduction, as an interest payment would be. It simply adds to the cost of the home.

A mortgage can be considered a "simple loan." Each payment consists of an advanced payment of one month's interest at 1/12 of the annual rate on the remaining balance of the loan. The rest of the payment is applied to the principal—i.e., the loan itself. Each month the loan is being reduced and the owner's equity (paid-up share) in the property is being increased. The amount to be paid each month, which includes interest and payment towards the principal, is the same throughout the life of the mortgage, unless it is refinanced.

If all goes well, your income will increase as your career advances, and the mortgage payment will gradually represent a smaller portion of your income than it did when you were first starting out. A "graduated rate" mortgage could then be an advantage. This arrangement calls for a lower payment in the early years and a correspondingly higher payment later on.

BUYING AND SELLING PROPERTY

Let us assume that you wish to buy another house, but have not yet sold your present home. If you qualify financially and the bank is not exposed to an above normal risk, you may be able to obtain a "blanket mortgage." This means that the bank will cover both pieces of property—the new mortgage and the balance of the mortgage on the original property. When the property is sold, the proceeds will be used to pay off the old mortgage and serve as all or part of the down payment on the new home. Until the first property is sold, taxes, insurance, and mortgage payments must be made on both homes. The blanket mortgage enables you to purchase the home you want when it is on the market without waiting for your old home to be sold.

Supposing you own your home "free and clear," and suppose that you are looking for ways to supplement your retirement income. You could investigate a "reverse mortgage" or "mortgage annuity." In this case you would receive a monthly income against a lender pre-approved mortgage with your home as collateral. When you were paying off your mortgage, each of your payments whittled down the debt. When you receive income, each payment to you represents a mortgage debt. The home can still be sold at any time, even when it is fully mortgaged. At the retirement period of life, a "reverse mortgage" or "mortgage annuity" can be a source of income.

With the exception of the "straight" or "level" mortgage, not all types of mortgages are approved in all states. More and more types of mortgages are being approved as time goes on, however, and prospective homeowners would do well to find out what kinds of mortgages are approved by their states.

Land Contract

Historically, the oldest means for buying real estate with or without a down payment is by land contract. The seller of the property remains the owner of record until sufficient funds have been accumulated through payments by the buyer to equal a down payment, and thus make the buyer eligible for a conventional mortgage. The periodic payments to the owner include both a charge for the use of the property and a sum designated to go toward the down payment. Should prospective buyers violate any of the contract provisions, they may forfeit their down payment allocation.

A land contract arrangement may benefit buyers by launching them on their way to being homeowners. The periodic payments represent rent and an enforced savings plan which enable them to accumulate enough money to be eligible for a mortgage from a lending institution. A land contract gives sellers income without their having to deed over the property.

Land contract provisions, however, can lead to many abuses that can be harmful to the buyer. In some states, land contract sales are illegal. No land contract arrangements should be entered into without advice from an attorney.

TYPES OF MORTGAGES

The Seller as Mortgagee

Suppose that as the seller of the property you have money to lend or want to defer the tax liability on the profit generated by the sale of your property. You could be the mortgagee and finance the sale yourself. You know the underlying collateral and, of course, should know the qualifications of the buyer. Such an arrangement will give you a systematic and consistent income over the length of the mortgage. Your income would consist of interest, capital gain, and return of the principal. This "purchase money" mortgage must consist of at least 70% of the net sales price or the installment purchase cannot apply and the tax liability cannot be deferred.

Variable Mortgage

During a period of rising interest rates, lenders look for some profit protection. Their profit is the difference between what they can charge for a loan and what they pay out as interest for money deposited with them. The interest rate charged does not change during the life of the mortgage, except in the case of a "variable mortgage." In a variable mortgage, lenders may change the rate when their cost of money changes. If they must pay a higher rate of interest to their depositors, they will raise the interest charged on their variable mortgages. Of course, when the cost of money drops, the interest charged for these mortgages should also drop.

Roll-over Mortgage

A roll-over provision in a mortgage permits mortgagors to request a reduction in their mortgage interest when such interest is lower than the rate of their current mortgage. The savings come from lower payments and the absence of closing costs. Some banks now reserve the same right for themselves to increase the interest rate.

Wrap-around Mortgage

This type of mortgage, especially in a large commercial real estate transaction, can be advantageous to mortgagors as well as to mortgagees. When such a piece of real estate is to be financed due to a sale or refinanced by the owner, the lender will assume the original mortgage and issue a second mortgage on the property. In this way, the lower interest rate of the first mortgage is still effective and the lender has assumed a conceivably lower risk by controlling all the financing and may be able to issue the "wrap-around" mortgage at a lower rate. Not all property lends itself to such an arrangement.

Anyone selling a home to purchase another may defer paying taxes on the profit (if any). If the new home is purchased within 18 months of the sale of the old residence and the proceeds are used to buy the new residence, for tax purposes the cost of the old home plus the amount added to purchase the new home may be considered the cost for the new home. Such an exchange, residence for residence, may be done no more than once a year unless for a valid reason such as job change, health reasons, etc. After the age of 55, senior citizen privileges can be used.

Senior Citizen Privileges

If the seller or seller's spouse is 55 years of age or older, and if either has lived in the house three of the last five years, the first $100,000 of the profit is not subject to tax. Commissions and closing costs, as well as any expenses incurred in improving the property up to 90 days in advance of the sale can be deducted from the selling price to arrive at the net profit. Senior citizen privileges may become more liberal and more numerous in the future, and you should explore them as the opportunity arises. The $100,000 profit exemption is a "once-in-a-lifetime" privilege for both owners and cannot be used again.

HOW TO SELL YOUR REAL ESTATE

Selling real estate is like selling anything else: you need a buyer who can afford to pay. How do you find such a buyer? A buyer can be found for anything provided that what is being sold is wanted and the price is agreeable. The things that influence the sale of your real property are price, condition, size, location, and how it is presented to the potential qualified buyers.

Determining the Price

In the home real estate market it is sometimes said that all sellers give their houses away and all buyers pay too much. In other words, neither buyer nor seller is ever satisfied. Since the market value of a home is the price the buyer and seller agree upon, and since no two homes are exactly alike, the exact value cannot be established beforehand. Sale prices can only be estimated. One way is to compare the actual selling price of similar homes in the neighborhood and allow for the differences in amenities, condition, location, age, and inflation. Another way is to call in several knowledgeable people, such as professional appraisers and real estate agents from the area. Very often, a tax appraisal is not a reliable guide. No matter how you arrive at your selling price, you should allow a small margin for negotiation.

The easier it is for prospective buyers to pay for your house, the more attractive your house will be to them. You can check with your local mortgage lenders to find out what kind of financing is available. Ask how much they will lend on your house and at what interest, and what the down payment must be for a qualified buyer. You will not get a firm commitment from them, but you will get ball-park figures and will be able to give prospective buyers some advice. Ask if your lender will allow a qualified buyer to assume your present mortgage. At the present time, a house with a mortgage is easier to sell than one without. You may wish to consider the possibility of carrying the mortgage yourself. Check with lenders about a "blanket" mortgage (also known as a "bridge" or "swing" loan) which can temporarily help to pay for a new home before you sell your present house. It's good to know about the availability of such loans because it may also determine what kind of a house you can buy.

It is a good idea to make all cosmetic repairs on a house before putting it on the market so that the condition of the house will invite buyers to live there. Any repair or fix-up expenses incurred within 90 days of the sale are considered a sales expense and are deducted from the sale price when you figure your taxes.

Real Estate Brokers

Homeowners can advertise the house themselves or can engage the assistance of a real estate broker. The advantage of owner-selling is the savings of the sales commission, but there is more to selling a house than just getting a buyer and seller together. Financing must be secured, escrow arrangements, title searches and all manner of details must be handled, and unless both buyer and seller know beforehand what they are getting into, you should rely on the services of a good real estate broker.

The real estate broker is entitled to a commission payable by the seller. The commission rate is not set by law and should be established by the agent and the seller before negotiations go any further. The agent will bear the costs of advertising the home. If the broker belongs to a multiple listing service, the real estate agent or broker will note all pertinent facts about the house such as size, lot measurements, taxes, utility costs, etc., on a card with a picture of the house, and this card will be distributed to other real estate agents who are part of the listing service. In this manner, as many prospective buyers as possible are made aware that the home is available. The more people who know about your home, the more likely you will be to find a buyer—and the right buyer.

How do you pick a real estate agent to represent you in selling your home? Obviously there must be mutual respect between the seller and the agent. The agent should represent a real estate company that is active in your area or belong to a multiple listing service that has an active real estate office in your area. A company that has a backlog of buyers has the best chance to sell your house.

The same agents who sell your house can also find a home for you to buy. They are compensated for their efforts by the seller. The licensing of real estate agents and brokers is done by the real estate commission of each state, and there are now very strict laws governing the buying and selling of homes and other real estate. Before a permanent license is granted, an applicant must pass several tests on the pertinent laws and ethics. An agent may only act in the name of the broker, and brokers are responsible for the action and conduct of the agents associated with them. Both agents and brokers must be bonded.

It is very important that the purchase agreement be properly drawn up. Real estate agents usually use an agreement approved by the real estate board in their area, but any agreement can be signed between buyer and seller as long as it contains all the necessary facts and provisions. If you are acting on your own, most stationery stores carry blank agreement forms you can use.

When a buyer makes an offer, the listing agent will meet with the seller to negotiate the price. If the price cannot be agreed upon, the sale is not concluded and no commission is due the agent. If the sale is made, the agent must make every effort to get the necessary financing arranged so that the buyer can take possession.

The Sale

The commission is divided among the broker, the agent who listed the home for sale, and the agent who actually made the sale. The split-up may be 50%, 20%, and 30%, respectively, but may vary with each real estate company. If the listing agent and the selling agent are from two different brokers, the commission is divided equitably, but only one commission is payable by the seller.

Before assuming responsibility, the real estate agent will ask you to sign a listing agreement. The standard effective period is from 60 to 90 days. It is to the seller's benefit to know as much about the agent and his or her home office as possible. If the seller does not think that the agent is doing enough to sell the house, a call to an officer of the real estate company may be in order. On the other hand, if the seller is unreasonable, if the price is too high, if the home is uninviting, if it was built specifically to satisfy the taste of the owner, it may not be competitive with other similarly priced homes on the market. All of these possibilities must be analyzed and the proper adjustments made.

Who must sign. If the owner-seller of the property is married, the spouse must also sign all documents, even if only one name appears on the deed. According to the law, in many states a wife has "dower" rights on the husband's property, which means that her position as legal wife entitles her to all the protection the law allows a legal wife. The husband has "courtesy" rights on his wife's real estate property. Because the law sees a marriage contract as involving both parties to it, both spouses may have to sign real estate documents.

Taxes

If you plan to purchase another home of a value equal to or greater than that of your present home, some or all of your profit may be subject to income taxes. Ask your accountant or a tax adviser about all possible implications of your sale. If you are buying another home and you are under age fifty-five, the tax on your profit (if any) can be postponed. If you are over fifty-five, up to $100,000 of profit can be excluded from taxation on a once-in-a-lifetime basis.

RATING SERVICES

Standard & Poor • *Moody* • *A. M. Best*

In Chapter 18 I talked about investment strategies and the role played by securities analysts. I have referred several times to Dow Jones averages, and Standard and Poor and other rating services, and talked about such things as "AAA bonds." In this chapter I will define the various classifications of stocks and bonds according to several rating services. The information that follows is reproduced from material put out by the rating services and is used with their permission. In Table 20–1 I have compared the ratings definitions of some of the best-known rating services with each other and with insurance companies in general.

Insurance companies are rated according to A. M. Best Company's analysis. Best's ratings are based on an analysis of the financial condition and operating performance of each insurance company. Five ratings are given: A+ and A (excellent); B+ (very good); B (good); C+ (fairly good); C (fair). These ratings reflect the relative financial strength of a company in comparison to the life/health insurance industry performance in such vital areas as: competent underwriting, control of expenses, adequate reserves, and sound investments.

Table 20-1

Comparison of Some Analytical Service Ratings

Standard & Poor (common stocks)		Standard & Poor (preferred stocks)		Standard & Poor (municipal and corporate bonds)		Moody's (municipal and corporate bonds)		A. M. Best Company (insurance analysts)	
A+	Highest	AAA	Prime	AAA	Prime	Aaa	Prime	A+ and A	Excellent
A	High	AA	High grade	AA	Excellent	Aa	Excellent	B+	Very good
A-	Average	A	Sound	A	Upper medium	A, A-1	Upper medium	B	Good
B	Below average	BBB	Medium grade	BBB	Lower medium	Baa, Baa-1	Lower medium	C+	Fairly good
B-	Lower	B	Speculative	BB	Marginally speculative	Ba	Marginally speculative	C	Fair
C	Lowest	CCC, CC, C	Non-paying	B	Very speculative	B, Caa	Very speculative		
				CCC, CC, C	No interest	Ca, C	Default		
D	In reorganization	D	Default	D	Default				

The criteria used by two major bond rating services are given below, through page 239. Financial analysts at Standard & Poor's and Moody's follow these guidelines in judging the quality of stocks and bonds.

STANDARD & POOR: MUNICIPAL AND CORPORATE BOND RATING DEFINITIONS

A Standard & Poor's corporate or municipal bond rating is a current assessment of the credit-worthiness of an obligor with respect to a specific debt obligation. This assessment may take into consideration obligors such as guarantors, insurers, or lessees.

The bond rating is not a recommendation to purchase, sell or hold a security, inasmuch as it does not comment as to market price or suitability for a particular investor.

The ratings are based on current information furnished by the issuer or obtained by Standard & Poor's from other sources we consider reliable. We do not perform an audit in connection with any rating and may, on occasion, rely on unaudited financial information. The ratings may be changed, suspended, or withdrawn as a result of changes in, or unavailability of, such information, or for other circumstances.

The ratings are based, in varying degrees, on the following considerations:

1. Likelihood of default—capacity and willingness of the obligor as to the timely payment of interest and repayment of principal in accordance with the terms of the obligation;

2. Nature of and provisions of the obligation;

3. Protection afforded by, and relative position of, the obligation in the event of bankruptcy, reorganization, or other arrangement under the laws of bankruptcy and other laws affecting creditors' rights.

AAA Bonds rated "AAA" have the highest rating assigned by Standard & Poor's to a debt obligation. Capacity to pay interest and repay principal is extremely strong.

AA Bonds rated "AA" have a very strong capacity to pay interest and repay principal and differ from the highest-rated issues only in a small degree.

A Bonds rated "A" have a strong capacity to pay interest and repay principal, although they are somewhat more susceptible to the adverse effects of changes in circumstances and economic conditions than bonds in higher-rated categories.

BBB Bonds rated "BBB" are regarded as having an adequate capacity to pay interest and repay principal. Whereas they normally exhibit adequate protection parameters, adverse economic conditions or changing circumstances are more likely to lead to a weakened capacity to pay interest and repay principal for bonds in this category than for bonds in higher-rated categories.

BB Bonds rated "BB," "CCC," and "CC" are regarded, on balance, as pre-
B dominantly speculative with respect to capacity to pay interest and
CCC repay principal in accordance with the terms of the obligation. "BB"
CC indicates the lowest degree of speculation and "CC" the highest degree of speculation. While bonds will likely have some quality and protective characteristics, these are outweighed by large uncertainties or major risk exposures to adverse conditions.

C The rating "C" is reserved for income bonds on which no interest is being paid.

D Bonds rated "D" are in default, and payment of interest and/or repayment of principal is in arrears.

Plus (+) or Minus (–): The ratings from "AA" to "BB" may be modified by the addition of a plus or minus sign to show relative standing within the major rating categories.

Provisional Ratings: The letter "p" indicates that the rating is provisional. A provisional rating assumes the successful completion of the project being financed by the bonds being rated and indicates that payment of debt service requirements is largely or entirely dependent upon the successful and timely completion of the project. This rating, however, while addressing credit quality subsequent to completion of the project, makes no comment on the likelihood of, or the risk of default upon failure of, such completion. The investor should exercise his own judgment with respect to such likelihood and risk.

NR Indicates that no rating has been requested, that there is insufficient information on which to base a rating or that Standard & Poor's does not rate a particular type of obligation as a matter of policy.

Debt Obligations of issuers outside the United States and its territories are rated on the same basis as domestic corporate and municipal issues. The ratings measure the creditworthiness of the obligor but do not take into account currency exchange and other uncertainties.

Bond Investment Quality Standards: Under present commercial bank regulations issued by the Comptroller of the Currency, bonds rated in the top four categories (AAA, AA, A, BBB, commonly known as "Investment Grade" ratings) are generally regarded as eligible for bank investment. In addition, the Legal Investment Laws of various states impose certain rating or other standards for obligations eligible for investment by savings banks, trust companies, insurance companies, and fiduciaries generally.

STANDARD & POOR: PREFERRED STOCK RATING DEFINITIONS

A Standard & Poor's preferred stock rating is an assessment of the capacity and willingness of an issuer to pay preferred stock dividends and any applicable sinking fund obligations. A preferred stock rating differs from a bond rating inasmuch as it is assigned to an equity issue, which issue is intrinsically different from, and subordinated to, a debt issue. Therefore, to reflect this difference, the preferred stock rating symbol will normally not be higher than the bond rating symbol assigned to, or that would be assigned to, the senior debt of the same issuer.

The preferred stock ratings are based on the following considerations:

1. Likelihood of payment-capacity and willingness of the issuer to meet the timely payment of preferred stock dividends and any applicable sinking fund requirements in accordance with the terms of the obligation.
2. Nature of, and provisions of, the issue.
3. Relative position of the issue in the event of bankruptcy, reorganization, or other arrangements affecting creditors' rights.

AAA   This is the highest rating that may be assigned by Standard & Poor's to a preferred stock issue and indicates an extremely strong capacity to pay the preferred stock obligations.

AA   A preferred stock issue rated "AA" also qualifies as a high-quality fixed income security. The capacity to pay preferred stock obligations is very strong, although not as overwhelming as for issues rated "AAA."

A   An issue rated "A·" is backed by a sound capacity to pay the preferred stock obligations, although it is somewhat more susceptible to the adverse effects of changes in circumstances and economic conditions.

BBB   An issue rated, "BBB" is regarded as backed by an adequate capacity to pay the preferred stock obligations. Whereas it normally exhibits adequate protection parameters, adverse economic conditions or changing circumstances are more likely to lead to a weakened capacity to make payments for a preferred stock in this category than for issues in the "A" category.

BB   Preferred stock rated "BB," "B," and "CCC" are regarded, on balance,
B   as predominately speculative with respect to the issuer's capacity to pay
CCC   preferred stock obligations. "BB" indicates the lowest degree of specula-
          tion and "CCC" the highest degree of speculation. While such issues will
          likely have some quality and protective characteristics, these are out-
          weighed by large uncertainties or major risk exposures to adverse con-
          ditions.

CC   The rating "CC" is reserved for a preferred stock issue in arrears on divi-
          dends or sinking fund payments but that is currently paying.

C   A preferred stock rated "C" is a non-paying issue.

D   A preferred stock rated "D" is a non-paying issue with the issuer in de-
          fault on debt instruments.

NR   Indicates that no rating has been requested, that there is insufficient in-
          formation on which to base a rating, or that S&P does not rate a particu-
          lar type of obligation as a matter of policy.

          Plus (+) or Minus (–). To provide more detailed indications of preferred
          stock quality, the ratings from "AA" to "BB" may be modified by the
          addition of a plus or minus sign to show relative standing within the
          major rating categories.

          The preferred stock rating is not a recommendation to purchase or
          sell a security, inasmuch as market price is not considered in arriving at
          the rating. Preferred stock *ratings* are wholly unrelated to Standard &
          Poor's earnings and dividend *rankings* for common stocks.

          The ratings are based on current information furnished to Stan-
          dard & Poor's by the issuer, and obtained by Standard & Poor's from
          other sources it considers reliable. The ratings may be changed, sus-
          pended, or withdrawn as a result of changes in, or unavailability of, such
          information.

          Standard & Poor's Corporation receives compensation for rating
          securities. Such compensation is based on the work done and is paid
          either by the issuers of such securities or by the underwriters partici-
          pating in the distribution thereof. The fees generally vary from $500 to
          $15,000 for corporate securities.

STANDARD & POOR: COMMON STOCK
RATING DEFINITIONS

The investment process involves assessment of various factors—such as
product and industry position, corporate resources and financial policy—with
results that make some common stocks more highly esteemed than others. In

this assessment, Standard & Poor's believes that earnings and dividend performance is the end result of the interplay of these factors and that, over the long
run, the record of this performance has a considerable bearing on relative quality. The rankings, however, do not pretend to reflect all of the factors, tangible
or intangible, that bear on stock quality.

Relative quality of bonds or other debt, that is, degrees of protection for
principal and interest, called creditworthiness, cannot be applied to common
stocks, and therefore rankings are not to be confused with bond quality ratings
which are arrived at by a necessarily different approach.

Growth and stability of earnings and dividends are deemed key elements in
establishing Standard & Poor's earnings and dividend rankings for common
stocks, which are designed to capsulize the nature of this record in a single symbol. It should be noted, however, that the process also takes into consideration
adjustments and modifications deemed desirable in establishing such rankings.

The point of departure in arriving at these rankings is a computerized
working system based on per-share earnings and dividend records of the most
recent ten years—a period deemed long enough to measure significant time
segments of secular growth, to capture indications of basic change in trend as
they develop, and to encompass the full peak-to-peak range of the business
cycle. Basic scores are computed for earnings and dividends, then adjusted as
indicated by a set of predetermined modifiers for growth, stability within long-
term trend, and cyclicality. Adjusted scores for earnings and dividends are then
combined to yield a final score.

Further, the ranking system makes allowance for the fact that, in general,
corporate size imparts certain recognized advantages from an investment standpoint. Conversely, minimum size limits (in terms of corporate sales volume) are
set for the various rankings, but the system provides for making exceptions
where the score reflects an outstanding earnings-dividend record.

The final score for each stock is measured against a scoring matrix determined by analysis of the scores of a large and representative sample of stocks.
The range of scores in the array of this sample has been aligned with the following ladder of rankings:

A+	Highest	B+	Average	C	Lowest
A	High	B	Below Average	D	In Reorganization
A−	Above Average	B−	Lower		

Standard & Poor's present policy is not to rank stocks of most finance-
oriented companies such as banks, insurance companies, etc., and stocks of
foreign companies; these carry the three-dot (...) designation. NR signifies no
ranking because of insufficient data or because the stock is not amenable to the
ranking process.

The positions as determined above may be modified in some instances
by special considerations, such as natural disasters, massive strikes, and non-

recurring accounting adjustments. And in the oil industry, for example, "cash flow" is taken into account to avoid distortions that might be caused by differences in accounting practices.

Because of the special impact of regulation on earnings and dividends of public utilities, special parameters have been devised for this group, and such factors as capital structure, operating rates, growth potential of service area, regulatory environment, and rate of return are considered.

A ranking is not a forecast of future market price performance, but is basically an appraisal of past performance of earnings and dividends, and relative current standing. These rankings must not be used as market recommendations; a high-score stock may at times be so overpriced as to justify its sale, while a low-score stock may be attractively priced for purchase. Rankings based upon earnings and dividend records are no substitute for complete analysis. They cannot take into account potential effects of management changes, internal company policies not yet fully reflected in the earnings and dividend record, public relations standing, recent competitive shifts, and a host of other factors that may be relevant to investment status and decision.

MOODY'S INVESTMENT SERVICE, INC.: CORPORATE BOND RATING DEFINITIONS

Aaa   Bonds which are rated **Aaa** are judged to be of the best quality. They carry the smallest degree of investment risk and are generally referred to as "gilt edge." Interest payments are protected by a large or by an exceptionally stable margin and principal is secure. While the various protective elements are likely to change, such changes as can be visualized are most unlikely to impair the fundamentally strong position of such issues.

Aa   Bonds which are rated **Aa** are judged to be of high quality by all standards. Together with the **Aaa** group they comprise what are generally known as high grade bonds. They are rated lower than the best bonds because margins of protection may not be as large as in **Aaa** securities or fluctuation of protective elements may be of greater amplitude or there may be other elements present which make the long-term risks appear somewhat larger than in **Aaa** securities.

A   Bonds which are rated **A** possess many favorable investment attributes and are to be considered as upper medium grade obligations. Factors giving security to principal and interest are considered adequate, but elements may be present which suggest a susceptibility to impairment sometime in the future.

Baa   Bonds which are rated **Baa** are considered as medium grade obligations, i.e., they are neither highly protected nor poorly secured. Interest payments and principal security appear adequate for the present but certain protective elements may be lacking or may be characteristically unreliable over any great length of time. Such bonds lack outstanding investment characteristics and in fact have speculative characteristics as well.

Ba   Bonds which are rated **Ba** are judged to have speculative elements; their future cannot be considered as well-assured. Often the protection of interest and principal payments may be very moderate, and thereby not well safeguarded during both good and bad times over the future. Uncertainty of position characterizes bonds in this class.

B   Bonds which are rated **B** generally lack characteristics of the desirable investment. Assurance of interest and principal payments or of maintenance of other terms of the contract over any long period of time may be small.

Caa   Bonds which are rated **Caa** are of poor standing. Such issues may be in default or there may be present elements of danger with respect to principal or interest.

Ca   Bonds which are rated **Ca** represent obligations which are speculative in a high degree. Such issues are often in default or have other marked shortcomings.

C   Bonds which are rated **C** are the lowest rated class of bonds, and issues so rated can be regarded as having extremely poor prospects of ever attaining any real investment standing.

CON. (...)   Bonds for which the security depends upon the completion of some act or the fulfillment of some condition are rated conditionally. These are bonds secured by (a) earnings of projects under construction, (b) earnings of projects unseasoned in operating experience, (c) rentals which begin when facilities are completed, or (d) payments to which some other limiting condition attaches. Parenthetical rating denotes probable credit stature upon completion of construction of elimination of basis of condition.

     Those bonds in the A and Baa groups which Moody's believes possess the strongest investment attributes are designated by the symbols **A1** and **Baa 1.**

21

OWNERSHIPS AND MANAGEMENTS

Corporations ● *Partnerships* ● *Sole Proprietorships* ● *Subchapter S Corporations*

Throughout this book I have stressed the importance of obtaining as much information as you can about any investment before risking your money. Before investing in any enterprise, therefore, it might be helpful to know how companies are organized and how they operate. What exactly are corporations, partnerships, and sole ownerships? What is a proxy and what happens in a proxy fight?

CORPORATIONS

A corporation is made up of a group of people who have legal powers to own, buy, sell, borrow, and be liable within the limits of the corporation. A board of directors establishes the corporation's policy and the corporation's officers manage its affairs. These officers may sit on the board, along with others who can contribute to the success of the corporation. The corporation may be privately owned, which means that all the stock issued is owned by a small group of people and is traded among them. This is in contrast to a publicly-held corporation in which all the stock that is issued is held by many people and is traded on the open market.

Privately owned corporations need not meet all the requirements of the Securities and Exchange Commission(s) since the stock
is not traded publicly, but if the corporation wishes to go "public,"
it must meet all the SEC requirements.

A stockholder of both a public and private corporation has the
right to vote for the corporation directors from a slate proposed by
directors or officers of the corporation. Those who own a large
enough number of shares may have sufficient votes to elect a director
of their own choosing and to gain control of the company. Voting
may be done in person at a meeting called for the purpose or may be
done by proxy. Proxy means that shareholders have given someone
else the right to vote for them. Proxy fights in which a particular
group tries to convince other shareholders to turn over their voting
rights to it are not uncommon. There may be more than one such
group who wage the fight. There may sometimes be only one person
who tries to gain control of as many proxy votes as possible in order
to put someone on the board who has not been recommended by
the existing board. To wage a proxy fight requires a good deal of
money and, to be successful, a controlling portion of shareholder
votes must be cornered.

The board of directors has the authority to declare a dividend
quarterly, semiannually, or annually if the corporation has earned
enough money to pay all its expenses and has accumulated a surplus. The shareholder, who owns a fractional interest in the corporation, is entitled to that fractional proportion of the profits. The
corporation is not obligated to pay out any part of its profits—it
may choose to set profits aside for expansion or for the purchase of
new equipment.

Shareholders are not personally liable for debts incurred by the
corporation. The most they can lose is their investment as represented by the shares they own. A company that has been incorporated will have the designation "Corp." or "Inc." in its company
name. Those with "Co." as part of the name may or may not be
incorporated. If you are thinking of investing and wish to know the
structure of the business you are interested in, you can find out by
contacting a broker, who may be able to supply you with a research
report or a Standard & Poor report. If the broker cannot provide
these materials, you can go to a public library or write to the head-
quarters of the corporation. All this applies, however, only if the
corporation is publicly held. If it is privately held, that information
does not have to be made available.

PARTNERSHIPS

A partnership is an association of two or more people who conduct a business jointly. Their share in the concern may be on an equal basis or may be in accord with a mutual agreement. Partners are entitled to any profits and are also personally liable for any losses. Their share of profits is taxable as personal income. The death of one partner automatically terminates the partnership. To continue the business, a new partnership or sole proprietorship must be formed.

The death or withdrawal of one partner may cause problems for the others. As each partner is usually a contributor to the success of the partnership, his or her death or withdrawal places additional responsibilities upon the remaining owner(s). If a new partnership or sole proprietorship cannot be quickly formed, the heirs of the deceased partner may press for payment of the value of their rightful partnership benefits, and the association may have to be liquidated.

Farsighted partners usually have a "criss-cross" or "buy-out" agreement funded by life insurance. Here's how it works: after establishing the value of each share of the partnership, the partnership itself or each of the partners buys a life insurance policy on each partner's life. The partnership, which is a legal entity, is the beneficiary. The proceeds of the policy will enable the surviving partner(s) to buy back the deceased's share in the business by paying off the heirs. In this way, the family of the dead partner receives cash and the other partner(s) can continue in business.

When the legal papers are drawn up, a partnership is identified as: "A Partnership, DBA (name of business)." (DBA means "doing business as.") For example: J. Jones and M. Smith, A Partnership, Doing Business As Jones, Smith, and Associates.

A partnership business may be run by the partners themselves or they may have employees. The employees, of course, are not part of the partnership, but merely work for it.

SOLE PROPRIETORSHIPS

This is a business owned and operated by one person. Although the owner may have employees, he or she is the sole proprietor. All profits belong to the owner alone, as do all debts and liabilities. Income from the business (after expenses) is ordinary income, and the owner is taxed correspondingly. The owner's legal description is: Milton Smith, DBA Milton Smith and Associates.

SUBCHAPTER S CORPORATIONS

United States laws governing businesses have evolved in many ways to meet the needs of its business people. Subchapter S allows for a corporation to have some of the benefits of partnerships. As a corporation under this regulation, it may not have more than fifteen shareholders. The profit distribution and/or losses are applied to the income the shareowners receive by virtue of their shareownership. No more than 20% of the business's income may come from investment, and the corporation's gross receipts from foreign sources may not exceed 80%. A Subchapter S corporation must pay income tax on its profits, and shareholders must pay income tax as ordinary income on any dividends.

If you want to start a Subchapter S Corporation or have the opportunity to be one of the fifteen shareholders of one, you may want to know more about how such a corporation is regulated. Publication #589, "Tax Information on Subchapter S Corporations," may be obtained from the IRS or the Treasury Department.

SOME ADDITIONAL FINANCIAL TERMS AND PROCEDURES

Joint Ownership • *How to Select a Real Estate Agent, Stockbroker, or Insurance Agent* • *Default and Bankruptcy* • *Verifying Your Signature* • *Tangibles*

In this chapter, I have put together some answers to questions that should be asked before you transact any business. There are terms you should understand before you sign a contract or make a purchase. I have tried to include here those things you need to know about money matters that I haven't dealt with in other chapters. If you don't find what you are looking for here, you should check the Glossary that follows.

JOINT OWNERSHIP

Generally speaking, the first experience two people have in owning something together is when they open a joint checking or savings account. If the account is owned jointly and if one of the parties should die, the other automatically owns all the money in the account. Either party usually has the right to make withdrawals from a joint checking account without the permission of the other. But transactions involving joint accounts at brokerage houses (withdrawals, sales, or purchases) certificates of ownership of real estate or securities, may require the signatures of all co-owners. Whether or not two signatures are required depends upon the stipulations of the joint account. Identification is usually made at the time the account is set up. Different states have different regulations governing joint accounts. You should remember that, on the death of one owner of a joint account, the surviving party may not withdraw the funds until they have been through probate, even though the survivor is a joint owner and has survivor rights.

If the legend reads: "Tenancy in common," it means that the property is owned jointly but that the death or withdrawal of one owner terminates the arrangement. The share of a deceased co-owner goes to his or her heirs or estate, and not to the surviving co-owner.

When you consider owning something with someone else, be sure you understand the full meaning of the exact form of joint ownership involved, and know what your rights and limitations are when it comes time to withdraw the assets. If you are uncertain about any aspect of joint ownership, ask that it be explained to you. The answers you get can save you some anxious moments should one of the parties to the joint ownership die or wish to terminate the arrangement.

As I said earlier, each state has its own variations on joint ownership, and you should check with your stockbroker, insurance agent, bank, or lawyer to find out what applies in your state.

HOW TO SELECT A REAL ESTATE
AGENT, STOCKBROKER, OR
INSURANCE AGENT

Real estate agents, stockbrokers, and insurance agents all have one thing in common—they are salespeople. They are in the business of selling something, and their livelihood depends upon how good they are in their job. Good salespeople are usually committed to their products—that is, they believe in it and know a lot about it. But there are talented individuals who can sell anything, whether they believe in it or not.

On the other side are the customers who must be convinced to buy. They may already be half interested—that is, interested enough to seek out a salesperson or, in a variety of ways, a salesperson may seek out the customer as a "good prospect." In any event, buyer and seller must be brought together to effect a sale, and the intermediary is the salesperson.

Good salespeople know their product, can answer all questions, and give good service. Bad salespeople are careless with details, are not interested enough in their product to be able to answer all questions, and fade out of the picture as soon as the deal is concluded. A good salesperson can mean the difference between a satisfied customer and a highly disgruntled one.

It behooves a business to hire the best possible salespeople, and to offer many incentives to encourage them to go out and do their utmost. The image of a company can be enhanced or degraded by the quality of its salespeople. Potential buyers should exercise choice. But what criteria should they use to select a company and a salesperson they will be happy with?

Real estate agents or brokers are licensed by the state in which they do business. Although requirements may vary from state to state, each sets certain standards which real estate brokers and salespeople are required to meet. They will be granted a license only after they pass certain tests and meet certain responsibilities. Real estate brokers can operate as brokers or as a company. Real estate agents are salespeople working for a broker/company. Agents are also licensed, but may only conduct business in the name of the broker/company. Brokers are responsible for sales practices, ethics, and proper conduct of their agents.

Brokers normally bear the expenses of running an office and advertising. They also have the responsibility for keeping their sales personnel informed about changes in real estate laws, financing, local ordinances, and so on. They will also enter into reciprocating arrangements with other brokers so that their sales staffs can sell real estate listed with other brokers. They may also join regional and/or national organizations so they can be of service to companies and individuals outside their local area. Their share of the real estate sales commission earned is about 50% although there is no fixed rule about this.

The salesperson will make every effort to find out what is for sale and to put the owner of the real property under exclusive contract to allow their broker to offer it for sale. For their efforts, the salesperson (or "lister") will get about 20% of the gross commission when a sale is successful.

Real estate salespeople will also try to find homes for potential buyers. They may show their own listings first, but as their primary objective is to sell, they may also show property listed by others with their knowledge and consent. In this case they are a "selling," salesperson, and will receive about 30% of the gross commission. If the listing and selling salespeople are from two different brokers, the total gross commission is split equitably between them. Only one commission, however, is charged to the seller of the property.

Brokers and salespeople may also make arrangements whereby they divide office and business expenses among themselves. Each one, in effect, works independently in the hopes that commission income will far exceed business expenses. Even if such arrangements are made, the broker is still legally responsible for the actions of the salespeople.

How do you pick the right real estate agent for you if you want to sell your house? Obviously, mutual trust and respect are essential, but these abstract terms are difficult to define and are not the same for everyone in every situation. You can begin by selecting a broker who specializes in the area you live in or want to move to. Visit the office and have a preliminary talk with the broker or a member of the staff. You can also study a broker's ads to determine the quality of the homes listed. Although it may not always be possible to do so, talking with someone who has actually used the services of the broker in question can give you a lot of information about the quality of service you can expect from the company.

The first thing your real estate agent may do is to make an on-site visit to determine what your property can bring on the market. If you ask five different agents you may get five different appraisal values of the market price. Should you list your home with the agent who gives you the highest appraisal? Not necessarily. An agent might give you a high appraisal to get the listing, knowing that you will ultimately have to reduce your expectations to sell your home. The agent will get a portion of the commission, even though he or she quotes you an unrealistic figure. There is no reason why you cannot ask more than one agency to look at your house. You can then sign with the one that, in your judgment, has estimated the fairest market price and that you think can do the most for you. Ask each one to explain to you why and how they arrive at the market price they recommend. Talk does no harm (and may do a lot of good) to make salespeople work for their money by asking all the questions you need answers to. A good salesperson will be glad to answer all of them.

Life Insurance Agents

Most insurance companies are large organizations that operate nationwide. Local branches are headed by "general agents" whose function it is to run the agency, supervise the agents, and hire and train new ones. Their compensation is based upon the commission income their agency generates and this, of course, depends upon the caliber of the agents. In these national organizations, the agents sell only policies of the parent company.

Independent agents are in business for themselves and may represent several companies at once. While independents do not have the backing of a giant corporation or the benefit of national advertising, many do well enough to hire agents to work for them. They have the advantage of being able to offer clients a choice of policies from various companies, and can help them select a policy that best suits their needs.

Both kinds of agents receive a commission that is included in the premiums paid by the policyowner.

Because there is a rapid turnover among agents, the choice of an agent is not as critical as the choice of policy, but there are some things a buyer should know when talking to an insurance agent. If agents seem too aggressive, make them prove their claims. When you buy insurance, buy out of need, not because you like the agent or because he or she is a relative or friend. If you have five policies bought from five different agents, ask yourself why you have so many. Do you really need all those policies, or did you buy them because you were pressured to do so? Start out with an insurance plan and review it periodically. Discuss your coverage with your agent. Ask questions and make your agent show you how good your plan is. You need different kinds of protection at different times for different reasons (see Chapters 7 and 16). If you need to make a change in your insurance program, do not hesitate to make an appointment with your agent to find out what is available that would meet your new needs. Like other kinds of investments, insurance is not immutable—it can be changed, and if it needs to be changed, change it.

Stockbrokers

Before talking about choosing your stockbroker, I should describe how brokerage houses work. National houses are usually based in New York, where the NY and American Stock Exchanges are located. Most of these have offices all over the U.S. and its territories. There are also regional brokerage houses.

All national houses have seats on the various exchanges. So do most regional offices, but some may have only trading arrangements with houses that have seats. Other houses belong *only* to the National Association of Securities Dealers (NASD). Many of these are insurance agencies which sell mainly mutual funds.

Stockbrokers may call themselves by various names, such as "Registered Representatives" or "Account Executives." They are paid a percentage of the commission charged for each trade done by the brokerage house which employs them. The broker's share is about 25 to 45% of the commission charged.

How do you choose a stockbroker? Make an appointment with one. State your current financial situation and your future goal. If you like to speculate, admit it, and if you want income at a low risk, say so. If the stockbroker's reasoning and logic complements your own thinking, all well and good, but if there is a difference of opinion, seek out another broker. Do not be afraid to ask questions and make sure you understand the answers. Request financial reports and ask the broker to do some research for you. Don't look for get-rich-quick schemes, because there aren't any. But there are good investments and your stockbroker can help you select them.

DEFAULT AND BANKRUPTCY

Default simply means failure to pay when payment is due. It means failure to pay on any bill, be it an individual's rent or mortgage payment, or a city's failure to pay interest on a municipal bond because it is short on tax revenue. Default means that the bill-holder can lay claim to the collateral that was put up to secure the loan. In the case of failure to pay rent, the landlord may evict the renter. In the case of default on a mortgage payment, the mortgagee may foreclose on the property. A finance company may repossess the car or stereo. Any creditors can take legal action to collect the amount due them.

Should the debtor be unable to make arrangements to pay that are satisfactory to the courts and the creditor, the next step is to declare bankruptcy. The United States government, in exercising its role as protector of all its citizens, has recognized the position of both debtor and creditor and has regularized the legal aspects of bankruptcy. According to Chapter Ten of the bankruptcy code, the creditors take possession of all assets of the debtor and divide the proceeds among themselves. They may have to settle for pennies on the dollar, but once they have done so, the creditors have no more claim against the debtor. Debtors—who may be individuals or partnerships—who have had a judgment of bankruptcy declared against them may not go through another bankruptcy for seven years. Otherwise, there are no restrictions on their ability to seek credit and start up again, except for the prudence of the creditor.

Chapter Eleven of the Bankruptcy Code applies to businesses that cannot meet current financial obligations, perhaps because of economic conditions. Chapter Eleven allows for continued operations if the company is still viable, though perhaps with some reorganization. The company may appeal to its creditors for redress, such as an extension on loans due. Through judicial action, the creditors may even extend the company additional credit and ask the courts to supervise the daily operation of the company. The creditors take the chance that the company may be able to turn itself around and be in a position to make full repayment of outstanding loans. If all goes well, the creditors may realize a profit on their investment and can expect total repayment. The employees retain their jobs and suppliers (who may also be creditors) can continue to do business with the company. There have been many such successful turn arounds under Chapter Eleven, and both companies and creditors have benefitted. This would not have been the case if the nation's bankruptcy laws had not foresightedly permitted such arrangements.

Investing in companies or municipalities that are on the verge of default, that have already defaulted, or are under threat of bankruptcy can sometimes prove to be very profitable, but such investments are only for the very sophisticated who can afford the possible loss.

VERIFYING YOUR SIGNATURE

Your signature is a very important part of your existence, yet affixing it to a document can be very confusing if the document does not exactly spell out what is required in the way of verification. Does your signature have to be guaranteed? Do you need witnesses? Must your signature be notarized?

A document as important as a will needs the signature of a witness or witnesses to verify that the person signing was personally known to them as the person he or she claims to be. The number of witnesses to a will depends upon the state in which the will is signed. The witness(es) must be able to state that the signer was "of sound mind" and not "under duress" at the time of signing. A witness to a will can be anybody who is not personally affected by the contents of it.

When a signature must be notarized, you must seek out the services of a notary public. A notary is appointed by the governor of a state for a fixed period of time, but in some states only after passing an oral and written examination. In other countries, a notary public is a person of some importance who has semi-legal powers, but in the U.S. a notary's function is limited to verifying signatures by the administration of an oath. Notaries were very necessary in the early days of the United States, when people could not easily travel great distances to appear in court or to conduct business in person. Notaries cannot draw up legal documents, nor are they responsible for the contents of a document they are asked to notarize. What they do is take information from those who swear they are who they are and who believe in the validity of the statement they are signing. Deeds must normally be notarized as must some insurance claims forms. All forms or documents that have to be entered in county records must be notarized.

Signature guarantees are required by brokerage houses. A signature may be guaranteed by someone associated with the brokerage firm who is authorized to do so by filing a resolution with a stock exchange or with the National Association of Securities Dealers. An officer of a bank which is a member of the Federal Reserve System can also guarantee a signature.

Your signature represents you, and when you sign something, you commit yourself to the terms of whatever it was you signed.

Make sure you understand all parts of a document. If you do not, do not sign until you have asked the questions you need answers to.

TANGIBLES

"Tangibles"—that is, things that have value in themselves, have been much in the news recently. As inflation continues, and as the value of the U.S. dollar is low compared to what it was in relation to the Japanese yen or the West German mark, some nervous persons are looking around for other things to invest their money in. Whether this is a wise investment choice or not depends upon one crucial factor: a tangible cannot be converted into cash or even bartered for something unless there is a "taker." Locating this taker and negotiating the deal can be a complicated matter, and liquidity of the item should be of concern to the investor who is thinking of buying something in the hopes that it will appreciate in value. On the other hand, if the purchase is only secondarily for investment and primarily for love, then it may prove to be a good choice. Oriental carpets, antiques, stamps, works of art, even old comic books can provide pleasure and may even become more valuable as time goes on. If the tangible does not appreciate in value, you will always have the "something" that you bought simply because you wanted to, and that is satisfaction enough.

Investing in tangibles should not be undertaken without the guidance of experts. Not all art is valuable, not all antiques are genuine. Only a reputable diamond appraiser should evaluate a stone.

The first tangible an investor thinks of is gold. Gold has played an important part in finance throughout history. Besides its intrinsic value—it does not tarnish, is easily workable, is a good conductor of electricity, is appealing to the eye—it is the one thing that everyone has placed a value on. The value of gold has increased over time, and will probably always be high, if for no other reason than its rarity.

Only about 88,000 tons of gold have been mined since the beginning of recorded history. Only a few areas of the world have any gold deposits, and the mining of it is strictly controlled. It is in demand for jewelry and art objects, for space-age technology, industry, medicine, and dentistry.

Gold can be bought and sold as gold itself or as futures. Bullion delivery can be taken in gold bars or ingots. (The world's gold production is figured not in kilograms, but in "ounces.") Gold must be stored, safeguarded, and insured by whoever is in possession of it, and annual charges can be as high as 10 to 15 percent of the value of the gold. When it is sold, the gold must be assayed and the assayer's fee must be paid. It costs money to own gold and, during the time of possession, it earns no interest. The only gain can come from a rise in gold prices and the subsequent sale of the gold. The same applies to other precious metals.

Very often, gold and silver are found together in the same deposit, but the ore will contain a much higher percentage of silver than of gold. Silver is more plentiful than gold, but platinum is very scarce. Copper and uranium are also in great demand. It has been estimated that the world has only about thirty years of copper production left. Uranium, of course, is the element upon which nuclear energy production, both peaceful and military, depends. The value of these and other precious metals is apparent because their amount is finite and we have, as yet, found no substitutes for them.

Some people have made a great deal of money buying and selling works of art. Some pension funds have gone into investing in art. The British Rail Superannuation Pension Fund, for example, sank $58 million into works of art. But buying paintings and sculptures and reselling them for a profit is not as simple as it seems. The works must be good and the chance of appreciation must be excellent. These are things very few people are qualified to judge. Old masterworks will surely increase in value because they are scarce, but not all old paintings are necessarily masterworks. Most of these are already in museums where they will remain—never appearing on the open market. The cost of any high quality masterpiece that did appear on the open market would be beyond almost anyone's private means.

There is a current rage for, of all things, old comic books and it is true that a first edition of Superman or a copy of the first Marvel comics can fetch a handsome price. But before you scurry to your attic, remember that only copies in mint condition can command high prices. If you do shell out a lot of money to buy one, ask yourself who, if the bottom drops out of the economy, will pay $15,000 for an old comic book?

Whether it is art, coins, stamps, or antiques, the cost of protecting such valuables is high. They will not earn interest. If you can live with it and enjoy it (works of art, antiques, oriental carpets), then your investment is worth it to you. If it must be kept in a vault (diamonds, gold, stamps, coins), then you may want to think twice. As investments, too much depends on who wants what and what price they are willing to pay.

Appendix A

U.S. GOVERNMENT PAMPHLETS

The United States government has compiled information on a variety of subjects that it feels would help its citizens. The following pamphlets are on subjects of interest to investors, retirees, and taxpayers in general. They are obtainable without charge from your district Internal Revenue Service Office.

For a list of other free and useful U.S. government publications, write Consumer Information Center, Dept. 23, Pueblo, CO 81009.

Appendix B

PENSION SERVICE: PS 58 TABLE

The rates below are used in computing the cost of pure life insurance that is taxable to the employed under qualified pension and profit-sharing plans.

Table B-1

One Year Term Premiums for $1,000 of
Life Insurance Protection

Age	Premium	Age	Premium	Age	Premium
15	$1.27	37	$ 3.63	59	$ 19.08
16	1.38	38	3.87	60	20.73
17	1.48	39	4.14	61	22.53
18	1.52	40	4.42	62	24.50
19	1.56	41	4.73	63	26.63
20	1.61	42	5.07	64	28.98
21	1.67	43	5.44	65	31.51
22	1.73	44	5.85	66	34.28
23	1.79	45	6.30	67	37.31
24	1.86	46	6.78	68	40.59
25	1.93	47	7.32	69	44.17
26	2.02	48	7.89	70	48.06
27	2.11	49	8.53	71	52.29
28	2.20	50	9.22	72	56.89
29	2.31	51	9.97	73	61.89
30	2.43	52	10.79	74	67.33

Table B-1—*Cont.*

One Year Term Premiums for $1,000 of Life Insurance Protection

Age	Premium	Age	Premium	Age	Premium
31	2.57	53	11.69	75	73.23
32	2.70	54	12.67	76	79.63
33	2.86	55	13.74	77	86.57
34	3.02	56	14.91	78	94.09
35	3.21	57	16.18	79	102.23
36	3.41	58	17.56	80	111.04
				81	120.57

Appendix C

COMPOUND INTEREST TABLES

Table C-1 shows how investing one dollar a year, every year, compounded annually will grow over a given number of years at specific interest rates. Thus, if each year one dollar is invested at 5½% interest, at the end of ten years the ten dollars will have grown to $13.58.

Table C-2 shows how much that same dollar, if not added to and left alone, can amount to at the end of a fixed period of time. At 5½%, that one dollar will increase to $1.708 at the end of ten years.

For figuring interest compounded daily, monthly, or quarterly see: *Thorndike Encyclopedia of Banking and Financial Tables,* compiled by David Thorndike (Boston: Warren, Gorham, and Lamont, 1973).

Table C-3 shows the amount needed today, if invested at a given annual compounded interest rate for a fixed number of years, to total one dollar. For example, if $1,000 is to be accumulated ten years from now, $585 must be invested today at 5½% interest compounded annually (.585 × 1,000). Or, $485 must be invested today at 7½% interest compounded annually (.485 × 1,000). Semiannual, quarterly, or daily compounding requires a correspondingly lower investment. Also, the higher the interest rate, the lower the investment needed.

Table C-4 shows the annual investment needed, if invested at a given annual compound interest rate for a fixed number of years, to withdraw one dollar each year. For instance, if $1,000 is to be

Table C-1

ONE DOLLAR PER ANNUM IN ADVANCE

The sum to which One Dollar per annum, paid in the beginning of each year, will increase at compound interest.

Years	2½%	3%	3½%	4%	4½%	5%	5½%	6%	6½%	7%	7½%	8%	8½%	9%	9½%	10%
1	1.025	1.030	1.035	1.040	1.045	1.050	1.055	1.060	1.065	1.070	1.075	1.080	1.085	1.090	1.095	1.100
2	2.076	2.091	2.106	2.122	2.137	2.153	2.168	2.184	2.199	2.215	2.231	2.246	2.262	2.278	2.294	2.310
3	3.153	3.184	3.215	3.246	3.278	3.310	3.342	3.375	3.407	3.440	3.473	3.506	3.540	3.573	3.607	3.641
4	4.256	4.309	4.362	4.416	4.471	4.526	4.581	4.637	4.694	4.751	4.808	4.867	4.925	4.985	5.045	5.105
5	5.388	5.468	5.550	5.633	5.717	5.802	5.888	5.975	6.064	6.153	6.244	6.336	6.429	6.523	6.619	6.716
6	6.547	6.662	6.779	6.898	7.019	7.142	7.267	7.394	7.523	7.654	7.787	7.923	8.060	8.200	8.343	8.487
7	7.736	7.892	8.052	8.214	8.380	8.549	8.722	8.897	9.077	9.260	9.446	9.637	9.831	10.028	10.230	10.436
8	8.955	9.159	9.368	9.583	9.802	10.027	10.256	10.491	10.732	10.978	11.230	11.488	11.751	12.021	12.297	12.579
9	10.203	10.464	10.731	11.006	11.288	11.578	11.875	12.181	12.494	12.816	13.147	13.487	13.835	14.193	14.560	14.937
10	11.483	11.808	12.142	12.486	12.841	13.207	13.583	13.972	14.372	14.784	15.208	15.645	16.096	16.560	17.039	17.531
11	12.796	13.192	13.602	14.026	14.464	14.917	15.386	15.870	16.371	16.888	17.424	17.977	18.549	19.141	19.752	20.384
12	14.140	14.618	15.113	15.627	16.160	16.713	17.287	17.882	18.500	19.141	19.806	20.495	21.211	21.953	22.724	23.523
13	15.519	16.086	16.677	17.292	17.932	18.599	19.293	20.015	20.767	21.550	22.366	23.215	24.099	25.019	25.977	26.975
14	16.932	17.599	18.296	19.024	19.784	20.579	21.409	22.276	23.182	24.129	25.118	26.152	27.232	28.361	29.540	30.772
15	18.380	19.157	19.971	20.825	21.719	22.657	23.641	24.673	25.754	26.888	28.077	29.324	30.632	32.003	33.442	34.950
16	19.865	20.762	21.705	22.698	23.742	24.840	25.996	27.213	28.493	29.840	31.258	32.750	34.321	35.974	37.714	39.545
17	21.386	22.414	23.500	24.645	25.855	27.132	28.481	29.906	31.410	32.999	34.677	36.450	38.323	40.301	42.391	44.599
18	22.946	24.117	25.357	26.671	28.064	29.539	31.103	32.760	34.517	36.379	38.353	40.446	42.665	45.018	47.513	50.159
19	24.545	25.870	27.280	28.778	30.371	32.066	33.868	35.786	37.825	39.995	42.305	44.762	47.377	50.160	53.122	56.275
20	26.183	27.676	29.269	30.969	32.783	34.719	36.786	38.993	41.349	43.865	46.553	49.423	52.489	55.765	59.264	63.002
21	27.863	29.537	31.329	33.249	35.303	37.505	39.864	42.392	45.102	48.006	51.119	54.457	58.036	61.873	65.989	70.403
22	29.584	31.453	33.460	35.618	37.937	40.430	43.112	45.996	49.098	52.436	56.028	59.893	64.054	68.532	73.353	78.543
23	31.349	33.426	35.667	38.083	40.689	43.502	46.538	49.816	53.355	57.177	61.305	65.765	70.583	75.790	81.416	87.497
24	33.158	35.459	37.950	40.646	43.565	46.727	50.153	53.865	57.888	62.249	66.978	72.106	77.668	83.701	90.246	97.347
25	35.012	37.553	40.313	43.312	46.571	50.113	53.966	58.156	62.715	67.676	73.076	78.954	85.355	92.324	99.914	108.182
26	36.912	39.710	42.759	46.084	49.711	53.669	57.989	62.706	67.857	73.484	79.632	86.351	93.695	101.723	110.501	120.100
27	38.860	41.931	45.291	48.968	52.993	57.403	62.234	67.528	73.333	79.698	86.679	94.339	102.744	111.968	122.094	133.210
28	40.856	44.219	47.911	51.966	56.423	61.323	66.711	72.640	79.164	86.347	94.255	102.966	112.562	123.135	134.788	147.631
29	42.903	46.575	50.623	55.085	60.007	65.439	71.435	78.058	85.375	93.461	102.399	112.283	123.215	135.308	148.688	163.494
30	45.000	49.003	53.429	58.328	63.752	69.761	76.419	83.802	91.989	101.073	111.154	122.346	134.773	148.575	163.908	180.943
31	47.150	51.503	56.335	61.701	67.666	74.299	81.677	89.890	99.034	109.218	120.566	133.214	147.314	163.037	180.574	200.138
32	49.354	54.078	59.341	65.210	71.756	79.064	87.225	96.343	106.536	117.933	130.683	144.951	160.920	178.800	198.824	221.252
33	51.613	56.730	62.453	68.858	76.030	84.067	93.077	103.184	114.526	127.259	141.560	157.627	175.684	195.982	218.807	244.477
34	53.928	59.462	65.674	72.652	80.497	89.320	99.251	110.435	123.035	137.237	153.252	171.317	191.702	214.711	240.688	270.024
35	56.301	62.276	69.008	76.598	85.164	94.836	105.765	118.121	132.097	147.913	165.820	186.102	209.081	235.125	264.649	298.127
36	58.734	65.174	72.458	80.702	90.041	100.628	112.637	126.268	141.748	159.337	179.332	202.070	227.938	257.376	290.886	329.039
37	61.227	68.159	76.029	84.970	95.138	106.710	119.887	134.904	152.627	171.561	193.857	219.316	248.398	281.630	319.615	363.043
38	63.783	71.234	79.725	89.409	100.484	113.095	127.536	144.058	162.974	184.640	209.471	237.941	270.597	308.066	351.073	400.448
39	66.403	74.401	83.550	94.026	106.030	119.800	135.606	153.762	174.632	198.635	226.257	258.057	294.683	336.882	385.520	441.593
40	69.088	77.663	87.510	98.827	111.847	126.840	144.119	164.048	187.048	213.610	244.301	279.781	320.816	368.292	423.239	486.852
41	71.840	81.023	91.607	103.820	117.925	134.232	153.100	174.951	200.271	229.632	263.698	303.244	349.170	402.528	464.542	536.637
42	74.661	84.484	95.849	109.012	124.276	141.993	162.576	186.508	214.354	246.776	284.551	328.583	379.934	439.846	509.769	591.401
43	77.552	88.048	100.238	114.413	130.914	150.143	172.573	198.758	229.352	265.121	306.967	355.950	413.314	480.522	559.292	651.641
44	80.516	91.720	104.782	120.029	137.850	158.700	183.119	211.744	245.325	284.749	331.065	385.506	449.530	524.859	613.519	717.905
45	83.554	95.501	109.484	125.871	145.098	167.685	194.246	225.508	262.336	305.752	356.969	417.426	488.825	573.186	672.899	790.795

Table C-2

ONE DOLLAR PRINCIPAL

The sum to which One Dollar Principal will increase at compound interest.

Years	2½%	3%	3½%	4%	4½%	5%	5½%	6%	6½%	7%	7½%	8%	8½%	9%	9½%	10%
1	1.025	1.030	1.035	1.040	1.045	1.050	1.055	1.060	1.065	1.070	1.075	1.080	1.085	1.090	1.095	1.100
2	1.051	1.061	1.071	1.082	1.092	1.103	1.113	1.124	1.134	1.145	1.156	1.166	1.177	1.188	1.199	1.210
3	1.077	1.093	1.109	1.125	1.141	1.158	1.174	1.191	1.208	1.225	1.242	1.260	1.277	1.295	1.313	1.331
4	1.104	1.126	1.148	1.170	1.193	1.216	1.239	1.262	1.286	1.311	1.335	1.360	1.386	1.412	1.438	1.464
5	1.131	1.159	1.188	1.217	1.246	1.276	1.307	1.338	1.370	1.403	1.436	1.469	1.504	1.539	1.574	1.611
6	1.160	1.194	1.229	1.265	1.302	1.340	1.379	1.419	1.459	1.501	1.543	1.587	1.631	1.677	1.724	1.772
7	1.189	1.230	1.272	1.316	1.361	1.407	1.455	1.504	1.554	1.606	1.659	1.714	1.770	1.828	1.888	1.949
8	1.218	1.267	1.317	1.369	1.422	1.477	1.535	1.594	1.655	1.718	1.783	1.851	1.921	1.993	2.067	2.144
9	1.249	1.305	1.363	1.423	1.486	1.551	1.619	1.689	1.763	1.838	1.917	1.999	2.084	2.172	2.263	2.358
10	1.280	1.344	1.411	1.480	1.553	1.629	1.708	1.791	1.877	1.967	2.061	2.159	2.261	2.367	2.478	2.594
11	1.312	1.384	1.460	1.539	1.623	1.710	1.802	1.898	1.999	2.105	2.216	2.332	2.453	2.580	2.714	2.853
12	1.345	1.426	1.511	1.601	1.696	1.796	1.901	2.012	2.129	2.252	2.382	2.518	2.662	2.813	2.971	3.138
13	1.379	1.469	1.564	1.665	1.772	1.886	2.006	2.133	2.267	2.410	2.560	2.720	2.888	3.066	3.254	3.452
14	1.413	1.513	1.619	1.732	1.852	1.980	2.116	2.261	2.415	2.579	2.752	2.937	3.133	3.342	3.563	3.797
15	1.448	1.558	1.675	1.801	1.935	2.079	2.232	2.397	2.572	2.759	2.959	3.172	3.400	3.642	3.901	4.177
16	1.485	1.605	1.734	1.873	2.022	2.183	2.355	2.540	2.739	2.952	3.181	3.426	3.689	3.970	4.272	4.595
17	1.522	1.653	1.795	1.948	2.113	2.292	2.485	2.693	2.917	3.159	3.419	3.700	4.002	4.328	4.678	5.054
18	1.560	1.702	1.857	2.026	2.208	2.407	2.621	2.854	3.107	3.380	3.676	3.996	4.342	4.717	5.122	5.560
19	1.599	1.754	1.923	2.107	2.308	2.527	2.766	3.026	3.309	3.617	3.951	4.316	4.712	5.142	5.609	6.116
20	1.639	1.806	1.990	2.191	2.412	2.653	2.918	3.207	3.524	3.870	4.248	4.661	5.112	5.604	6.142	6.727
21	1.680	1.860	2.059	2.279	2.520	2.786	3.078	3.400	3.753	4.141	4.566	5.034	5.547	6.109	6.725	7.400
22	1.722	1.916	2.132	2.370	2.634	2.925	3.248	3.604	3.997	4.430	4.909	5.437	6.018	6.659	7.364	8.140
23	1.765	1.974	2.206	2.465	2.752	3.072	3.426	3.820	4.256	4.741	5.277	5.871	6.530	7.258	8.064	8.954
24	1.809	2.033	2.283	2.563	2.876	3.225	3.615	4.049	4.533	5.072	5.673	6.341	7.085	7.911	8.830	9.850
25	1.854	2.094	2.363	2.666	3.005	3.386	3.813	4.292	4.828	5.427	6.098	6.848	7.687	8.623	9.668	10.835
26	1.900	2.157	2.446	2.772	3.141	3.556	4.023	4.549	5.141	5.807	6.556	7.396	8.340	9.399	10.587	11.918
27	1.948	2.221	2.532	2.883	3.282	3.733	4.244	4.822	5.476	6.214	7.047	7.988	9.049	10.245	11.593	13.110
28	1.996	2.288	2.620	2.999	3.430	3.920	4.478	5.112	5.832	6.649	7.576	8.627	9.818	11.167	12.694	14.421
29	2.046	2.357	2.712	3.119	3.584	4.116	4.724	5.418	6.211	7.114	8.144	9.317	10.653	12.172	13.900	15.863
30	2.098	2.427	2.807	3.243	3.745	4.322	4.984	5.743	6.614	7.612	8.755	10.063	11.558	13.268	15.220	17.449
31	2.160	2.500	2.905	3.373	3.914	4.538	5.258	6.088	7.044	8.145	9.412	10.868	12.541	14.462	16.666	19.194
32	2.204	2.575	3.007	3.508	4.090	4.765	5.547	6.453	7.502	8.715	10.117	11.737	13.607	15.763	18.250	21.114
33	2.259	2.652	3.112	3.648	4.274	5.003	5.852	6.841	7.990	9.325	10.876	12.676	14.763	17.182	19.983	23.225
34	2.315	2.732	3.221	3.794	4.466	5.253	6.174	7.251	8.509	9.978	11.692	13.690	16.018	18.728	21.882	25.548
35	2.373	2.814	3.334	3.946	4.667	5.516	6.514	7.686	9.062	10.677	12.569	14.785	17.380	20.414	23.960	28.102
36	2.433	2.898	3.450	4.104	4.877	5.792	6.872	8.147	9.651	11.424	13.512	15.968	18.857	22.251	26.237	30.913
37	2.493	2.985	3.571	4.268	5.097	6.081	7.250	8.636	10.279	12.224	14.425	17.246	20.460	24.254	28.729	34.004
38	2.556	3.075	3.696	4.439	5.326	6.385	7.649	9.154	10.947	13.079	15.614	18.625	22.199	26.437	31.458	37.404
39	2.620	3.167	3.825	4.616	5.566	6.705	8.069	9.704	11.658	13.995	16.785	20.115	24.086	28.816	34.447	41.145
40	2.685	3.262	3.959	4.801	5.816	7.040	8.513	10.286	12.416	14.974	18.044	21.725	26.133	31.409	37.719	45.259
41	2.752	3.360	4.098	4.993	6.078	7.392	8.982	10.903	13.223	16.023	19.398	23.462	28.354	34.236	41.303	49.785
42	2.821	3.461	4.241	5.193	6.352	7.762	9.476	11.557	14.083	17.144	20.852	25.339	30.764	37.318	45.227	54.764
43	2.892	3.565	4.390	5.400	6.637	8.150	9.997	12.250	14.998	18.344	22.416	27.367	33.379	40.676	49.523	60.240
44	2.964	3.671	4.543	5.617	6.936	8.557	10.546	12.985	15.973	19.628	24.098	29.556	36.217	44.337	54.228	66.264
45	3.038	3.782	4.702	5.841	7.248	8.985	11.127	13.765	17.011	21.002	25.905	31.920	39.295	48.327	59.379	72.890

Table C-3

ONE DOLLAR PER ANNUM

The present value of an annuity of One Dollar (Annuity payable at the end of each year).

Years	2½%	2¾%	3%	3½%	4%	4½%	5%	5½%	6%	6½%	7%	7½%	8%	8½%	9%	9½%	10%
1	.976	.973	.971	.966	.962	.957	.952	.948	.943	.939	.935	.930	.926	.922	.917	.913	.909
2	1.927	1.920	1.913	1.900	1.886	1.873	1.859	1.846	1.833	1.821	1.808	1.796	1.783	1.771	1.759	1.747	1.736
3	2.856	2.842	2.829	2.802	2.775	2.749	2.723	2.698	2.673	2.648	2.624	2.601	2.577	2.554	2.531	2.509	2.487
4	3.762	3.739	3.717	3.673	3.630	3.588	3.546	3.505	3.465	3.426	3.387	3.349	3.312	3.276	3.240	3.204	3.170
5	4.646	4.613	4.580	4.515	4.452	4.390	4.329	4.270	4.212	4.156	4.100	4.046	3.993	3.941	3.890	3.840	3.791
6	5.508	5.462	5.417	5.329	5.242	5.158	5.076	4.996	4.917	4.841	4.767	4.694	4.623	4.554	4.486	4.420	4.355
7	6.349	6.289	6.230	6.115	6.002	5.893	5.786	5.683	5.582	5.485	5.389	5.297	5.206	5.119	5.033	4.950	4.868
8	7.170	7.094	7.020	6.874	6.733	6.596	6.463	6.335	6.210	6.089	5.971	5.857	5.747	5.639	5.535	5.433	5.335
9	7.971	7.878	7.786	7.608	7.435	7.269	7.108	6.952	6.802	6.656	6.515	6.379	6.247	6.119	5.995	5.875	5.759
10	8.752	8.640	8.530	8.317	8.111	7.913	7.722	7.538	7.360	7.189	7.024	6.864	6.710	6.561	6.418	6.279	6.145
11	9.514	9.382	9.253	9.002	8.760	8.529	8.306	8.093	7.887	7.689	7.499	7.315	7.139	6.969	6.805	6.647	6.495
12	10.258	10.104	9.954	9.663	9.385	9.119	8.863	8.619	8.384	8.159	7.943	7.735	7.536	7.345	7.161	6.984	6.814
13	10.983	10.807	10.635	10.303	9.986	9.683	9.394	9.117	8.853	8.600	8.358	8.126	7.904	7.691	7.487	7.291	7.103
14	11.691	11.491	11.296	10.921	10.563	10.223	9.899	9.590	9.295	9.014	8.745	8.489	8.244	8.010	7.786	7.572	7.367
15	12.381	12.157	11.938	11.517	11.118	10.740	10.380	10.038	9.712	9.403	9.108	8.827	8.559	8.304	8.061	7.828	7.606
16	13.055	12.805	12.561	12.094	11.652	11.234	10.838	10.462	10.106	9.768	9.447	9.142	8.851	8.575	8.313	8.062	7.824
17	13.712	13.435	13.166	12.651	12.166	11.707	11.274	10.865	10.477	10.111	9.763	9.434	9.122	8.825	8.544	8.276	8.022
18	14.353	14.049	13.754	13.190	12.659	12.160	11.690	11.246	10.828	10.432	10.059	9.706	9.372	9.055	8.756	8.471	8.201
19	14.979	14.646	14.324	13.710	13.134	12.593	12.085	11.608	11.158	10.735	10.336	9.959	9.604	9.268	8.950	8.650	8.365
20	15.589	15.227	14.877	14.212	13.590	13.008	12.462	11.950	11.470	11.019	10.594	10.194	9.818	9.463	9.129	8.812	8.514
21	16.185	15.793	15.415	14.698	14.029	13.405	12.821	12.275	11.764	11.285	10.836	10.413	10.017	9.644	9.292	8.961	8.649
22	16.765	16.343	15.937	15.167	14.451	13.784	13.163	12.583	12.042	11.535	11.061	10.617	10.201	9.810	9.442	9.097	8.772
23	17.332	16.879	16.444	15.620	14.857	14.148	13.489	12.875	12.303	11.770	11.272	10.807	10.371	9.963	9.580	9.221	8.883
24	17.885	17.401	16.936	16.058	15.247	14.495	13.799	13.152	12.550	11.991	11.469	10.983	10.529	10.104	9.707	9.334	8.985
25	18.424	17.908	17.413	16.482	15.622	14.828	14.094	13.414	12.783	12.198	11.654	11.147	10.675	10.234	9.823	9.438	9.077
26	18.951	18.402	17.877	16.890	15.983	15.147	14.375	13.662	13.003	12.392	11.826	11.299	10.810	10.354	9.929	9.532	9.161
27	19.464	18.883	18.327	17.285	16.330	15.451	14.643	13.898	13.211	12.575	11.987	11.441	10.935	10.465	10.027	9.618	9.237
28	19.965	19.351	18.764	17.667	16.663	15.743	14.898	14.121	13.406	12.746	12.137	11.573	11.051	10.566	10.116	9.697	9.307
29	20.454	19.806	19.188	18.036	16.984	16.022	15.141	14.333	13.591	12.907	12.278	11.696	11.158	10.660	10.198	9.769	9.370
30	20.930	20.249	19.600	18.392	17.292	16.289	15.372	14.534	13.765	13.059	12.409	11.810	11.258	10.747	10.274	9.835	9.427
31	21.395	20.681	20.000	18.736	17.588	16.544	15.593	14.724	13.929	13.201	12.532	11.917	11.350	10.827	10.343	9.895	9.479
32	21.849	21.100	20.389	19.069	17.874	16.789	15.803	14.904	14.084	13.334	12.647	12.015	11.435	10.900	10.406	9.950	9.526
33	22.292	21.509	20.766	19.390	18.148	17.023	16.003	15.075	14.230	13.459	12.754	12.107	11.514	10.968	10.464	10.000	9.569
34	22.724	21.906	21.132	19.701	18.411	17.247	16.193	15.237	14.368	13.577	12.854	12.193	11.587	11.030	10.518	10.045	9.609
35	23.145	22.293	21.487	20.001	18.665	17.461	16.374	15.391	14.498	13.687	12.948	12.273	11.655	11.088	10.567	10.087	9.644
36	23.556	22.670	21.832	20.290	18.908	17.666	16.547	15.536	14.621	13.791	13.035	12.347	11.717	11.141	10.612	10.125	9.677
37	23.957	23.036	22.167	20.571	19.143	17.862	16.711	15.674	14.737	13.888	13.117	12.415	11.775	11.190	10.653	10.160	9.706
38	24.349	23.393	22.492	20.841	19.368	18.050	16.868	15.805	14.846	13.979	13.193	12.479	11.829	11.235	10.691	10.192	9.733
39	24.730	23.740	22.808	21.103	19.584	18.230	17.017	15.929	14.949	14.065	13.265	12.539	11.879	11.276	10.726	10.221	9.757
40	25.103	24.078	23.115	21.355	19.793	18.402	17.159	16.046	15.046	14.146	13.332	12.594	11.925	11.315	10.757	10.247	9.779
41	25.466	24.407	23.412	21.599	19.993	18.566	17.294	16.157	15.138	14.221	13.394	12.646	11.967	11.350	10.787	10.271	9.799
42	25.821	24.727	23.701	21.835	20.186	18.724	17.423	16.263	15.225	14.292	13.452	12.694	12.007	11.382	10.813	10.294	9.817
43	26.166	25.038	23.982	22.063	20.371	18.874	17.546	16.363	15.306	14.359	13.507	12.739	12.043	11.412	10.838	10.314	9.834
44	26.504	25.341	24.254	22.283	20.549	19.018	17.663	16.458	15.383	14.421	13.558	12.780	12.077	11.440	10.861	10.332	9.849
45	26.833	25.636	24.519	22.495	20.720	19.156	17.774	16.548	15.456	14.480	13.606	12.819	12.108	11.465	10.881	10.349	9.863

Table C-4

ONE DOLLAR PRINCIPAL

The present value of One Dollar to be received at the end of a specified number of years.

Years	2½%	3%	3½%	4%	4½%	5%	5½%	6%	6½%	7%	7½%	8%	8½%	9%	9½%	10%
1	.976	.971	.966	.962	.957	.952	.948	.943	.939	.935	.930	.926	.922	.917	.913	.909
2	.952	.943	.934	.925	.916	.907	.898	.890	.882	.873	.865	.857	.849	.842	.834	.826
3	.929	.915	.902	.889	.876	.864	.852	.840	.828	.816	.805	.794	.783	.772	.762	.751
4	.906	.888	.871	.855	.839	.823	.807	.792	.777	.763	.749	.735	.722	.708	.696	.683
5	.884	.863	.842	.822	.802	.784	.765	.747	.730	.713	.697	.681	.665	.650	.635	.621
6	.862	.837	.814	.790	.768	.746	.725	.705	.685	.666	.648	.630	.613	.596	.580	.564
7	.841	.813	.786	.760	.735	.711	.687	.665	.644	.623	.603	.583	.565	.547	.530	.513
8	.821	.789	.759	.731	.703	.677	.652	.627	.604	.582	.561	.540	.521	.502	.484	.467
9	.801	.766	.734	.703	.673	.645	.618	.592	.567	.544	.522	.500	.480	.460	.442	.424
10	.781	.744	.709	.676	.644	.614	.585	.558	.533	.508	.485	.463	.442	.422	.404	.386
11	.762	.722	.685	.650	.616	.585	.555	.527	.500	.475	.451	.429	.408	.388	.369	.350
12	.744	.701	.662	.625	.590	.557	.526	.497	.470	.444	.420	.397	.376	.356	.337	.319
13	.725	.681	.639	.601	.564	.530	.499	.469	.441	.415	.391	.368	.346	.326	.307	.290
14	.708	.661	.618	.577	.540	.505	.473	.442	.414	.388	.363	.340	.319	.299	.281	.263
15	.690	.642	.597	.555	.517	.481	.448	.417	.389	.362	.338	.315	.294	.275	.256	.239
16	.674	.623	.577	.534	.494	.458	.425	.394	.365	.339	.314	.292	.271	.252	.234	.218
17	.657	.605	.557	.513	.473	.436	.402	.371	.343	.317	.292	.270	.250	.231	.214	.198
18	.641	.587	.538	.494	.453	.416	.381	.350	.322	.296	.272	.250	.230	.212	.195	.180
19	.626	.570	.520	.475	.433	.396	.362	.331	.302	.277	.253	.232	.212	.194	.178	.164
20	.610	.554	.503	.456	.415	.377	.343	.312	.284	.258	.235	.215	.196	.178	.163	.149
21	.595	.538	.486	.439	.397	.359	.325	.294	.266	.242	.219	.199	.180	.164	.149	.135
22	.581	.522	.469	.422	.380	.342	.308	.278	.250	.226	.204	.184	.166	.150	.136	.123
23	.567	.507	.453	.406	.363	.326	.292	.262	.235	.211	.189	.170	.153	.138	.124	.112
24	.553	.492	.438	.390	.348	.310	.277	.247	.221	.197	.176	.158	.141	.126	.113	.102
25	.539	.478	.423	.375	.333	.295	.263	.233	.207	.184	.164	.146	.130	.116	.103	.092
26	.526	.464	.409	.361	.318	.281	.249	.220	.194	.172	.153	.135	.120	.106	.094	.084
27	.513	.450	.395	.347	.305	.268	.236	.207	.183	.161	.142	.125	.111	.098	.086	.076
28	.501	.437	.382	.333	.292	.255	.223	.196	.171	.150	.132	.116	.102	.090	.079	.069
29	.489	.424	.369	.321	.279	.243	.212	.185	.161	.141	.123	.107	.094	.082	.072	.063
30	.477	.412	.356	.308	.267	.231	.201	.174	.151	.131	.114	.099	.087	.075	.066	.057
31	.465	.400	.345	.296	.256	.220	.190	.164	.142	.123	.106	.092	.080	.069	.060	.052
32	.454	.388	.333	.285	.244	.210	.180	.155	.133	.115	.099	.085	.073	.063	.055	.047
33	.443	.377	.321	.274	.234	.200	.171	.146	.125	.107	.092	.079	.068	.058	.050	.043
34	.432	.366	.310	.264	.224	.190	.162	.138	.118	.100	.086	.073	.062	.053	.046	.039
35	.421	.355	.300	.253	.214	.181	.154	.130	.110	.094	.080	.068	.058	.049	.042	.036
36	.411	.345	.290	.244	.205	.173	.146	.123	.104	.088	.074	.063	.053	.044	.038	.032
37	.401	.335	.280	.234	.196	.164	.138	.116	.097	.082	.069	.058	.049	.041	.035	.029
38	.391	.325	.271	.225	.188	.157	.131	.109	.091	.076	.064	.054	.045	.038	.032	.027
39	.382	.316	.261	.217	.180	.149	.124	.103	.086	.071	.060	.050	.041	.035	.029	.024
40	.372	.307	.253	.208	.172	.142	.117	.097	.081	.067	.055	.046	.038	.032	.027	.022
41	.363	.298	.244	.200	.165	.135	.111	.092	.076	.062	.052	.043	.035	.029	.024	.020
42	.354	.289	.236	.193	.157	.129	.106	.087	.071	.058	.048	.039	.033	.027	.022	.018
43	.346	.281	.228	.185	.151	.123	.100	.082	.067	.055	.045	.037	.030	.025	.020	.017
44	.337	.272	.220	.178	.144	.117	.095	.077	.063	.051	.041	.034	.028	.023	.018	.015
45	.329	.264	.213	.171	.138	.111	.090	.073	.059	.048	.039	.031	.025	.021	.017	.014

265

withdrawn at the end of each year for ten years, $7,538 must be invested today at 5½% interest compounded annually (7.538 X 1,000). Or, $6,864 must be invested today at 7½% interest compounded annually (6.864 X 1,000). Again, semiannual, quarterly, or daily compounding requires a correspondingly lower investment. The higher the interest rate, the lower the investment needed.

Appendix D

MORTALITY TABLE

Table D-1 shows the average number of years a person of a given age can expect to live. The average life expectancy for women is approximately three years more than for men. As a result, life insurance premiums for women of the same age are computed at three years less than the same age rate for men. Since the life expectancy of a woman is longer than that of a man, the annuity income rate is correspondingly lower, as more money is required to guarantee her the same lifetime income.

The table on page 268 is the Commissioners 1958 Standard Mortality Table, showing average "future lifetime" or "expectation of life" and death rates per 1000 persons. Most insurance companies have updated this table in accordance with their own more current actuarial experience by also adjusting premium rates. The premium rate of a female is the same as that of a male but three years younger. Since the life expectancy of a woman is longer than that of a man, the annuity income rate is correspondingly lower, as more money is required to guarantee her the same lifetime income.

Table D-1

Age Last Birthday	Number Living at Beginning of Year	Number Dying During the Year	Death Rate Per 1000	Average Expectation of Life in Years
0	9,964,600	44,138	4.43	68.04
1	9,920,462	16,270	1.64	67.34
2	9,904,192	14,758	1.49	66.45
3	9,889,434	14,142	1.43	65.55
4	9,875,292	13,578	1.37	64.64
5	9,861,714	13,067	1.33	63.73
6	9,848,647	12,607	1.28	62.81
7	9,836,040	12,246	1.25	61.89
8	9,823,794	11,984	1.22	60.97
9	9,811,810	11,872	1.21	60.04
10	9,799,938	11,956	1.22	59.12
11	9,787,982	12,186	1.24	58.19
12	9,775,796	12,611	1.29	57.26
13	9,763,185	13,229	1.35	56.33
14	9,749,956	13,894	1.43	55.41
15	9,736,062	14,604	1.50	54.49
16	9,721,458	15,360	1.58	53.57
17	9,706,098	16,063	1.65	52.65
18	9,690,035	16,618	1.71	51.74
19	9,673,417	17,073	1.76	50.83
20	9,656,344	17,478	1.81	49.92
21	9,638,866	17,783	1.84	49.00
22	9,621,083	18,039	1.87	48.09
23	9,603,044	18,246	1.90	47.18
24	9,584,798	18,402	1.92	46.27
25	9,566,396	18,607	1.95	45.36
26	9,547,789	18,857	1.98	44.45
27	9,528,932	19,152	2.01	43.54
28	9,509,780	19,542	2.05	42.62
29	9,490,238	19,976	2.10	41.71
30	9,470,262	20,456	2.16	40.80
31	9,449,806	20,978	2.22	39.88
32	9,428,828	21,545	2.29	38.97
33	9,407,283	22,201	2.36	38.06
34	9,385,082	23,039	2.45	37.15
35	9,362,043	24,107	2.57	36.24
36	9,337,936	25,398	2.72	35.33
37	9,312,538	27,052	2.90	34.42
38	9,285,486	29,061	3.13	33.52
39	9,256,425	31,377	3.39	32.63
40	9,225,048	33,992	3.68	31.74
41	9,191,056	36,808	4.00	30.85
42	9,154,248	39,817	4.35	29.97
43	9,114,431	43,061	4.72	29.10
44	9,071,370	46,577	5.13	28.24
45	9,024,793	50,443	5.59	27.38
46	8,974,350	54,691	6.09	26.53
47	8,919,659	59,352	6.65	25.69
48	8,860,307	64,449	7.27	24.86
49	8,795,858	70,003	7.96	24.04

Age Last Birthday	Number Living at Beginning of Year	Number Dying During the Year	Death Rate Per 1000	Average Expectation of Life in Years
50	8,725,855	76,031	8.71	23.23
51	8,649,824	82,459	9.53	22.43
52	8,567,365	89,295	10.42	21.64
53	8,478,070	96,584	11.39	20.86
54	8,381,486	104,322	12.45	20.10
55	8,277,164	112,578	13.60	19.34
56	8,164,586	121,410	14.87	18.60
57	8,043,176	130,816	16.26	17.88
58	7,912,360	140,747	17.79	17.16
59	7,771,613	151,211	19.46	16.47
60	7,620,402	162,164	21.28	15.78
61	7,458,238	173,504	23.26	15.12
62	7,284,734	185,222	25.43	14.46
63	7,099,512	197,284	27.79	13.83
64	6,902,228	209,656	30.38	13.21
65	6,692,572	222,332	33.22	12.61
66	6,470,240	235,264	36.36	12.02
67	6,234,976	248,306	39.82	11.46
68	5,986,670	261,038	43.60	10.91
69	5,725,632	272,833	47.65	10.39
70	5,452,799	283,079	51.91	9.88
71	5,169,720	291,248	56.34	9.39
72	4,878,472	297,028	60.89	8.93
73	4,581,444	300,591	65.61	8.47
74	4,280,853	302,453	70.65	8.03
75	3,978,400	303,012	76.16	7.60
76	3,675,388	302,506	82.31	7.19
77	3,372,882	300,912	89.22	6.79
78	3,071,970	297,756	96.93	6.41
79	2,774,214	292,266	105.35	6.04
80	2,481,948	283,916	114.39	5.69
81	2,198,032	277,442	123.95	5.36
82	1,925,590	257,880	133.92	5.05
83	1,667,710	240,646	144.30	4.76
84	1,427,064	221,372	155.12	4.47
85	1,205,692	200,709	166.47	4.20
86	1,004,983	179,281	178.39	3.94
87	825,702	157,726	191.02	3.69
88	667,976	136,650	204.57	3.44
89	531,326	116,556	219.37	3.20
90	414,770	97,812	235.82	2.96
91	316,958	80,646	254.44	2.72
92	236,312	65,180	275.82	2.47
93	171,132	51,454	300.67	2.22
94	119,678	39,577	330.70	1.96
95	80,101	29,689	370.64	1.69
96	50,412	21,853	433.49	1.39
97	28,559	15,686	549.25	1.06
98	12,873	9,665	750.80	.75
99	3,208	3,208	1000.00	.50

GLOSSARY

Account executive. Someone who has met the requirements of a securities exchange, and who has an unblemished personal background and has proved knowledge of the securities business. Also known as a "registered representative" or "customer's broker."

Accrued interest. Interest accumulated since the last interest payment.

Ad valorem tax. A tax based on added value of the assessed value of property.

Agency bonds. See authority bonds.

AMEX. The American Stock Exchange, the second largest exchange in the United States.

Amortization. Accounting for expenses or charges gradually, in advance of maturity of the obligation. Includes such practices as depreciation, depletion, write-off of intangibles, prepaid expenses, and deferred charges.

Annual report. The formal financial statement issued yearly by a corporation. The annual report shows assets, liabilities, earnings, and how the company stood at the close of the business year. It may also contain other information of interest to shareowners.

Annuity. A contract to pay (or receive) a sum of money at regular intervals.

Annuity mortgage. A periodic return (income) from mortgaging property as collateral as the payments are being made—which increases the mortgage debt.

Assets. Everything an individual or corporation owns that is not a liability.

Auction market. The system of trading securities through brokers or agents on an exchange. Buyers compete with other buyers and sellers compete with other sellers.

Authority and agency bonds. Authorities and agencies are created by states or their subdivisions to perform specific functions, such as the operation of waterways, sewage, or electric systems, bridges, tunnels, highways, etc. Called "authority" because the first words in the documents are "Authority is invested in...".

Averages. Various ways of measuring the trend of securities prices. One measure is the Dow Jones Industrial Averages.

Balance sheet. A condensed financial statement showing the nature and amount of a company's assets, liabilities, and capital on a given date.

Bankers acceptances. Negotiable bank-backed business credit instruments, typically financing an import order.

Basis book. A book of mathematical tables used to convert yield percentages to equivalent dollar prices.

Basis point. One one-hundredth (1/100) of one percent.

Basis price. Price expressed in yield or percentage of return on an investment.

Bearer bond. A bond which does not have the owner's name registered on the books of the issuer, and which is payable to whoever has physical possession of it.

Bear market. A declining market.

Beta coefficient. A term used by Value-Line Investment Survey for measuring a stock's sensitivity to the fluctuation of about 1700 selected stocks which make up their averages.

Bid and asked. The bid is the highest price anyone has declared that he or she is willing to pay for a security at a given time. The asked price is the lowest price anyone will take at the same time. (see Quotation).

Blanket mortgage. One mortgage which covers both the property to be sold and the property to be bought.

Block. A large holding or transaction of stock—usually 10,000 or more shares.

Blue chip. Describes a company or its stock that has demonstrated its past ability to make money and pay dividends.

Blue sky laws. A popular name for laws various states have enacted to protect the public against securities frauds. The term is believed to have originated when a judge ruled that a particular stock "had about the same value as a patch of blue sky."

Bond. A written promise by the issuer to repay on a specified date a fixed amount of borrowed money and to pay a set annual rate of interest during the life of the bond, generally at semiannual intervals.

Bond Anticipation Notes (BANs). May be backed by the issuer's full faith and credit, and are sold in anticipation of a bond sale. They thus provide the issuer with funds prior to a bond sale.

Bond funds. Registered investment companies whose assets are invested in diversified portfolios of bonds.

Bond swap. Exchanging a bond with a coupon yield lower than the current yield for a bond with a coupon yield equal to or higher than the current yield.

Book. A notebook in which stock specialists keep a record of the buy and sell orders at specified prices, in sequence of receipt, which are left with them by other brokers.

Book value. The book value of a stock is determined from a company's records by adding all assets and deducting all debts and other liabilities, including the liquidation price of any preferred issues. The sum is divided by the number of common shares outstanding, and the result is the book value per common share.

Bridge mortgage loan. See Blanket mortgage.

Broker. An agent who handles customers' orders to buy and sell.

Brokers' loans. Money borrowed by brokers from banks or other brokers. It may be used by specialists to help finance inventories of stock they deal in; by brokerage firms to finance the underwriting of new issues of corporate and municipal securities; to help finance a firm's own investments; and to help finance the purchase of securities for customers who prefer to use the broker's credit when they buy securities (see Margin).

Bull market. An advancing market.

Buy-out agreement. An agreement made by partnerships to enable one to buy another under specified circumstances.

Call. The right to buy a fixed number of shares of stock at a stated price within a specified period of time. Sometimes referred to as a call option.

Callable. Refers to a bond issue all or part of which may be redeemed by the issuing corporation under definite conditions be-before maturity. Also applies to preferred shares which may be redeemed by the issuing corporation.

Call date. The date or dates a security may be called for redemption by the issuer.

Called bonds. Bonds redeemed prior to maturity.

Call money. The charge on loans to brokers on stock exchange collateral.

Call option. The right to buy a fixed number of shares of stock at a stated price within a specified time. Sometimes referred to simply as "a call."

Call provision. The terms designated by the issuer for redeeming a security prior to its maturity.

Call spread. Buying and selling a call on the same security. The strike price and/or expiration date are different for each transaction.

Call writer. One who sells the right to call in a fixed number of securities at a specified price within a definite period of time.

Capital gain/loss. Profit or loss for the sale of a capital asset. Under current tax laws, a capital gain or loss may be either short-term (twelve months or less) or long-term (more than twelve months). A short-term capital gain is taxed at the reporting individual's full income tax rate. A long-term capital gain is subject to a lower tax. A loss is a deduction from gross income and, therefore, reduces the taxes to be paid.

Capitalization. Total amount of the various securities issued by a corporation. May include bonds, debentures, preferred and common stock, and surplus.

Capital stock. All shares representing ownership of a business, including preferred and common stocks.

Cash flow. Reported net income plus amounts charged off for depreciation, depletion, amortization, and extraordinary charges to reserves which are bookkeeping deductions not paid out in actual dollars and cents.

Cash sale. A transaction on the floor of the Stock Exchange which calls for delivery of the securities the next day. These are contrasted with "regular way" trades, in which the seller is to deliver on the fifth business day (except for bonds which have "next day" delivery).

Cash settlement. Same day settlement of accounts.

Certificate. The actual piece of paper which is evidence of ownership. Usually elaborately engraved on watermarked paper to discourage forgery.

Certificate of deposit. A certificate representing a deposit in a bank which shows amount, interest rate, and maturity date. The interest rate varies with the amount deposited and the length of maturity.

Chattel. Any property other than real estate.

Chattel mortgage. A document using any property except real estate as collateral for a loan.

Closed-end investment company/mutual funds. An investment company (mutual fund) whose capitalization remains constant because the initial capital is obtained by selling only a fixed number of shares.

Closed lien. A pledge made solely to one issue which prohibits further pledging of the resource.

Collateral. Whatever is pledged to secure repayment of a loan. Can be securities, real estate, bank account, automobile, etc.

Collateral trust bond. A bond secured by collateral deposited with a trustee.

Combination call and put. Buying a call and put on the same security, or selling a call and put at the same time on the same security with the same expiration date and the same strike price.

Commercial paper. Extremely short-term corporate IOUs due, generally, in less than a year.

Commission. An agent's basic fee for buying and selling a commodity or securities for a client.

Commission broker. An agent who executes the public's orders for the purchase or sale of securities or commodities.

Commodity. Anything that can be bought or sold for profit.

Common stock. Securities which represent an ownership interest in a corporation. Claims are junior to claims of preferred stockholders, bondholders, or other creditors of a company. Common stock represents the greater risk but generally exercises the greater control, and may gain the greater reward in the form of dividends and capital appreciation. The terms "common stock" and "capital stock" are often used interchangeably when a company issues no preferred stock.

Competitive traders. Members of an exchange who trade in stocks for accounts in which they have an interest. Also known as a "registered trader."

Compound interest. Interest paid on interest.

Condominium. An individually owned unit in a multi-unit structure or the structure itself.

Conglomerate. A corporation that has diversified its operations, usually by acquiring enterprises in widely varied industries.

Consolidated balance sheet. A balance sheet showing the financial condition of a corporation and all its subsidiaries.

Consolidated Tape. Under the Consolidated Tape Plan, the NYSE and AMEX ticker systems became a consolidated network (Network A and Network B, respectively). Network A reports transactions in NYSE-listed securities that place on the NYSE or any of the participating regional stock exchanges and other markets. Each transaction is identified according to its originating market. Similarly, transactions in AMEX-listed securities and certain other securities listed on regional stock exchanges, are reported and identified on Network B.

Convertible. A bond, debenture, or preferred share which may be exchanged by the owner for common stock or another security, usually from the same company, in accordance with the terms of issue.

Co-op. A multi-unit structure owned cooperatively. Ownership in a co-op means part ownership in a corporation set up to control the structure.

Co-ops. Banks of cooperatives providing service loans to eligible agricultural cooperative associations owned and controlled by individual farmers.

Corporate settlement. Five business day settlement, usually associated with corporate bonds.

Corporation. A legal entity unto itself formed for a specific purpose and registered in the state in which it is doing business.

Correspondent. A securities firm, bank, or other financial organization which regularly performs services for another in a place or market to which the other does not have direct access.

Coupon. The portion of a security certificate that shows the interest due on the payable date, and which is presented by the holder for payment. Also: the stated rate of periodic interest payments.

Coupon bond. Bond with interest coupons attached. The coupons are clipped as they become due, and are presented by the holder for payment of interest.

Courtesy rights. The rights, under common law, that a husband has to his wife's property (see Dower rights).

Coverage. A term usually connected with revenue bonds. It indicates the margin of safety for payment of debt service by reflecting the number of times or percentage by which earnings for a period of time exceed debt service payable in such period.

Covered option. An option for which the seller actually owns the underlying stock. See Naked option.

Covering. Buying a security previously sold short.

Crisscross agreement. Buy-out agreement in a partnership.

Cumulative preferred. A stock having a provision that if one or more dividends are omitted, the omitted dividends must be paid before dividends may be paid on the company's common stock.

Cumulative voting. A method of voting for corporate directors which enables shareholders to multiply the number of their shares by the number of directorships being voted on and cast the total for one director or a selected group of directors.

Curb Exchange. The former name of the American Stock Exchange.

Current assets. Assets of a company which can be reasonably expected to be realized in cash or sold or consumed during the normal operating cycle of the business. Includes cash, U.S. government bonds, inventories, receivables, and usually money due within one year.

Current liabilities. Debts owed and payable by a company, usually within one year.

Current return. See Current yield.

Current yield. The ratio of interest to the actual market price of a bond. It is obtained by dividing the current dollar income by the current market price for the security, expressed in %.

Customer's broker. See Account executive.

Customer's man. See Registered representative.

Day order. An order to buy or sell which, if not executed, expires at the end of the trading day on which it was entered.

Dealers. Individuals or firms acting as principals rather than as agents. Dealers may buy for their own account and sell to customers from their own inventory.

Debenture. A promissory note backed by the general credit of a company and usually not secured by a mortgage or lien on any specific property.

Debit balance. In a customer's margin account a debit balance is that portion of the purchase price of stock, bonds, or commodities covered by credit extended by the broker to the margin customer; or balance owed.

Debt limit. The statutory or constitutional maximum debt that a municipal bond issuer can legally incur.

Debt ratio. The ratio of the issuer's debt to a measure of value such as assessed valuation, real value, etc.

Debt service. Refers to the payments required for interest and retirement of the principal amount of a debt.

Deep discount bonds. Bonds with a lower than BB rating.

Default. Failure to pay principal or interest when due.

Denomination. The face amount or par value of a bond which the issuer promises to pay on the bond's maturity date.

Depletion. An accounting allowance for the reduction of natural resources such as oil and gas, metals, timber, etc., which can conceivably be reduced to zero over the years. It does not represent any cash outlay, nor are any funds earmarked for the purpose. It is simply a bookkeeping entry of charges against earnings based upon the amount of the asset taken out of the total reserves in the period for which the accounting was made.

Depository Trust Company (DTC). A central securities certificate depository through which members effect security deliveries among each other via computerized bookkeeping entries, thereby reducing the number of physical transfers of stock certificates.

Depreciation. Charges against earnings to write off the cost, less salvage value, of an asset over its estimated useful life. A bookkeeping entry which does not represent any cash outlay, nor are any funds earmarked for it.

Diagonal spread. Buying and selling the same security with a different strike price and a different expiration date for each.

Director. The person elected by shareholders to establish company policies. The directors appoint the president, vice-president, and all other operating officers. Among other matters, directors decide if and when dividends shall be paid.

Discount. The amount by which something sells below its listed value.

Discount rate. The interest rate the Federal Reserve charges its member banks for borrowing money from it.

Discretionary account. An account in which the customer gives the broker or someone else discretion, which may be complete or within specific limits, either for the purchase or sale of securities or commodities. The discretion provides for selection, timing, amount, and price to be paid or received.

Diversification. Spreading investments among different companies or municipalities in different fields or geographical locations.

Dividend. The payment designated by the board of directors of a company to be distributed among the shares outstanding. Also refers to excess premium return on an insurance policy.

Dollar bond. A bond that is quoted and traded in dollar prices rather than in terms of yield.

Dollar cost averaging. A system of buying securities with a fixed dollar amount at regular intervals. Under this system, the investor buys by the dollars' worth rather than by the number of shares.

Double-barrelled bond. A bond secured by the pledge of two or more sources of repayment—that is, it is secured by taxes and also revenues.

Double exemption. Securities that are exempt from state as well as federal income taxes are said to have double exemption.

Double taxation of dividends. The federal government taxes corporate profits once as corporate income. Any part of the profits distributed as dividends to stockholders may be taxed again as income to the recipient stockholder.

Dower rights. The rights, under common law, that a wife has on her husband's property (see Courtesy rights).

Dow theory. The theory of market analysis based upon the performance of the Dow Jones industrial and transportation stock price averages. The theory says that the market is in a basic upward trend if one of these averages advances above a previous important high, accompanied or followed by a similar advance in the other. When the averages both dip below previous important lows, this is regarded as confirmation of a basic downward trend. The theory does not attempt to predict how long either trend will continue, although it is widely misinterpreted as a method of forecasting future action.

Earnings report. A statement—also called an income statement—issued by a company showing its earnings or losses over a given period (see Balance sheet).

ERISA (Employee Retirement Income Securities Act).

Equity. Owner's portion. Also refers to excess of value of securities over the debit balance in a margin account.

Equipment trust certificate. A type of security, generally issued by a railroad, to pay for new equipment. Title to the equipment is held by a trustee until the notes are paid off.

Escrow. A situation where property is held or exchanged for the benefit of interested persons until certain conditions are met.

ESOT/ESOP (Employee Stock Ownership Trust or Plan). Also sometimes referred to as Employee Stock Option Trust or Plan.

Eurodollars. U.S. dollar deposits in foreign banks, usually in amounts of $100,000 or more.

Excess interest. Interest paid to an insurance policyholder in excess of the guaranteed interest.

Exchange acquisition. A method of filling an order to buy a large block of stock on the floor of the Exchange. Under certain circumstances, a member-broker can facilitate the purchase of a block by soliciting orders to sell. All orders to sell the security are lumped together and crossed with the buy order in the regular auction market.

Exchange distribution. A method of selling large blocks of stock on the floor of the Exchange. Under certain circumstances, a member-broker can facilitate the sale of a block of stock by soliciting and getting other member-brokers to solicit orders to buy. Individual buy orders are lumped together and crossed with the sell order in the regular auction market.

Ex-dividend. Without dividend. The buyer of a stock selling ex-dividend does not receive the recently declared dividend.

Extra. The short form of "extra dividend." A dividend in the form of stock or cash in addition to the regular or usual dividend a company has been paying.

Face amount. The principal or maturity value of a security appearing on the face of the instrument.

Fannie Mae (Federal National Mortgage Association, FNMA). A government-sponsored corporation owned entirely by private stockholders. The Association provides liquidity for mortgage investments by buying mortgages when normal sources of funds are in short supply and selling mortgages when funds are plentiful.

FDIC. (Federal Deposit Insurance Corporation). Created by Congress to insure bank deposits of a member of the Federal Reserve Bank System up to $100,000.

Federal Home Loan Banks. Credit reserve institutions for savings and loan banks which finance home ownership. Organized in 1932.

Federal funds. Reserves traded among commercial banks for overnight use in amounts of one million dollars or more.

Federal land banks. These banks make first mortgage loans to farmers for rural real estate for agriculture or credit needs. Organized in 1917.

FHA (Federal Housing Administration). An agency created by Congress to make it possible to purchase certain real estate with a minimum or no down payment.

FICBs (Federal Intermediate Credit Banks). Provide loans to institutions which, in turn, lend to farmers and ranchers. Organized in 1923.

Fiduciary. A person or an act of trust.

Firm. Another name for company or corporation but, in investment jargon, a commitment to buy or sell a security at a fixed price for a specified period of time.

Fiscal agents. Financial officers who represent specific governmental agencies and act on behalf of these agencies in financing and other fiscal matters.

Fiscal year. A company's accounting year. Usually July 1 to June 30, but may also follow the calendar year of January 1 to December 31. It can be any period of 365 days.

Fixed charges. A company's fixed expenses. These are deducted from income before earnings on equity capital can be computed.

Flat income bond. The price at which a bond is traded includes consideration for all unpaid accruals of interest. Bonds which are in default of interest or principal are traded "flat." Income bonds which pay interest only to the extent earned are usually traded flat. All other bonds are usually dealt in "and interest," which means that the buyer pays to the seller the market price plus interest accrued since the last payment date.

Floor broker. A member of the stock exchange who executes orders on the floor of the exchange to buy and sell listed securities.

Formula investing. An investment technique. One formula calls for the shifting of funds from common shares to preferred shares or bonds as the market, on average, rises above a certain predetermined point, and for the return of funds to common share investments as the market average declines.

Free and open market. A market in which supply and demand are freely expressed in terms of price. Contrasts with a controlled market, in which supply and price may be regulated.

Front-end load. A charge when a payment is made for a purchase, such as in an annuity, or some open-end mutual funds.

FOMC (Federal Open Market Committee). Responsible for determining what transactions the Federal Reserve bank will conduct in the open market by selling and buying government securities.

FSLIC (Federal Savings and Loan Insurance Corporation). Created by Congress to insure deposits up to $100,000 per account.

Fundamental analyst. Someone who examines the operations and management of various industries, the position of particular companies within their industry, and tries to make judgments about their possible future performance.

Fundamental research. Analysis of industries and companies based on such factors as sales, assets, earnings, products or services, markets, and management. As applied to the economy, fundamental research includes consideration of gross national produce, interest rates, unemployment, inventories, savings, etc.

Funded debt. Usually interest-bearing bonds or debentures of a company, but can include long-term bank loans. Does *not* include short-term loans or preferred or common stock.

Future. A contract to buy or sell a commodity that is to be delivered at some future time.

General mortgage bond. A bond which is secured by a blanket mortgage on the company's property, but which may be outranked by one or more other mortgages.

General obligation bond. A bond secured by the pledge of the issuer's full faith, credit, and taxing power. Such bonds are usually issued to finance public projects that do not produce revenues.

Gilt-edged bond. High-grade bond issued by a company which has demonstrated its ability to earn a comfortable profit over a period of years and pay its bondholders their interest without interruption. So-called because they are generally printed on high-quality paper and in the past had gilt decoration on the edges of the certificate.

Ginnie Maes (Government National Mortgage Association, GNMA). Was empowered to assume certain functions of the Federal National Mortgage Association (FNMA). Its main purpose is to help finance more housing by making real estate mortgage investments more attractive to all types of investors. In substance, Ginnie Mae investors own a government security collateralized by government-backed mortgages of thirty-year stated life and approximately twelve-year average life. An issuer, normally a mortgage banker, guarantees mortgages to a savings and loan or commercial bank, places them in the custody of a bank, and through GNMA, issues a Ginnie Mae pass-through security collaterized by the mortgages.

Good delivery. Certain basic qualifications must be met before a security sold on the exchange may be delivered. The security must be in proper form to comply with the contract of sale and to transfer title to the purchaser—to make a good delivery.

Good 'Til Cancelled Order (GTC). Also called open order. An order to buy or sell which remains in effect until it is either executed or cancelled.

Government bonds. Obligations of the U.S. government, regarded as the highest grade issues in existence.

Graduated rate mortgage. Lower payments in early years of the life of the mortgage and correspondingly higher payments toward the end.

Gross debt. The sum total of a debtor's obligations.

Growth stock. Stock of a company with a record of growth in earnings at a relatively rapid rate, but which is not guaranteed for the future.

Guaranteed bond. A bond which has interest or principal (or both) guaranteed by a company other than the issuer. Usually found in the railroad industry when large roads, leasing sections of trackage owned by small railroads, may guarantee the bonds of the smaller road.

Guaranteed stock. Usually preferred stock on which dividends are guaranteed by another company under much the same circumstances as a bond is guaranteed.

Hedge. A term used to describe an action to safeguard as much as possible against another action.

Holding company. A corporation which owns the securities of another, and in most cases has voting control.

House call. A call for additional down payment when the value of a margined security is below the (brokerage) house minimum margin.

HR 10 (Keogh). A qualified retirement plan for self-employed persons and their employees.

Hypothecation. The pledging of securities as collateral—for example, to secure the debit balance in a margin account or loan with a bank.

Inactive stock. An issue traded on an exchange or in the over-the-counter market in which there is a relatively low volume of transactions. Volume may be no more than a few hundred shares a week, and could be even less. On the New York Stock Exchange, many inactive stocks are traded in ten-share units rather than the customary one hundred-share units.

In-and-out. Purchase and sale of the same security within a short period of a day, week, or month. An in-and-out trader is generally more interested in day-to-day price fluctuations than in dividends or long-term growth.

Indenture. A written agreement under which bonds and debentures are issued, setting forth maturity date, interest rate, and other terms.

Independent brokers. Members on the floor of the NYSE who execute orders for other brokers having more business at that time than they can handle themselves, or for firms who do not have their Exchange member on the floor. Formerly known as two-dollar brokers from the time they received $2 per hundred shares for executing such orders.

Index. A statistical yardstick expressed in terms of percentages of a base year or years. For instance, the Federal Reserve Board's index of industrial production is based on 1967 as 100. An index is not an average.

Industrial Revenue Bond. A security backed by private enterprises that have been financed by a municipal issue. The credit quality of these bonds is based on the credit rating of the corporation, not of the municipality.

Institutional investors. Organizations whose primary purpose is to invest their own assets or those held in trust by it for others. Includes pension funds, investment companies, insurance companies, universities, and banks.

Interest. Payments borrowers pay lenders for the use of their money. A corporation pays interest on its bonds to its bondholders, banks to their depositors.

Interest-adjusted cost. A common denominator for comparing costs of the various insurance policies by hypothetically investing the annual premium at compounded interest and computing the net cost.

Interest dates. The dates on which interest is payable to the holders of securities.

Investment. The use of money for the purpose of making more money, to gain income, increase capital, or both.

Investment adviser. A person registered with the SEC, federal and state, who is engaged in the business of advising others, directly or in writing, regarding investing in, analysis or value of securities, for compensation.

Investment bankers. Also known as underwriters. They are the go-betweens connecting corporations issuing new securities with the public. The usual practice is for one or more investment bankers to buy a new issue of stocks or bonds outright from a corporation. The group forms a syndicate to sell the securities to the public. Investment bankers also distribute very large blocks of stocks or bonds, such as in an estate.

Investment company. A company or trust which uses its capital to invest in other companies. There are two principal types: closed-end, and open-end mutual funds and trusts.

Investment counsel. A person whose principal business consists of acting as an investment adviser. A substantial part of his or her business consists of rendering investment supervisory services.

Investment Service Bureau. A facility of the New York Stock Exchange which answers written inquiries from individual investors on all aspects of securities investing: for example, local brokerage firms which take small orders or accounts; investing methods and listed securities; Exchange operations; and tracing dubious securities.

IRA (Individual Retirement Account). A qualified plan for those who are gainfully employed who do not qualify for or participate in any other qualified retirement plan.

IRA roll-over. An individual retirement account that can continue to hold tax-free funds from discontinued qualified retirement plans.

Issue. Any of a company's securities or the act of distributing such securities.

Issuer. Any entity that offers its own securities for sale.

Keogh (HR-10). Pronounced Key-oh. Named after the senator who introduced the legislation. A qualified retirement plan for self-employed persons and their employees.

Land contract. A contract between an owner and a potential buyer whereby periodic payments are made by the buyer to the seller until a predetermined amount has been paid, whereupon ownership is transferred to the buyer.

Lease-secured bonds. Lease-secured bonds are backed by a pledge of a party other than the issuer to make fixed payments to the issuer over the life of the bonds to cover principal and interest requirements. Normally the payment is made pursuant to a lease and trust agreement. Often the lessee's credit background is superior to that of the issuer.

Legal list. A list of investments, selected by various states, in which certain institutions and fiduciaries, such as insurance companies and banks, may invest. Legal lists are often restricted to high quality securities meeting certain specifications.

Legal opinion. An opinion concerning the legality of a bond issue, usually written by a recognized law firm specializing in public borrowings.

Leverage. The effect on the per-share earnings of the common stock of a company when large sums must be paid for bond interest or preferred stock dividends, or both, before the common stock is entitled to share in the earnings.

Liabilities. All the claims against assets. They can include accounts and wages and salaries payable; dividends declared payable; accrued taxes payable; fixed or long-term liabilities such as mortgage bonds; debentures; and bank loans.

Lien. A claim against property. Can be a mechanic's lien against property newly constructed or some other form of claim. A bond is usually secured by a lien against specific property of a company.

Limit, limited order, or limited price order. An order to buy or sell a stated amount of a security at a specified price, or at a better price if obtainable after the order is represented on the exchanges.

Limited and special tax bonds. Bonds payable from a pledge of the proceeds derived by the issuer from a specific tax, such as an ad valorem tax levied at a fixed rate, a gasoline tax, or some special assessment.

Limited tax bond. A bond secured by a pledge of a tax or a group of taxes limited as to rate or amount.

Liquidation. The process of converting securities or other property into cash. The dissolution of a company, with any cash remaining after sale of its assets and payment of all indebtedness being distributed to the shareholders.

Liquidity. Refers to how readily an asset can be converted to cash with a minimum of risk. The market in a particular security must be able to absorb a reasonable amount of buying or selling at reasonable price changes.

Listed stock. The stock of a company which is traded on a securities exchange.

Load. The portion of the offering price of shares of open-end investment companies in excess of the value of the underlying assets. It covers sales commissions and all other costs of distribution. The load is usually incurred only on purchase; in most cases there is no charge when the shares are sold (redeemed).

Long. Signifies ownership of securities: "I am long 100 General Motors" means the investor owns 100 shares of General Motors stock.

Manipulation. An illegal operation involving the buying or selling of a security to create false or misleading market activity for the purpose of raising or depressing the price to induce purchase or sale by others.

Margin. The amount paid by customers when they use their broker's credit to buy a security. Under Federal Reserve regulations, the initial margin required ranged from 50% of the purchase price all the way to 100%.

Margin call. The demand upon a customer to put up additional money or securities with the broker. Calls are made when a purchase is made, and also if a customer's equity in a margin account declines below a minimum standard set by the exchange or by the brokerage firm.

Marketability. A measure of the ease with which a security can be sold in the secondary market.

Market order. An order to buy or sell a stated amount of a security at the most advantageous price obtainable after the order is represented at the exchanges.

Market price. The last reported price at which the stock or bond is sold.

Maturity. The date on which a loan or a bond or debenture comes due and is to be paid off.

Member corporation. A securities brokerage firm, organized as a corporation with at least one member of the New York Stock Exchange, Inc., or another exchange, who is an officer and a holder of voting stock in the corporation.

Member firm. A securities brokerage firm organized as a partnership and having at least one general partner who is a member of a stock exchange.

Money market certificate. A bank certificate funded by short-term treasury bills—usually twenty-six weeks (six months).

Money market fund. A mutual fund investing in short-term securities—usually not to exceed six months.

Mortgage (Mortgage deed). A document using real estate as collateral for a loan.

Mortgage bond. A bond secured by a mortgage on a property. The value of the property may or may not equal the value of the so-called mortgage bonds issued against it.

Mortgagee. The lender to whom property has been pledged as collateral for a loan.

Mortgagor. The owner of the property which has been used as collateral for a loan.

Multiple. See P/E ratio.

Municipal bond. A bond issued by a state or a political subdivision such as a county, city, township, or village. The term also designates bonds issued by state agencies and authorities. In general, interest paid on municipal bonds is exempt from federal income taxes, and from state and local income taxes within the state of issue.

Mutual funds. Investment companies that pool the funds of numerous investors who do not wish to manage their money themselves.

Naked option. An option written without owning the underlying security. See Covered option.

NASD (National Association of Securities Dealers). An association of brokers and dealers in the over-the-counter securities business.

NASDAQ (National Association of Securities Dealers Automated Quotations). An automated information network which provides brokers and dealers with price quotations on securities traded over-the-counter.

NAV (Net Asset Value). It is common practice for an investment company to compute its assets daily, or even twice daily, by totalling the market value of all securities owned. All liabilities are deducted and the balance divided by the number of shares outstanding. The resulting figure is the net asset value per share.

NCUA (National Credit Union Administration). An agency created by Congress to charter national credit unions and secure their deposits within a certain limit. Similar to FDIC and FSLIC.

Negotiable. Refers to a security, title to which is transferable by delivery of the security.

Net debt. Gross debt, minus sinking fund accumulations and all self-supporting debt.

Net change. The change in the price of a security from the closing price on one day and the closing price on the following day on which the stock is traded. The net change is ordinarily the last figure on the stock price list. The mark + 1-1/8 means up $1.125 a share from the last sale on the previous day the stock was traded.

New housing authority bonds. Also known as public housing authority bonds. These bonds are issued by a local public housing authority to finance public housing. They are backed by an assistance agreement which includes the solemn pledge of the U.S. government that payment will be made in full.

New issue. A stock or bond sold by a corporation for the first time. Proceeds may be issued to retire outstanding securities of the company, for new plant or equipment, or for additional working capital.

Noncumulative. A preferred stock on which unpaid dividends do not accrue. Omitted dividends are, as a rule, gone forever.

Notes. Short-term unsecured promises to pay specific amounts of money. For municipal notes, maturities generally range from six to twelve months.

NYSE (New York Stock Exchange).

NYSE common stock index. A composite index covering price movements of all common stocks listed on the "Big Board." It is based on the close of the market on December 31, 1965, using 50.00 as the base number. The index is computed continuously and is printed on ticker tape each half-hour. Point changes are converted to dollars and cents to provide a meaningful measure of changes in the average price of listed stocks.

Odd Lot. An amount of stock less than the established one-hundred-share unit or ten-share unit of trading; from one to ninety-nine shares for the great majority of issues, and one to nine for so-called inactive stocks. Can also be any amount of government securities less than $100,000.

Offer. The price at which a person is ready to sell. As opposed to bid, the price at which one is ready to buy.

Official statement. The official document prepared by an investment banker or the issuer which gives detailed information about the security and financial information related to the issue.

Open-end mutual funds. Funds which make a continuous offering of new shares to investors and redeem any shares at any time.

Option. The choice of buying or selling or not buying or selling. The right to buy (call) or sell (put) a fixed amount of a given stock at a specified price within a limited period of time.

Overbought. An opinion as to price levels. May refer to a security which has had a sharp rise or to the market as a whole after a period of vigorous buying, which it may be argued has left prices "too high."

Oversold. The reverse of overbought. A single security or a market which, it is believed, has declined to an unreasonable level.

Over-the-counter. A market for securities made up of securities dealers who may or may not be members of a securities exchange. Business is conducted by negotiation rather than through the use of an auction system as represented by a stock exchange.

Paper Profit. An unrealized profit on a security still held. Paper profits become real only when the security is sold.

Par. The full face value of a security. Prices are normally quoted on a scale with 100 representing par value.

Participating preferred. A preferred stock which is entitled to its stated dividend and also to additional dividends on a specified basis upon payment of dividends on the common stock.

Participation certificate (P.C.P.). Participation certificates are issued by federal agencies and represent participation in a pool of assets held by these agencies. They carry a definite coupon and maturity date and are treated as securities in the money market.

Partnership. Ownership by legal agreement of two or more persons.

Passed dividend. Omission of a regular or scheduled dividend.

Paydown. When the dollar value of a new issue of government securities is less than the maturing issue it replaces, the difference is called the paydown.

Paying agent. The place where the principal and interest is payable. Usually a designated bank or the treasurer's office of the issuer.

PBGC (Pension Benefit Guaranty Corporation). Enacted by Congress to protect pension benefits of certain qualified pension programs.

Penny stocks. Low-priced issues, often highly speculative, selling at less than $1 per share. Frequently used as a term of derision, although some penny stocks have developed into investment-caliber issues.

P/E ratio (Price/earning ratio). Sometimes called the "multiple." It is the price of a stock divided by its actual current earnings per share. A stock selling for $50 a share and earning $5 a share is said to be selling at a price/earnings ratio of 10 to 1.

Percentage order. A limited price order to buy (or sell) a stated amount of a specified stock after a fixed number of shares of such stock have been traded.

Point. In *bond prices* a point is $10, since bond prices are quoted as a percentage of $1,000 par value. In *stock prices,* a point means $1. In *real estate* terminology, one point is 1% of the mortgage debt. A one-time payment to compensate for interest rate adjustment.

Portfolio. Holdings of securities by an individual or institution.

Preferred stocks. Stocks whose dividends are fixed and must be paid before any dividends are paid out to common shareholders.

Premium. The amount, if any, by which the price of a security exceeds its principal amount—that is, the amount by which a preferred stock, bond, or option may sell above its par value. In insurance, a premium is the fixed amount as stated on the policy that the policyholder pays at scheduled intervals to the insurance carrier.

Primary distribution. Also called primary offering. The original sale of a company's securities. The first offering to the public must be accompanied by a prospectus.

Prime rate. The interest rate banks charge their most favored customers.

Principal. The face amount of a bond exclusive of accrued interest. Also refers to the person for whom a broker executes an order or a dealer who is buying or selling for his or her own account. Can also refer to a person's capital.

Probate. Transfer by a valid will, subject to judicial authority.

Profit-taking. Selling stock which has appreciated in value since purchase in order to realize the profit which has been made possible. The term is often used to explain a downturn in the market following a period of rising prices.

Project notes. Short-term obligations issued by local authorities under an agreement with the U.S. Department of Housing and Urban Development to finance federal programs for urban renewal.

Prospectus. A brochure giving all pertinent facts about a corporation making its first stock offer to the public. All prime offerings must be accompanied by a prospectus.

Proxy. Written authorization given by shareholders to someone else to represent them and vote their shares at a shareholders' meeting.

Proxy statement. Information required by the SEC to be given to stockholders as a prerequisite to solicitation of proxies for a security subject to the requirements of Securities Exchange Act.

Prudent man rule. An investment standard first ruled by Judge Samuel Putnam of Massachusetts over a hundred and fifty years ago which means that trustees must act with the same discretion and intelligence when acting for others as people would when acting for themselves to obtain a reasonable income and preserve capital.

PS 58 (Pension Service #58 Rate Table). Shows pure life insurance annual cost per $1,000 of death benefits. See Appendix.

Put. The right to sell a certain number of shares of stock at a specified price within a specified period of time.

Put option. Sellers of put options sell the right to *sell to them* a security at a specified price within a specified period of time. The seller of a put option has the right to buy and the buyer the obligation to sell.

Quit claim. A document relinquishing all rights to a piece of property. A quit claim deed transfers ownership of real estate, for instance.

Quotation. Often shortened to "quote." The highest bid to buy and the lowest offer to sell a security in a given market at a given time.

Quote. The bid and asked price of a security at a particular time.

Quote only. Used when a trader gives a market for an indication only and not a binding offer or bid.

Rally. A brisk rise following a decline in the general price level of the stock market or in an individual stock.

Ratings. Designations used by investors' services designed to give relative indications of the quality of a security or its issuer.

Record date. Date on which a shareholder must be registered on the stock book of a company in order to receive a declared dividend, or (among other things) to vote on company affairs.

Redemption. Payment on maturity date by the issuer of a bond at par value, or call price on or after a call date.

Redemption price. The price at which a bond may be redeemed before maturity at the option of the issuing company. Redemption value also applies to the price the company must pay to call in certain types of preferred stock.

Refinancing. Same as refunding. New securities are sold by a company and the money is used to retire existing securities. The object may be to save interest costs, extend the maturity of the loan, or both. In real estate, refinancing may be done with mortgage loans depending upon the restrictions of the lending institution.

Refunding. Same as refinancing (above). With bonds, the redemption of a bond issue by a new bond issue at conditions generally more favorable to the issuer.

Registered bond. On a registered bond, the name and address of the owner of the bond are registered with the issuer or its paying agent. The bond must be properly endorsed by the current owner before it can be transferred to another owner.

Registered representative. Present name for the older term "customer's man." Same as an account executive.

Registered traders. Members of an exchange who trade in stocks on the floor for an account in which they have an interest.

Registrar. Usually a trust company or bank charged with the responsibility of preventing the issuance of more stock than authorized by a company.

Registration. Before a public offering may be made of new securities by a company, or of outstanding securities by controlling stockholders, the securities must be registered under the Securities Act of 1933. The Registration Statement must be filed with the SEC by the issuer. Also, before a security may be admitted to dealings on a national securities exchange, it must be registered under the Securities Exchange Act of 1934. The Registration Statement must include pertinent information relating to the company's operation, securities, and management.

Regular way delivery. Unless otherwise specified, securities are delivered to the buying broker by the selling broker and payment made to the selling broker by the buying broker on the fifth business day after transaction. Regular way delivery for bonds is the following business day.

Regulation G. Federal Reserve Board limitations on the amount of credit that may be extended to lenders not covered by Regulation T.

Regulation T. Federal Reserve Board limitations on the amount of credit that may be extended to brokers or dealers for purchase of securities.

Regulation U. Federal Reserve Board limitations on the amount of credit that may be extended by banks to their customers for the purchase of listed stocks.

Regulation Z. A "truth in lending" regulation covering full disclosure of borrowing terms.

REIT (Real Estate Investment Trust). An organization, an investment company, which concentrates its holdings in real estate investment. REITs are required to distribute at least 90% of their income.

Repo or RP. Trading language for a repurchase agreement. A repurchase agreement is a sale of securities in which the seller agrees to buy the securities back at a future date for payment of the original principal plus interest at a predetermined rate.

Return. Dividend and interest from investments, expressed in dollars.

Revenue bonds. Bonds payable from revenues derived from tolls, charges, or rents paid by users of the facility constructed from the proceeds of the bond issue.

Reverse annuity. Same as Annuity mortgage.

Reverse Repo. Designates the act of the original sale of the securities in a repurchase agreement. The transaction is a "repo" for the investor and a "reverse repo" for the borrower.

Rider. A statement added to a document to modify in some way the conditions of the document.

Rights. When a company wishes to raise more money by issuing additional securities, it may give its stockholders the opportunity, ahead of others, to buy the new securities in proportion to the number of shares each owns. Rights have a market value of their own because the right to buy additional stock is usually offered to stockholders below the current market price. In most cases, rights must be exercised within a relatively short period of time and failure to do so may result in actual loss to the holder.

Round lot. A unit of trading or a multiple thereof. On the NYSE the unit of trading is generally 100 shares in stocks and $1,000 par value in bonds. In some inactive stocks, the unit of trading is 10 shares.

Rule of 45. Retirement provision whereby employees' vesting must be 50% if they have at least five years of service and are forty-five years old.

Rule of 72. A rule of thumb calculation. One dollar invested at 1% will double in seventy-two years. To arrive at the length of time an investment doubles, divide the interest rate into seventy-two.

Scale Order. An order to buy or sell a security which specifies the total amount to be bought or sold and the amount to be bought or sold at specified price variations.

Seat. Figure-of-speech meaning a membership on an exchange.

SEC (Securities and Exchange Commission). Established by Congress to help protect investors. The SEC administers the Securities Act of 1933, the Securities Exchange Act of 1934, the Securities Act Amendments of 1975, the Trust Indenture Act, the Investment Company Act, the Investment Advisers Act, and the Public Utility Holding Company Act.

Secondary distribution. Also known as a secondary offering. The redistribution of a block of stock some time after it has been sold by the issuing company. The block is usually a large one, such as may be involved in the settlement of an estate. The securities may be listed or unlisted.

Secondary market. All transactions in an issue once the distribution of a new issue has been completed.

Self-supporting debt. Debt incurred for a project or enterprise requiring no tax support other than the specific revenues earmarked for the purpose.

Seller's option. A special transaction which gives the seller the right to deliver the stock or bond at any time within a specified period, ranging from not less than six business days to not more than sixty days.

Serial bond. An issue which matures at periodic stated intervals, usually annually or semiannually.

Settlement. Conclusion of a securities transaction in which a customer pays a debit balance he or she owes a broker or receives from the broker the proceeds from a sale. The term also applies to continuous daily accounting of transactions among brokerage houses, usually through centralized securities clearing corporations.

Settlement date. The day a transaction is completed by transfer of funds from the buyer and delivery of securities to the buyer from the seller.

Short covering. Buying stock to return stock previously borrowed to make delivery on a short sale.

Short position. Stocks sold short and not covered as of a particular date.

Short sale. This is best explained by an example: suppose you believe that a stock will decline. You instruct your broker to sell short 100 shares of the stock *even though you do not own it.* Your broker borrows the stock so that he can deliver it to the buyer. The money value of the shares borrowed is deposited by your broker with the lender. Sooner or later you must cover your short sale by buying the same amount of stock you borrowed for return to the lender. If you are able to buy the stock for less money than you sold it for, your profit is the difference between the two transactions. But if you have to buy the stock for more than you sold it for, you have incurred a loss. Stock exchange and federal regulations govern and limit the conditions under which a short sale may be made. Sometimes people sell short a stock they already own in order to protect a paper profit. This is known as "selling short against the box." The sale of a security not owned by the seller.

SIAC (Securities Industry Automation Corporation). An independent organization established by the N.Y. and American Stock Exchanges as a jointly owned subsidiary to provide automation, data processing, clearing, and communications services.

Simple interest. Interest paid only once at the end of a transaction. It is computed by multiplying the principal by the percent of interest by the time period involved. In real estate, interest is computed monthly, or whenver payments are made.

Sinking fund. A fund accumulated over a period of time which can be applied to periodic retirement of debt.

SIPC (Securities Investor Protection Corporation). Provides funds, if necessary, to protect customers' cash and securities which may be on deposit with an SIPC member firm in the event the firm fails. SIPC is not a government agency. It is a nonprofit membership corporation created by an act of Congress.

Special bid. A method of filling an order to buy a large block of stock. In special bids, the bidders for the block of stock will pay a special commission to the broker who represents them in making the purchase.

Specialists. Members of a stock exchange who have two functions: to maintain an orderly market insofar as is reasonably practicable in the stocks in which they are registered as specialists, and to act as a broker's broker.

Special tax bond. A bond secured by a special tax such as a gasoline tax or utility franchise tax. If the bond also carries the issuer's pledge of full faith, credit, and taxing power, it is classed as a general obligation bond. Such bonds are often referred to as "double-barrelled bonds."

Speculation. The employment of funds by a speculator. Safety of principal is a secondary factor.

Speculator. One who is willing to assume a larger risk in the hope of gain.

Split. The division of the outstanding shares of a corporation into a larger number of shares. A 3-for-1 split by a company will result in each holder of 100 shares, for instance, having 300 shares, although each stockholder's proportionate equity in the company would remain the same.

Spread. The difference between bid and asked price, or the difference in yield in basis points between securities.

Stock dividend. A dividend paid in securities rather than cash. The dividend may be additional shares of the issuing company, or in shares of another company (usually a subsidiary).

Stockholder of record. A stockholder whose name is registered on the books of the issuing corporation.

Stock split. When a company splits its stock the number of shares outstanding is increased but the value of the capitalization is not increased (see Split).

Stop limit order. A stop order which becomes a limit order after the specified stop price has been reached.

Stop order. An order to buy at a price above or sell at a price below the current market.

Straddle. A call and put on the same stock.

Street name. Securities held in the name of a broker instead of the customer's name. This is done when the securities have been bought on margin or when the customer wishes the security to be held by the broker.

Strike price. Specified price of a security, as quoted in an option transaction.

Subscription. A bid to purchase all or part of an issuer's proposed offering of a security. This transaction is binding between the parties when accepted by either the issuer or its legal representatives.

Suitability limitations. Imposed by most states on potential investors in tax-sheltered investments.

Surrender charge. A charge imposed when a payment is made.

Switching. Selling one security and buying another.

Switch order, contingent order. An order for the purchase (sale) of one stock and the sale (purchase) of another stock at a stipulated price difference.

Syndicate. A group of investment bankers who together underwrite and distribute a new issue of securities or a large block of an outstanding issue.

Take-over. The acquisition of one corporation by another, usually in a friendly merger, but sometimes marked by a "proxy fight."

Tax and Revenue Anticipation Notes (TANS and RANS). Sold in anticipation of tax receipts and other revenues. They provide the issuer with funds prior to the actual receipt of taxes and revenues.

Tax base. The total resources available for taxation.

Tax-exempt bond. A bond whose interest payments are exempt from federal income tax.

Tax-exempt bond funds. Mutual funds whose assets are invested in a diversified portfolio of interest-bearing municipal bonds. The interest income from the funds is exempt from all federal income taxes.

Tax-sheltered annuity. Also referred to as a tax-deferred annuity. Defers payment of taxes on current interest income to a later time.

Technical analyst. A specialist who charts the performance of the overall stock market and/or the activities of particular companies.

Tender offer. A public offer to buy shares from existing stockholders of one public corporation by another company or other organization under specified terms good for a certain time period. Stockholders are asked to "tender" (surrender) their holdings for stated value, usually at a premium above current market price, sometimes subject to the tendering of a minimum and maximum number of shares.

Term bond. Bond of an issue which has a single maturity.

Thin market. A market in which there are comparatively few bids to buy, offers to sell, or both.

Third market. Trading of stock exchange-listed securities in the over-the-counter market by non-exchange member brokers and all types of investors.

Time order. An order which becomes a market or limited price order at a specified time.

Traders. Those who buy and sell for their own account for short-term profit.

Transfer. The delivery of a stock certificate from the seller's broker to the buyer's broker. Also refers to the recording of a change in stock ownership by the transfer agent on the books of a corporation.

Transfer agents. Keep a record of the name of each registered share-owner and see that certificates presented to their office for transfer are properly cancelled and new certificates issued in the name of the transferee.

Treasury bill. Short-term U.S. government bills sold at a discount from face value in units of $10,000 to $1 million for terms of thirteen weeks or twenty-six weeks.

Treasury stock. Stock issued by a company but later reacquired. It may be held in the company's treasury indefinitely, reissued to the public, or retired. Treasury stock receives no dividends and has no vote while held by the company.

Troy weight. Fine metals are measured by troy ounces. A troy ounce is equal to about 1.10 ounces avoirdupois, the unit of weight measure familiar to Americans. One kilo of gold contains approximately 32.15 troy ounces.

Trust. Legal title to property held by one party (the trustee) for the benefit of another party (the beneficiary).

Trustee. A person or institution designated as the custodian of funds, and who acts as the official representative of the beneficiary.

Underwriter. One who "underwrites" or guarantees the sale of new issues of securities. Also, a casualty insurance agent.

Unit investment trust. An investment company formed to obtain current income through investments in a diversified portfolio of municipal or corporate debt obligations and preferred stock. Each unit represents an undivided interest in the underlying securities.

Unlimited tax bond. A bond secured by pledge of taxes which may be levied in an unlimited amount or at an unlimited rate.

Unlisted. A security not listed on a stock exchange and traded over-the-counter.

Variable hedge. Selling one more call for each 100 shares owned.

Variable rate mortgage. Interest rate to borrow mortgage money is based upon a set number of percentage points above the cost of money to banks.

Vesting. Undisputed ownership of certain pension plan benefits.

Volume. The number of shares traded in a security or an entire market during a given period.

Voting right. The stockholders' right to vote their stock in the affairs of their company. Most common shares have one vote each. Preferred stock usually has the right to vote when preferred dividends are in default for a specified period. The right to vote may be delegated by the stockholder to another person by proxy.

Warrant. The right to purchase additional shares of a new issue of stocks or bonds within a specified time at a fixed price. Sometimes a warrant is offered with securities as an inducement to buy.

Warranty deed. A document transferring warranted ownership of real estate guaranteed by the seller to be free of any liens or encumbrances.

When issued. A short form of "when, as and if issued." The term indicates a conditional transaction in a security authorized for issuance but not as yet actually issued.

Wire house. A member firm of an exchange maintaining a communications network linking either its own branch offices, offices of correspondent firms, or a combination of such offices.

Working control. Ownership of 51% of a company's voting stock. Effective control can sometimes be exerted through individual or group ownership of less than 50% if the owners act in concert.

Yield. Dividend and interest from investments, expressed in percent (%).

Yield to maturity. The current income yield minus any premium above par or plus any discount from par in purchase price, with the adjustments spread over the period from the purchase date to the maturity date.

INDEX